The ORCHID

INTIMATE PORTRAITS OF A FASCINATING FLOWER

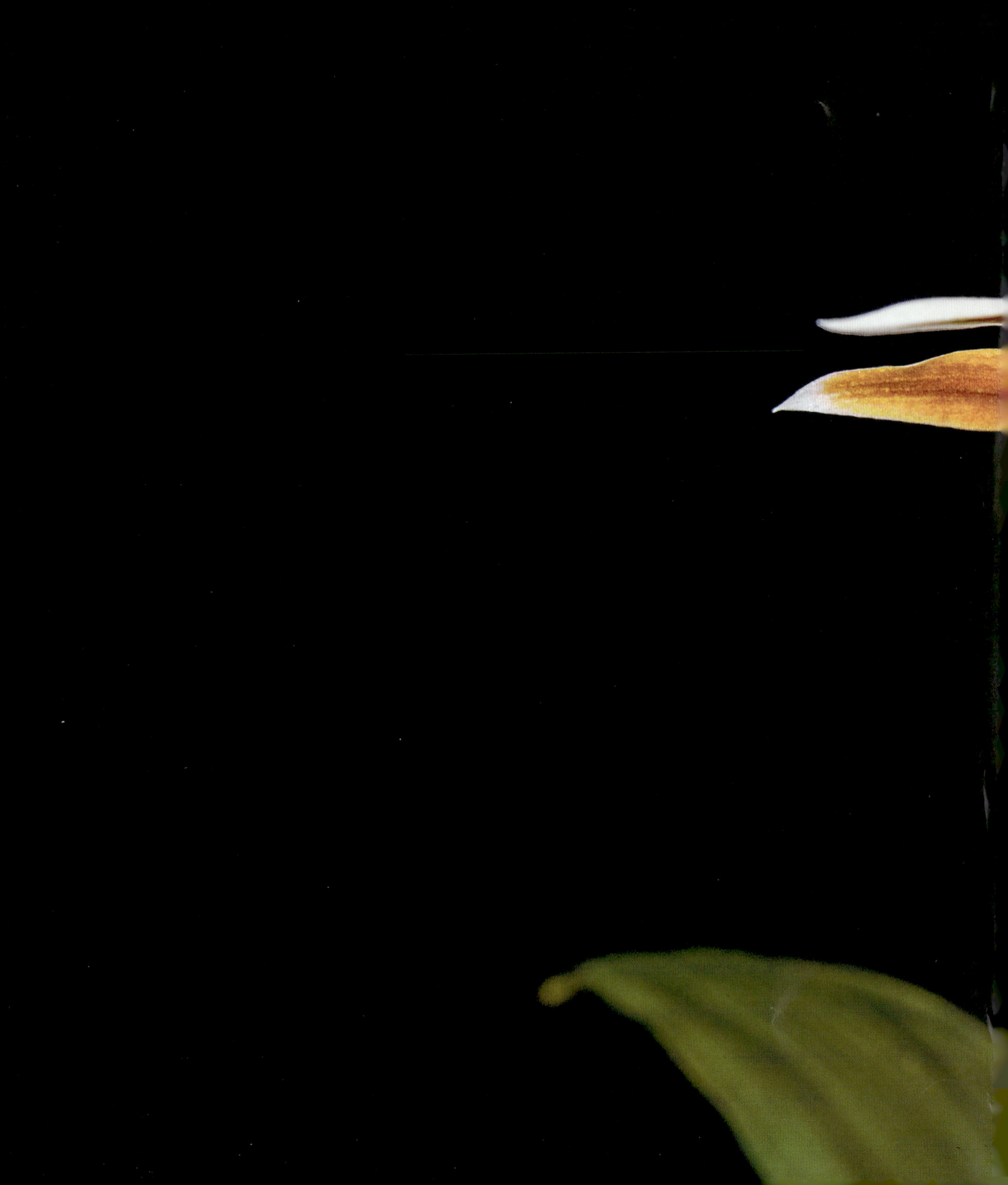

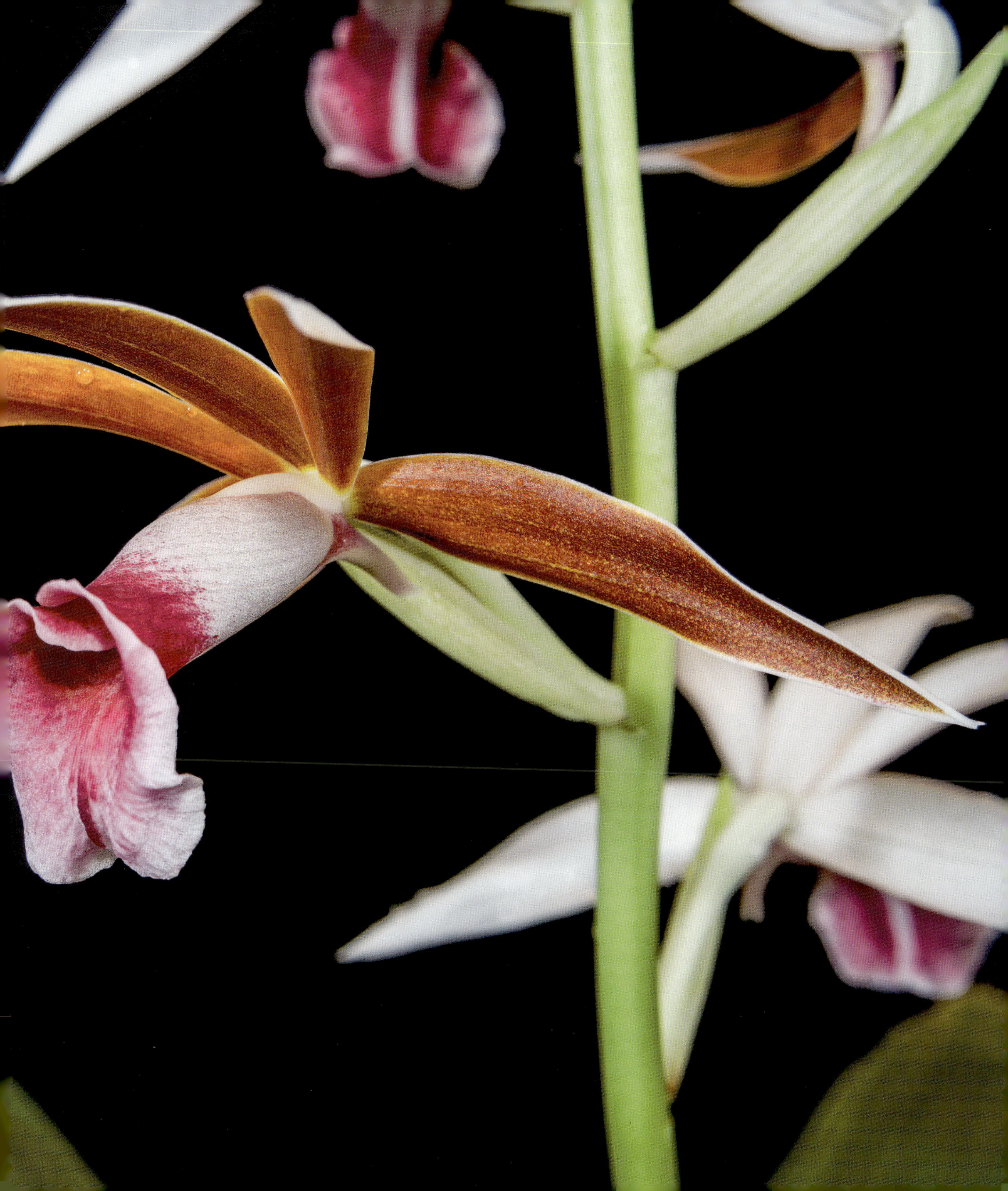

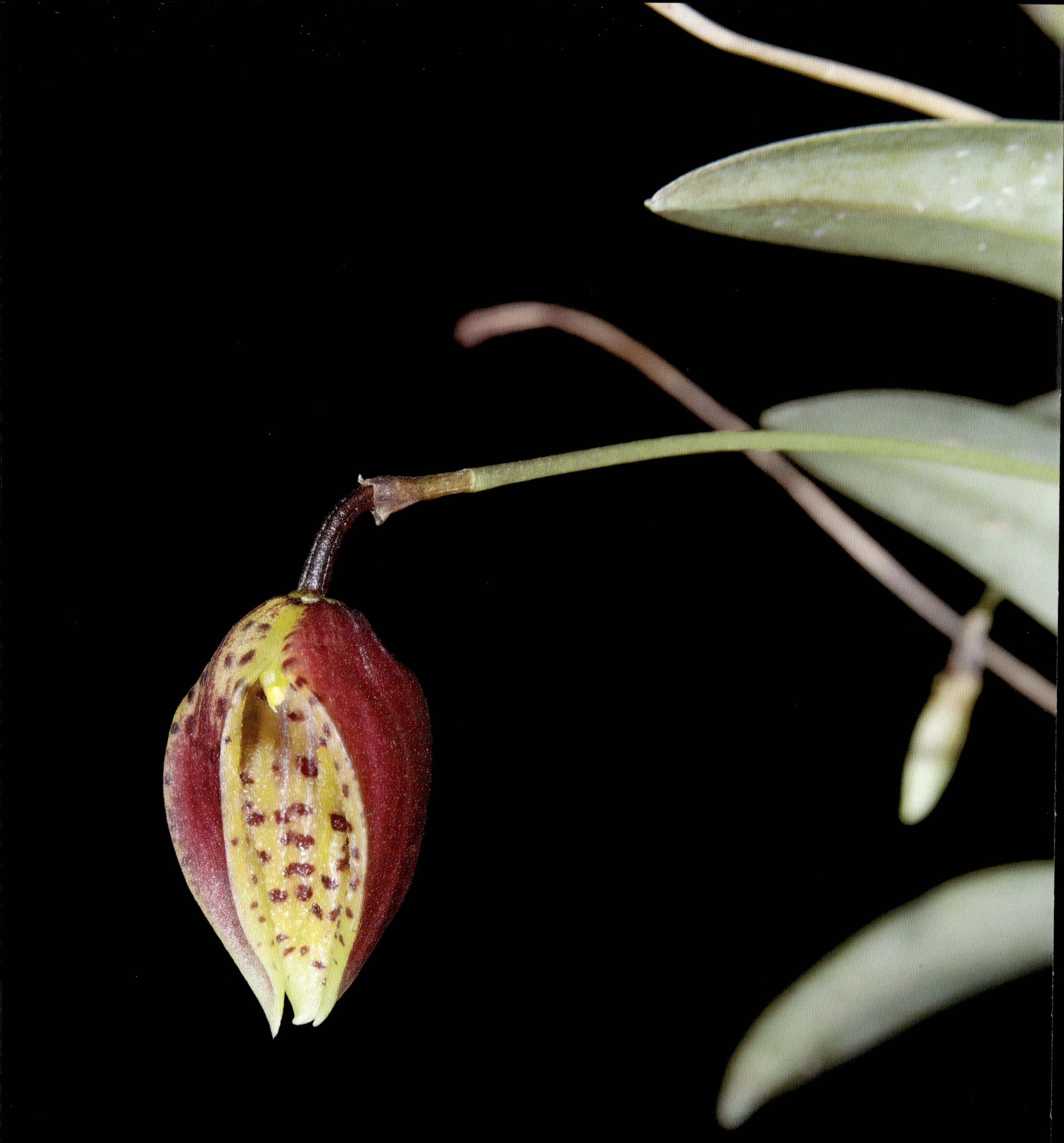

EDITED BY DAVID A. BERRY

The ORCHID

INTIMATE PORTRAITS OF A FASCINATING FLOWER

WITH CONTRIBUTIONS BY

TATIANA ARIAS, JEMMA FAGLER, BRUCE K. HOLST,

ANGEL LARA, SHAWN MCCOURT,

MIKE MCLAUGHLIN, AND JENNIFER O. ROMINIECKI

MARIE SELBY BOTANICAL GARDENS

SCALA

First published in 2026 by
Scala Arts Publishers, Inc.
c/o CohnReznick LLP
10th floor, 1301 Avenue of the Americas
New York, NY 10019, USA
www.scalapublishers.com
An imprint of B. T. Batsford Holdings Ltd.

In association with
Marie Selby Botanical Gardens
1534 Mound Street
Sarasota, FL 34236

ISBN 978 1 78551 651 1

This is a condensed, reduced-format edition of a book first published in 2023 as *Orchid*.

2026 edition managed by Tally de Orellana
Design: Joe Ewart
Editor: Susan Higman Larsen

Typeset in GT Alpina and HEX Franklin
Printed and bound in China
10 9 8 7 6 5 4 3 2 1

Scala is represented in UK and Europe by Abrams & Chronicle Books, 1st Floor, 22–24 Ely Place, London EC1N 6TE and 57 rue Gaston Tessier, 75166 Paris, France.
www.abramsandchronicle.co.uk
info@abramsandchronicle.co.uk

Cover: *Paphiopedilum callosum*
Back cover: *Gongora portentosa*

Library of Congress Cataloging-in-Publication Data:
Names: David A. Berry, editor | Marie Selby Botanical Gardens (Sarasota, FL)

Identifiers:
LCCN 2026937014 | ISBN 978 1 78551 651 1
Subjects: Orchids. Botany. Horticulture.
Marie Selby Botanical Gardens. Florida.

PHOTO CREDITS

Wade Collier: 2-3, *Phaius* sp.; 4, *Phloeophila pelecaniceps*; 8; 19; 171, *Encyclia cyperifolia*.
Aaron Fink: 172, *Dendrobium lindleyi*.
Lunardi Photography: 15, 16, 17, 18.
Sandra Robinson: 11.
© Trustees of the Natural History Museum, London: 10, 13.

MIX
Paper | Supporting responsible forestry
FSC® C104723
www.fsc.org

CONTENTS

INTRODUCTION

9

PLATES

21

CHECKLIST

164

GLOBAL PARTNERS

170

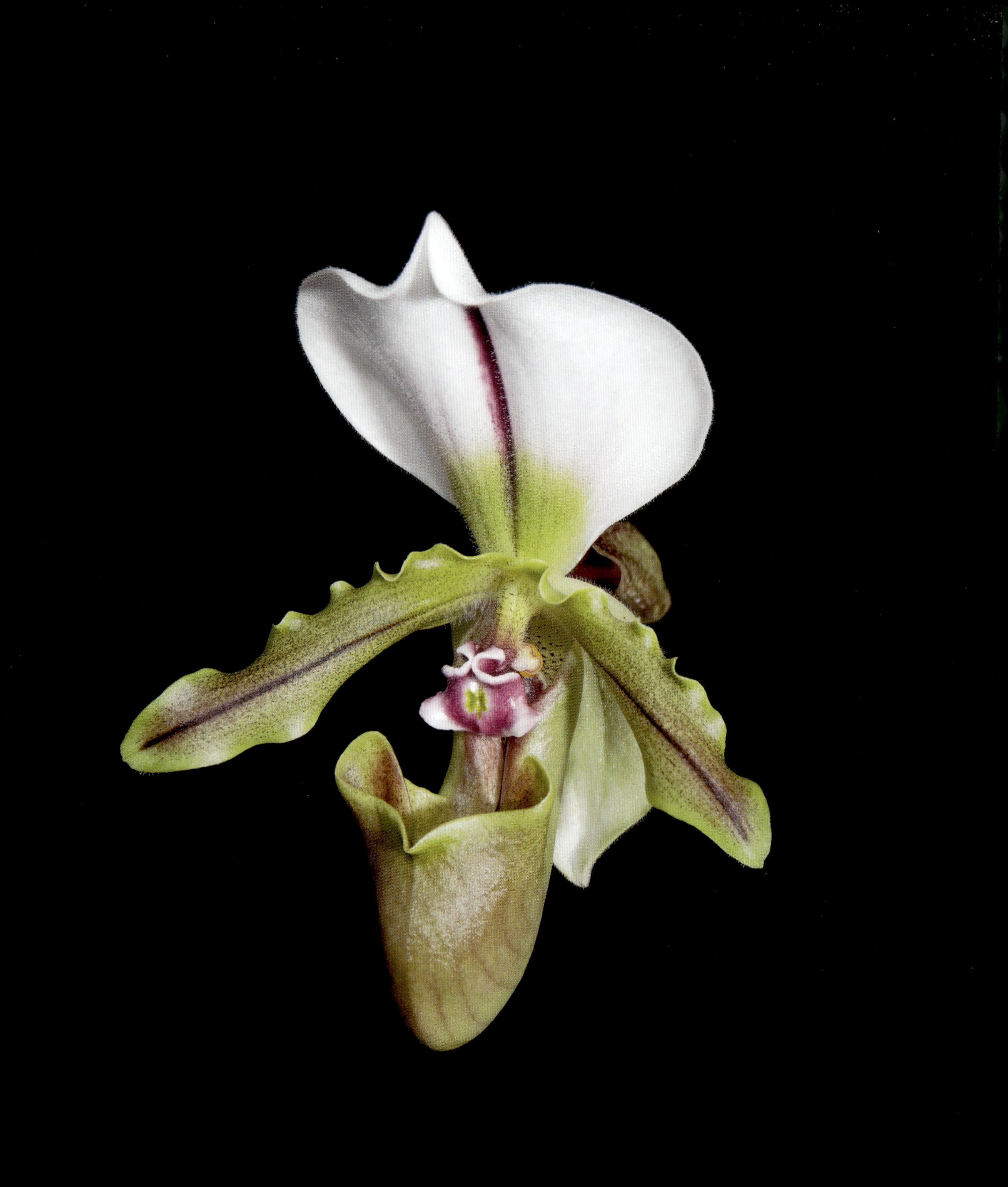

Orchids are amazing. They enchant us with their breathtaking beauty and astound us with their seemingly endless variety. They grow on six of the world's seven continents and at elevations ranging from sea level to mountain top. Orchids live in the soil (terrestrials), on rocks (lithophytes), and on other plants (epiphytes). While orchids have a reputation for being difficult to care for, some of these surprisingly resilient plants can, with the proper attention, thrive on your windowsill at home.

Paphiopedilum spicerianum

In the nineteenth century, orchids were considered luxury items and status symbols, reflecting the wealth and taste of their collectors, who spent huge sums competing for the most spectacular species. At the time, orchids were rare and thus quite expensive. The plants could not yet be grown from seed and had to be collected in the wild and shipped to market, sometimes halfway around the world. They became the subject of a popular craze known as "Orchidmania," which still affects orchid enthusiasts today as much as it did their predecessors more than a century ago. The only cure for "Orchidmania" is more orchids.

Since the development of modern propagation methods in the early twentieth century, orchids have become everyday commodities, accessible to the masses. Some of the orchids in this book might resemble, in color or form, those found in the local florist or supermarket, but most examples included here will be completely unfamiliar to the reader. A few specimens may even challenge the common perception of what an orchid can be, as their blossoms suggest an alien life-form from a distant planet or a creature from the deepest sea.

ORCHIDS

The orchid family, or Orchidaceae, is one of the largest of the flowering plants. The family comprises upwards of 28,000 species and counting. Orchids live in various climates and environments nearly the world over. Most are native to the tropics and subtropics, with the highest concentration and greatest diversity of orchids found in the rainforests of Central and South America. Orchids are integral to the ecosystem in supplying food and shelter to a diverse assortment of animals.

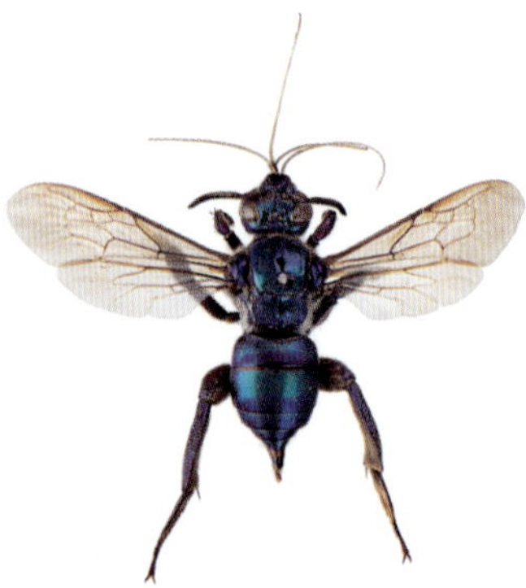

Orchid bee

The root tubers of certain terrestrial orchids are used to make a starchy flour called salep, which has been consumed as a beverage in parts of the Middle East for centuries. Tubers are also dried and pounded into edible cakes known as chikanda in Africa. The most widely known edible orchid is *Vanilla planifolia*, from which vanilla extract is derived. In addition to serving as a source of food, orchids are used as ingredients in medicines and in the making of cosmetics and perfumes.

Orchids have left little trace in the fossil record. As a result, they were once thought to have evolved in the more recent past. The lack of fossil evidence for orchids is due largely to the fact that they are herbaceous plants with no woody parts favorable to preservation that tend to live in tropical conditions not conducive to fossilization. Recent DNA analyses have shown that the orchid family originated between 80 and 95 million years ago, during the late Cretaceous period.

The orchid family is characterized by its remarkable variety and novelty, perhaps most clearly illustrated by the staggering diversity of flowers. Their various features are all effective in attracting pollinators, such as bees, wasps, beetles, flies,

PARTS OF AN ORCHID FLOWER

Encyclia cordigera

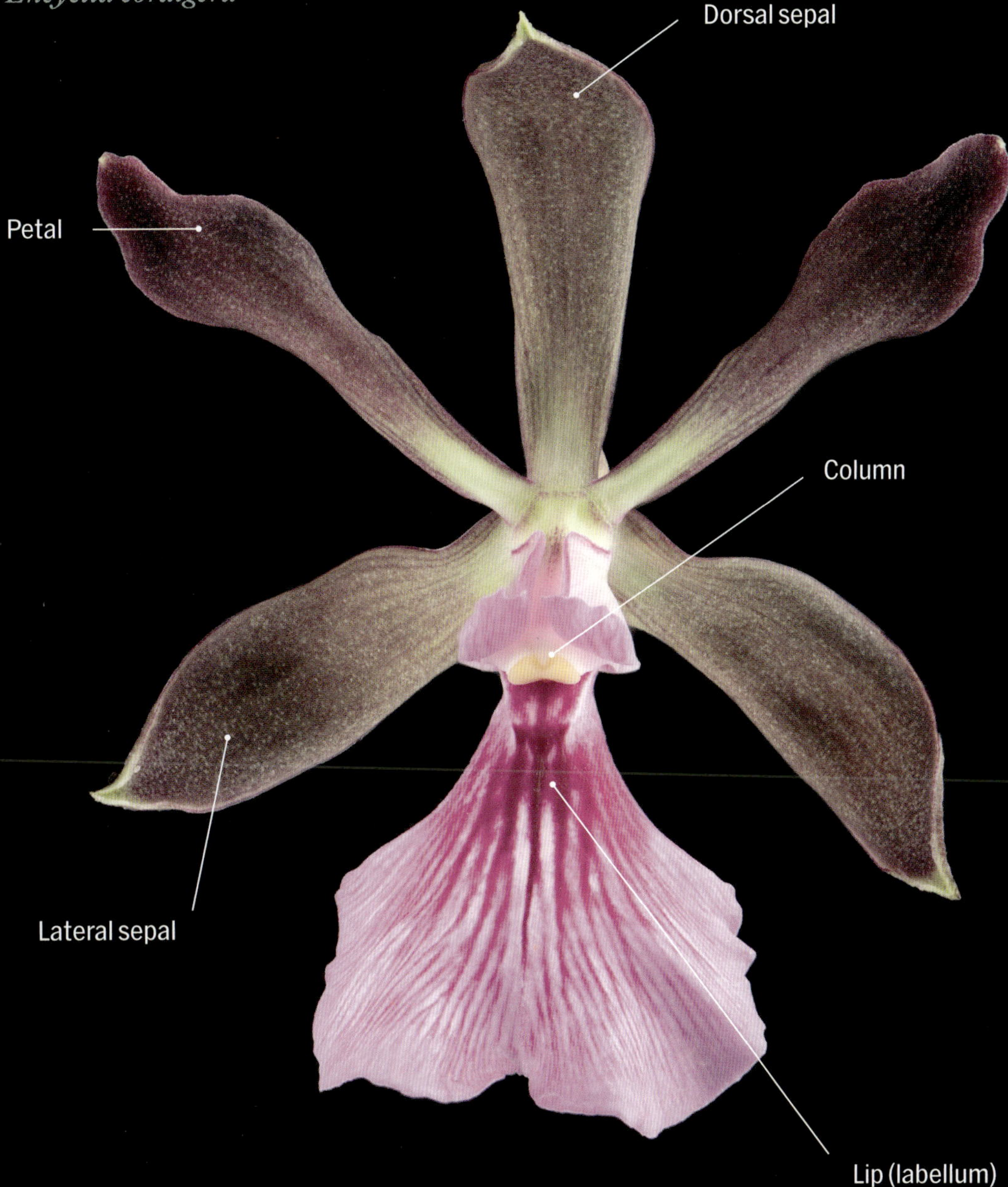

butterflies, and moths. Orchid flowers consist of three petals and three sepals. One of the petals is usually highly modified, forming a lip or labellum, designed to attract pollinators. A distinctive feature of most orchid flowers is the column, a reproductive structure derived from the fusion of both male (stamen) and female (carpel or pistil) parts into a single sexual organ. Most orchid flowers exhibit bilateral symmetry, which means that their two halves (left and right) mirror each other. During an early stage of their development, orchid flowers usually twist upside-down, resulting in the inversion of the positions of the labellum and column. This process is known as resupination.

The largest orchid flowers are about the size of a salad plate, while the smallest are as tiny as the head of a pin, with details only visible under magnification. Orchid flowers come in a multiplicity of colors and patterns, consisting of spots, stripes, or other exotic markings. The flowers can also have striking scents, ranging from pleasant to putrid (the latter proving irresistible to beetles and flies).

In their efforts to attract pollinators, many orchids have mastered the art of deception known as floral mimicry. Through certain features of their flowers, such as form and scent, these orchids lure particular insects by offering the false hope of either food to eat or a mate with which to reproduce. This might be unkind to the insects, but it is certainly beneficial to the orchids, helping to increase their chances of survival.

One of the first scientists to explore the complex relationship between orchids and pollinators was the English naturalist Charles Darwin, best known for his theory of evolution by means of natural selection, initially recorded in the book *On the Origin of Species*, published in 1859. Intended by

Darwin's sphinx moth

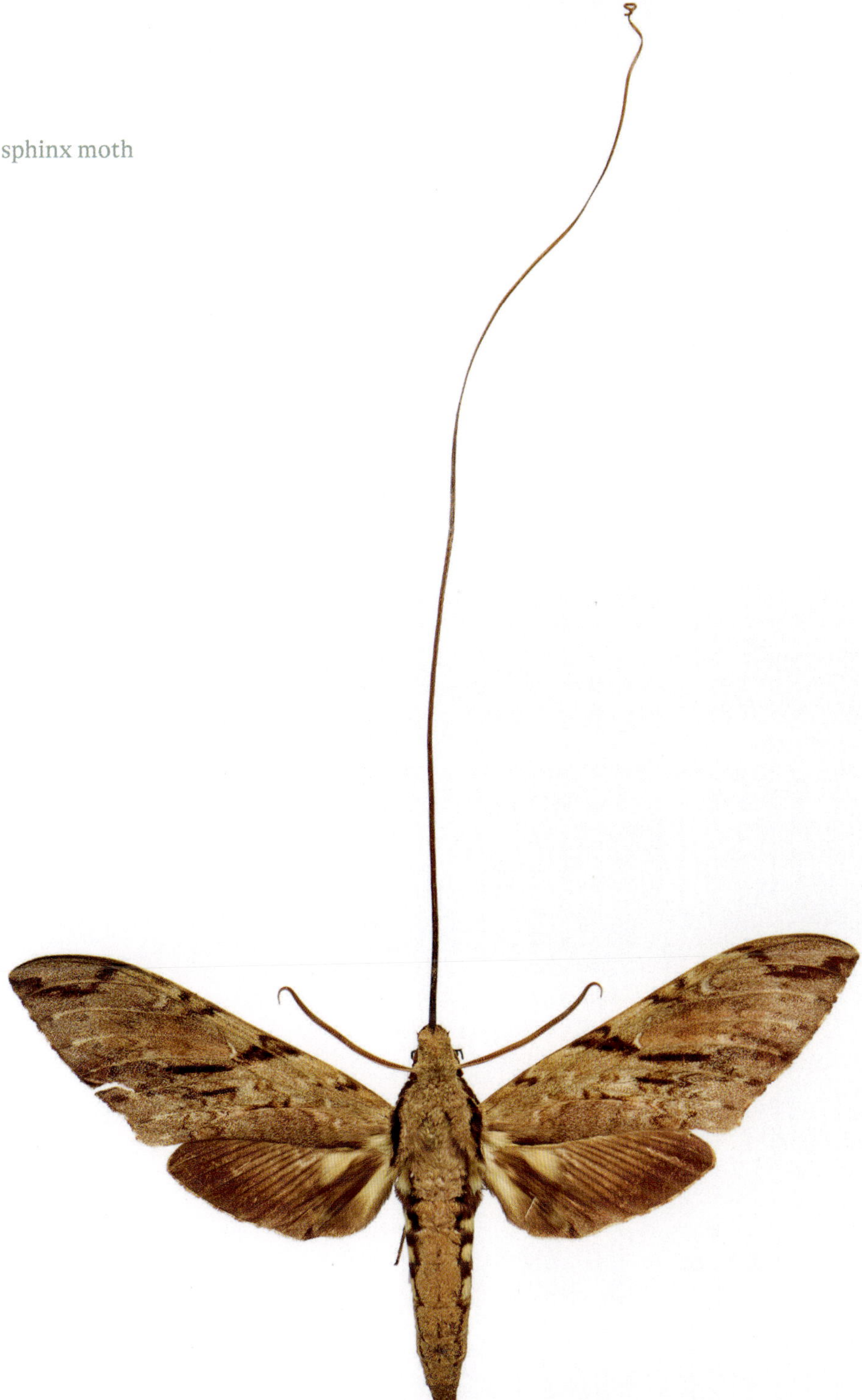

Darwin as the abstract to a larger work on evolution, the book was criticized for a lack of supporting evidence. Darwin used orchids to help substantiate his theory in his next major work, *On the Various Contrivances by which British and Foreign Orchids are Fertilised by Insects*, published in 1862.

Darwin studied native orchids that grew wild near his home at Downe in Kent. He also collected tropical orchids, which he either purchased from commercial nurseries or received as gifts from fellow naturalists. He described the function of the various parts of the plant, which had been something of a mystery. He discussed how orchids evolved to attract certain insects as pollinators and concluded that they had developed strategies to ensure cross-pollination, which benefits the orchids by producing greater numbers of viable seeds and healthy plants. By showing natural selection at work, Darwin's research on orchids laid the foundation of modern evolutionary thought.

A few months prior to the publication of his orchid book, Darwin received a specimen of the star orchid, *Angraecum sesquipedale*, from Madagascar. Darwin proposed that the orchid, which had a nectary of astonishing length, must be pollinated by a large moth with a long proboscis (feeding tube), despite no such insect yet having been found on the island. While Darwin was attacked by critics who rejected his theory, he was ultimately proven correct when a moth with a proboscis of 10 to 12 inches was discovered in Madagascar in 1903, more than 20 years after his death. The scientific name of the moth, *Xanthopan morgani praedicta*, includes a reference to Darwin's prediction that such an insect existed. Darwin knew that the discovery of the moth was inevitable, for in a coevolutionary relationship based on natural selection, the orchid could not reproduce without the insect to pollinate it.

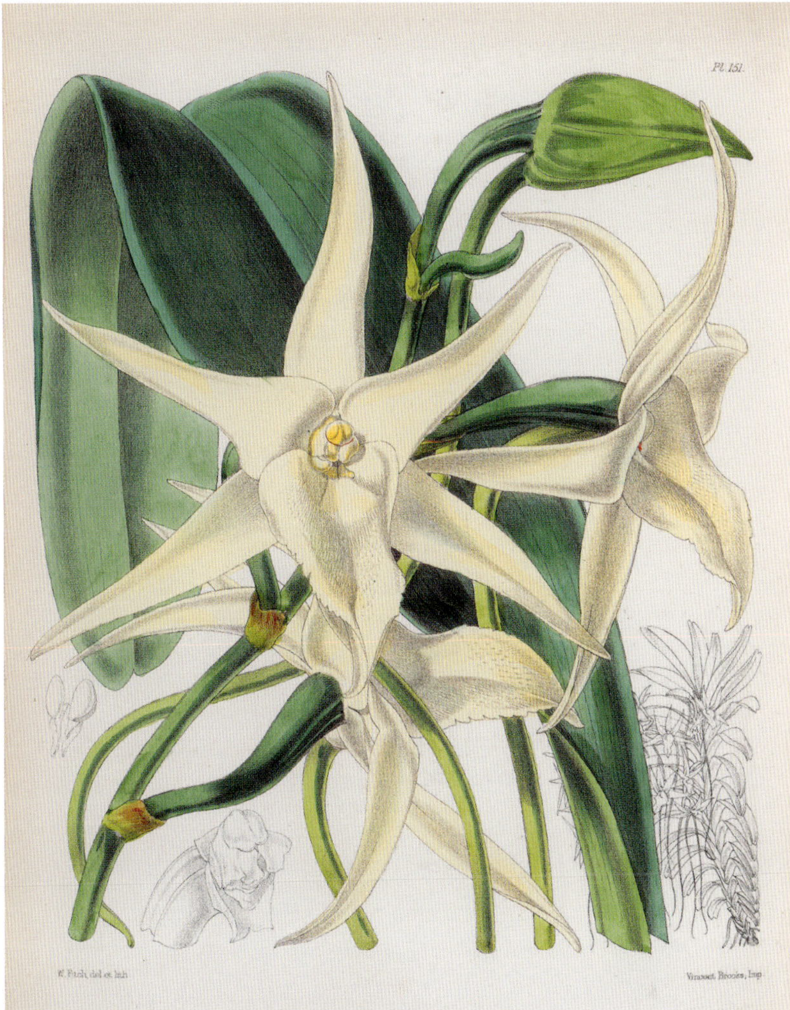

Illustration of *Angraecum sesquipedale* by Walter Hood Fitch from James Bateman's *A Second Century of Orchidaceous Plants*, 1867. Bateman presented a specimen of this orchid to Charles Darwin for his collection.

Autographed copy of Charles Darwin's "Notes on the Fertilization of Orchids," first printed in 1869

Selby Gardens is fortunate to possess an autographed copy of a pamphlet consisting of "Notes on the Fertilization of Orchids" prepared by Darwin for a French translation of his orchid book. The pamphlet is an offprint of the notes, first printed in *The Annals and Magazine of Natural History* in 1869. It is one of the treasures of the Nathalie McCulloch Research Library.

Orchids have been studied extensively by scientists since Darwin's day, but there is still much more to learn about them. A subject of ongoing investigation is the complex symbiotic relationship between orchids and mycorrhizae, a class of fungi. Orchids produce tiny, dust-like seeds that are too small to store the energy the plants require to grow on their own. Instead, these seeds receive the essential nutrients for germination from fungi that live in their developing roots. In return for providing the energy boost that orchids need to grow in their earliest stage of life, the fungi get a steady supply of moisture and food in the form of organic plant material. Some orchids retain their relationship with these fungi throughout their lives, although the benefits of this to both organisms are not entirely understood.

Illustration of the epiphyte house at Knypersley Hall in Staffordshire, England, from James Bateman's *The Orchidaceae of Mexico and Guatemala*, 1837–1843

EPIPHYTES

Epiphytes, or air plants, live on other plants without doing them harm. Most epiphytes have evolved to live in trees, high above the ground. Life in the trees gives them certain advantages. It provides them with greater access to sunlight, which is more plentiful in the branches of trees than on the shady forest floor. A higher perch keeps epiphytes out of the reach of most hungry herbivores in search of a snack. It also enables those epiphytes that produce tiny, wind-blown or bird-dispersed seeds to spread them from tree to tree.

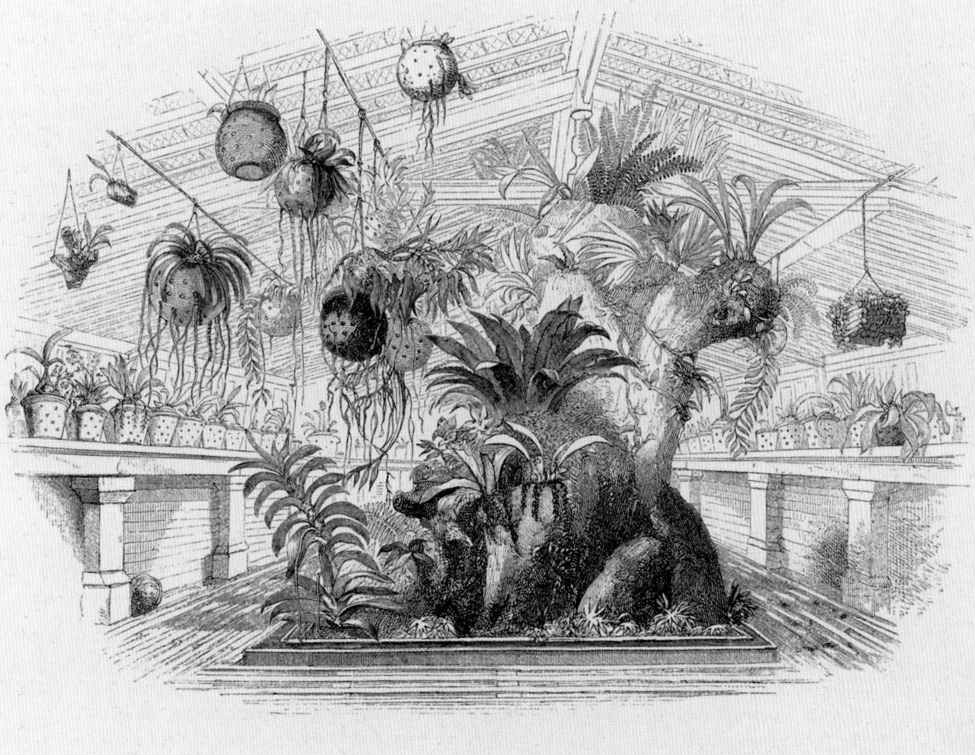

INTERIOR OF EPIPHYTE HOUSE, AT KNYPERSLEY.

Illustration of *Galeandra baueri* by Sarah Anne Drake from James Bateman's *The Orchidaceae of Mexico and Guatemala*, 1837–1843

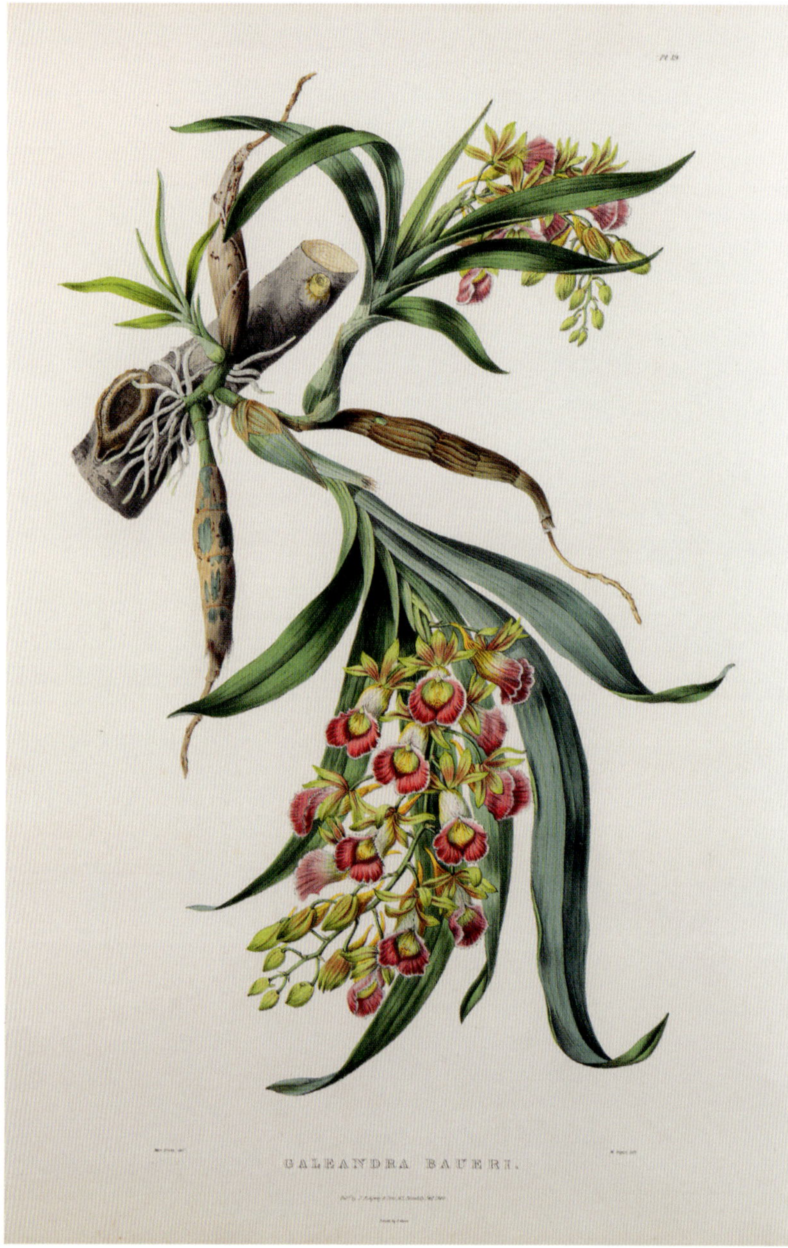

PARTS OF AN EPIPHYTIC ORCHID

Oncidium ornithorhynchum

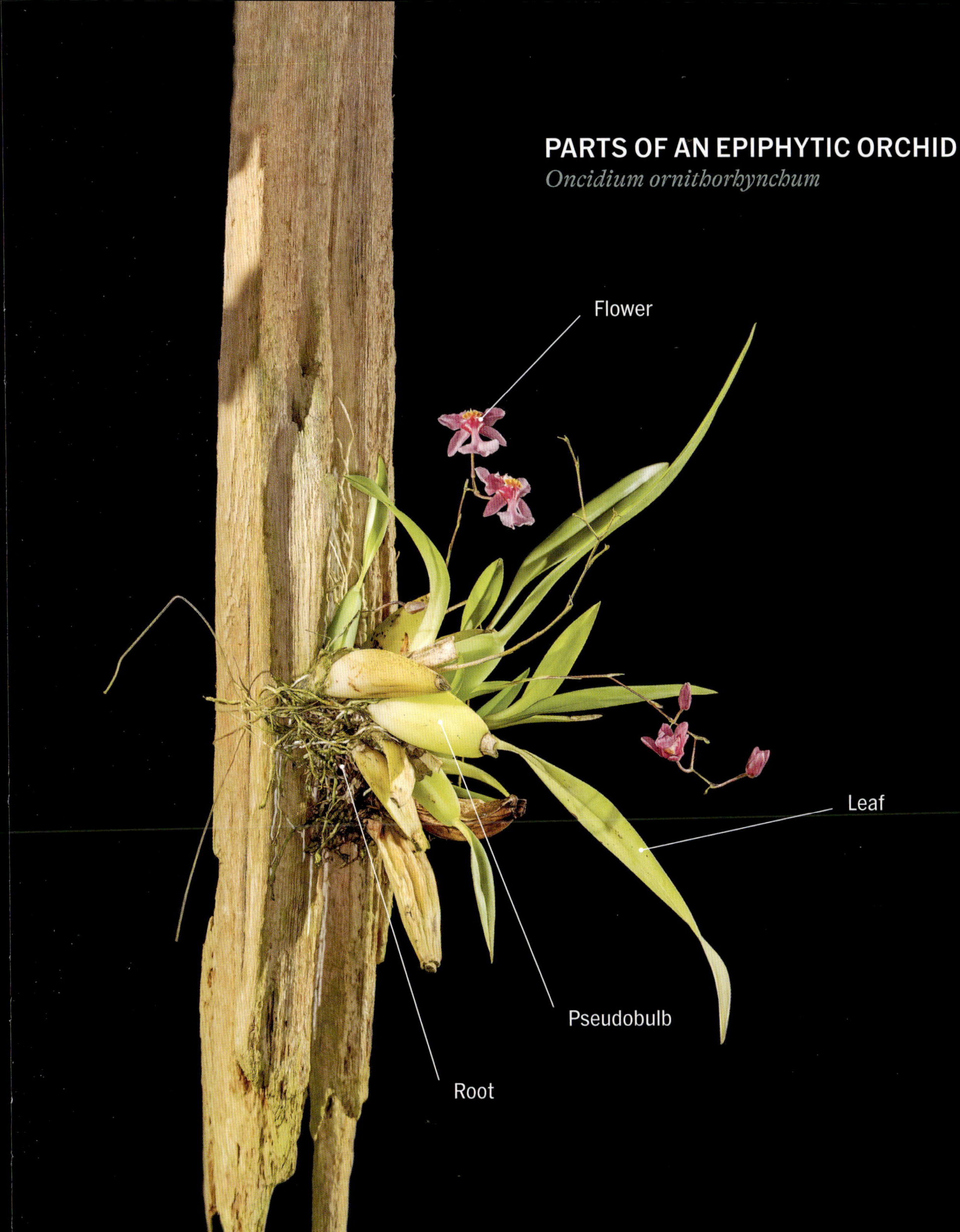

About 10% of all plant species worldwide are epiphytic. The best known of these are orchids, bromeliads, gesneriads, and ferns, but examples are present in every major family in the plant kingdom. Approximately 70% of orchids are epiphytic. Most of these are found in the tropics and subtropics, where they form a significant part of the biodiversity of these regions.

Epiphytic orchids do not have roots in the soil but have evolved other efficient ways of collecting water and nutrients. These orchids get water from rain or moisture that condenses on the surface of their hosts. They have roots with specialized tissue called velamen, which acts like a sponge to quickly absorb and retain moisture. Some epiphytic orchids can store water in thick stems, called pseudobulbs, which enable them to survive periods of drought. They draw nutrients from leaf litter, dust, and decaying organisms that fall into or near them. Certain orchids even draw nutrients from detritus accumulated by colonies of ants housed in their hollow pseudobulbs.

When tropical orchids and other epiphytes were first introduced into Europe in the nineteenth century, the concept of a plant that lives above the ground was hard to grasp, and it took growers years of trial and error to cultivate them successfully. An early misconception was that epiphytes are parasitic, drawing nutrients directly from their hosts instead of using them for physical support. Some growers mistakenly thought that because epiphytes are air plants, they could survive without water. Others misunderstood their growing conditions and potted them in soil. Thankfully, we have learned much about epiphytes over the last two centuries, so that the epiphytic orchids in Selby Gardens' living collection can be cultivated with great success.

PLATES

THE PHOTOGRAPHS THAT FOLLOW ILLUSTRATE THE BEAUTY AND DIVERSITY OF orchids from Selby Gardens' living collection and highlight the achievement of the volunteer photographers who have so successfully captured their character and complexity. The more than 90 different orchids featured here are native to various regions around the world. They range considerably in size and offer an astounding variety of colors, patterns, shapes, and forms. In presenting these exceptional orchids, we hope to promote appreciation of and respect for the incredible plants with which we are privileged to share the planet.

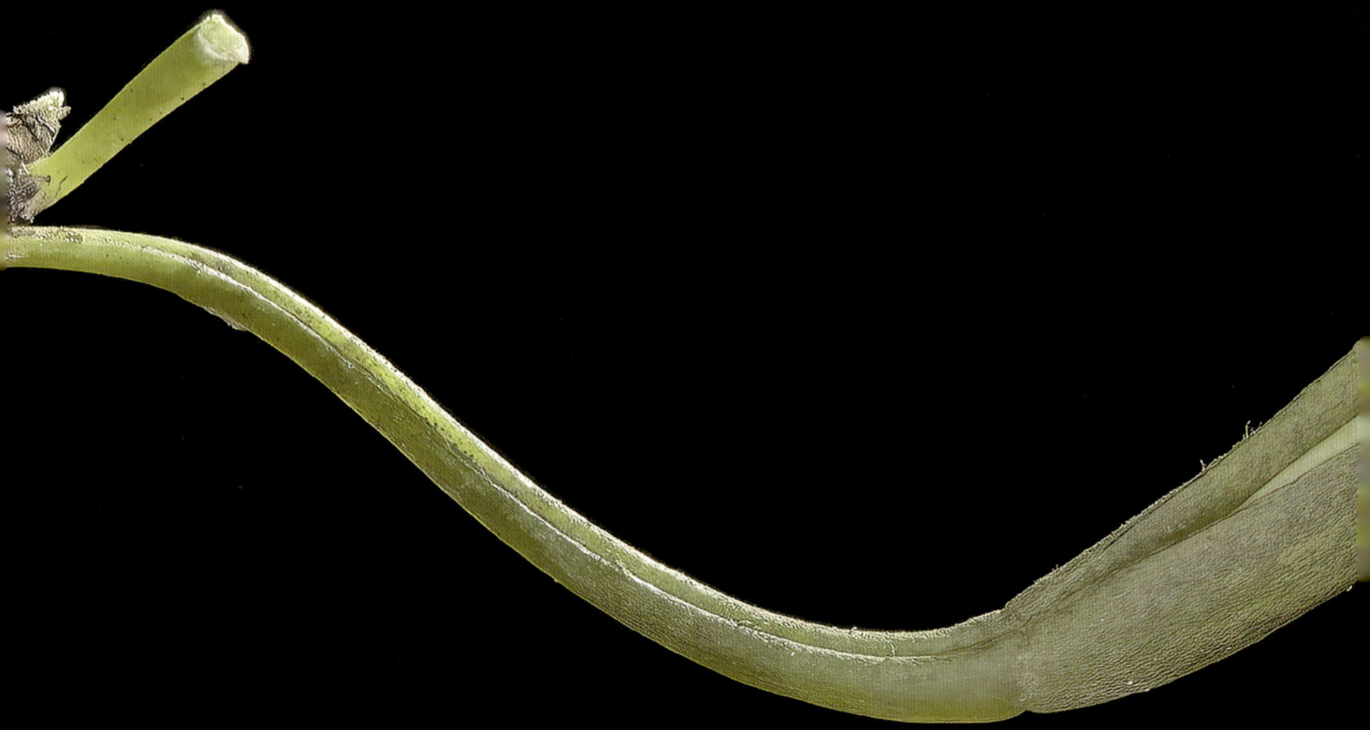

Acianthera sp.

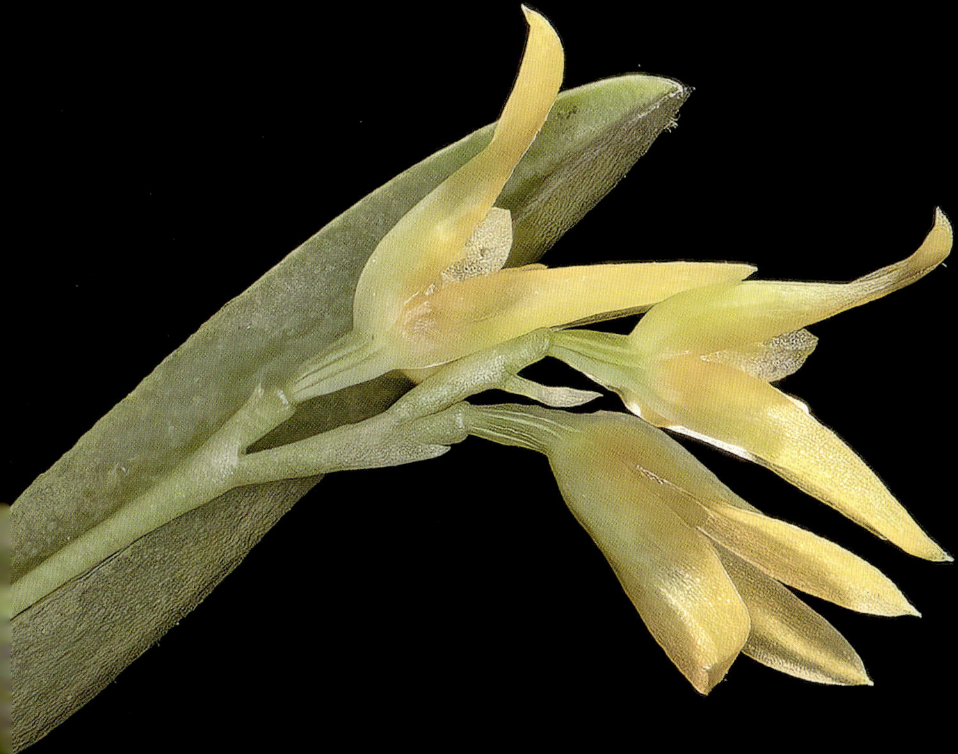

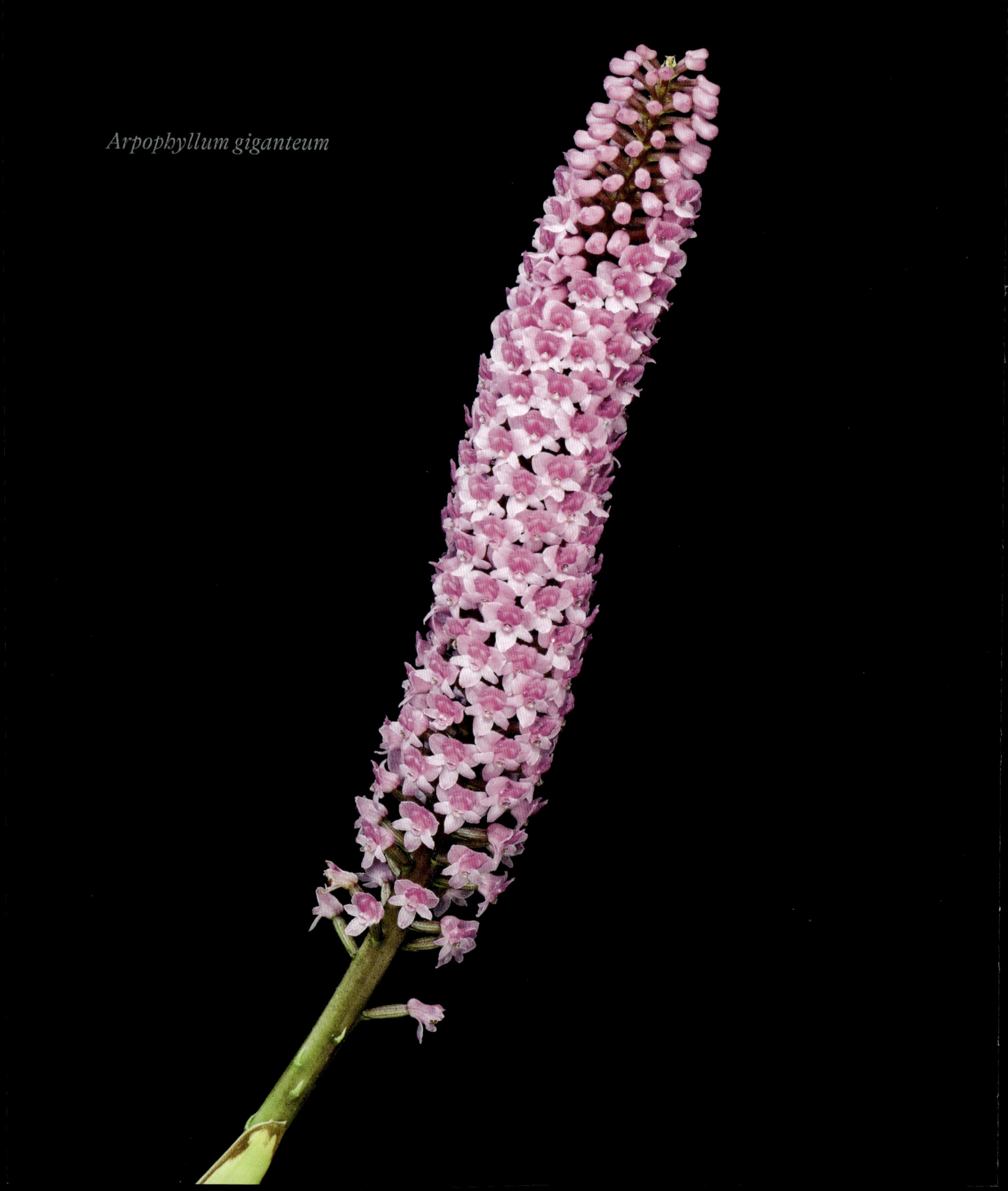

Arpophyllum giganteum

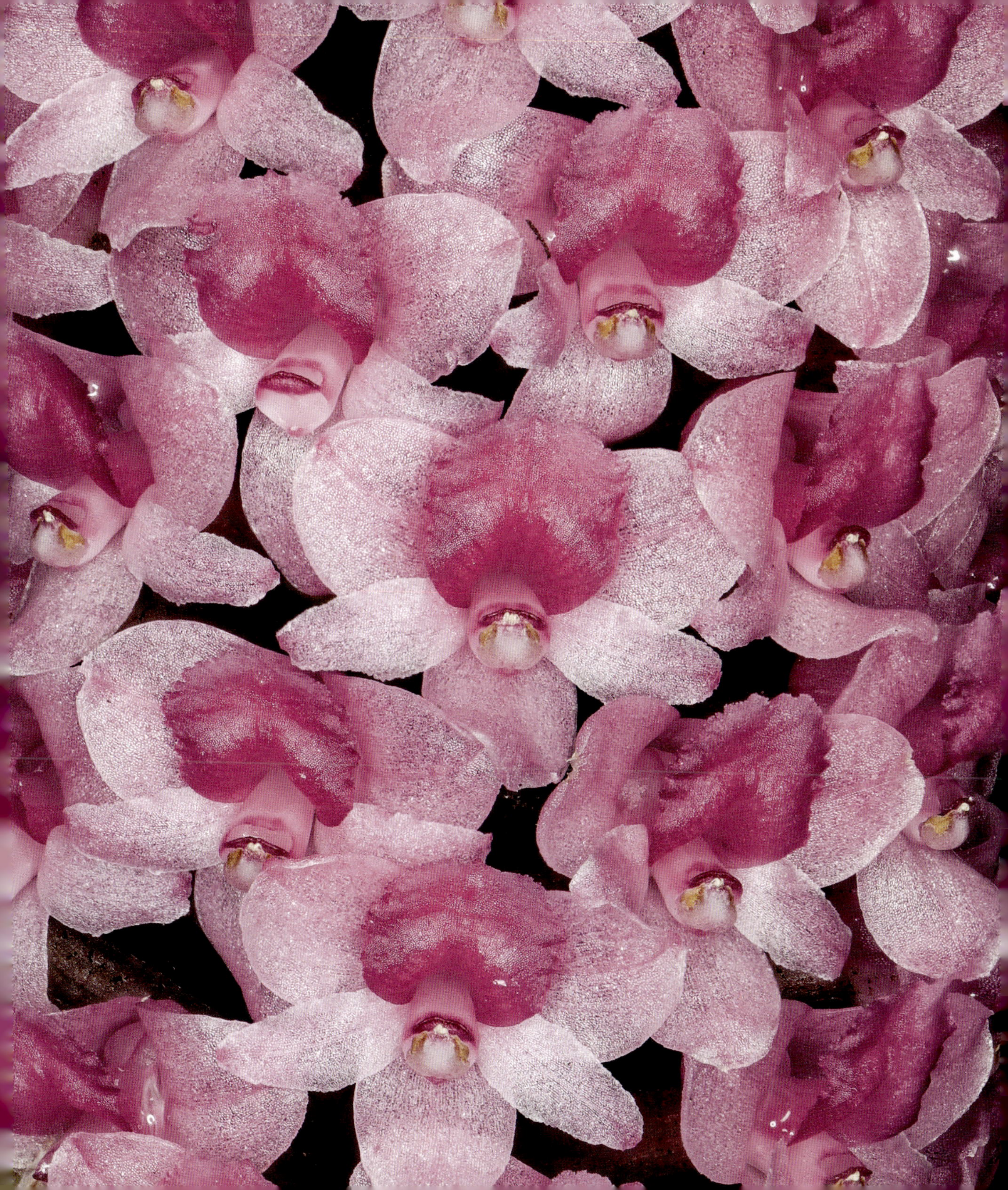

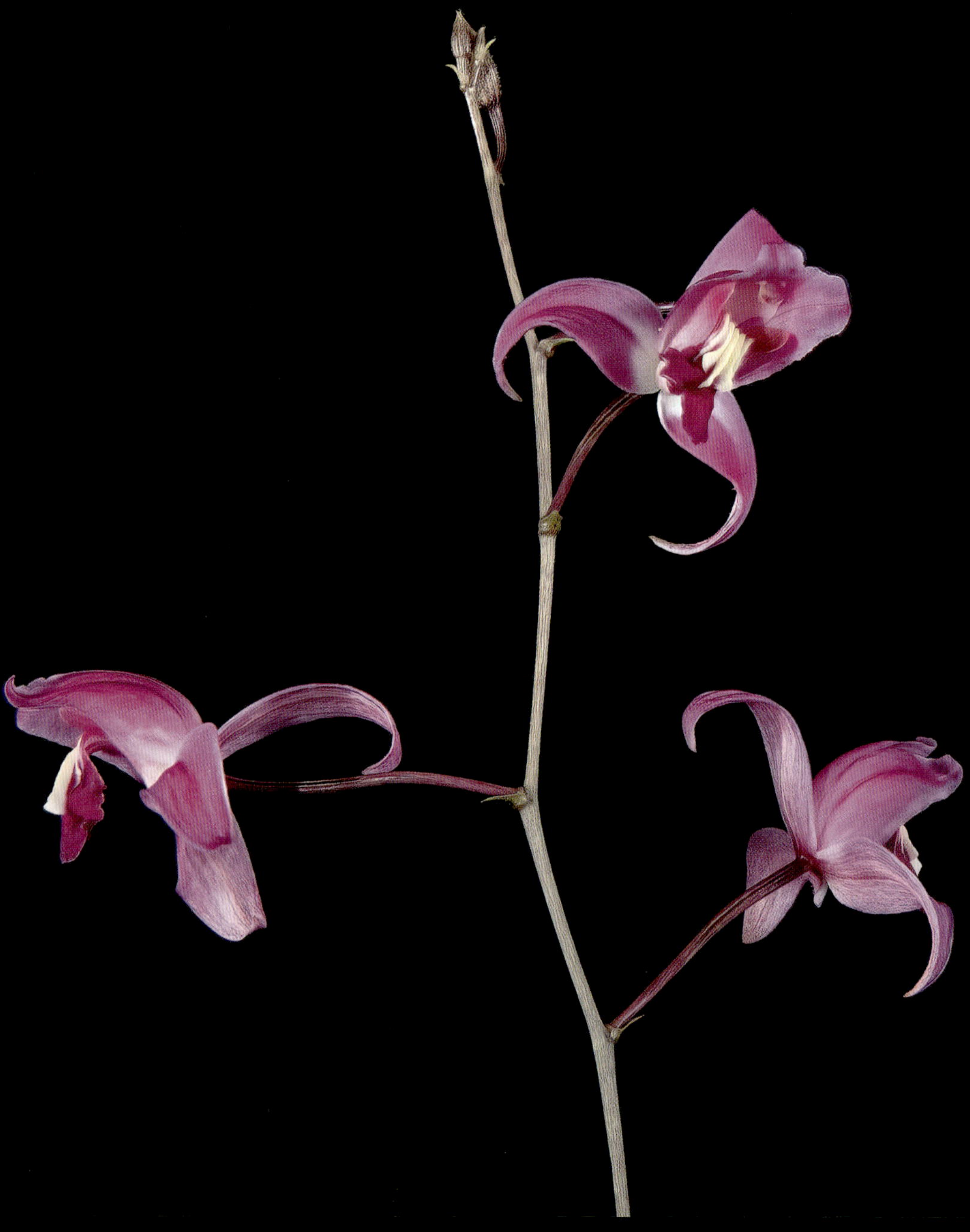

Bletia riparia

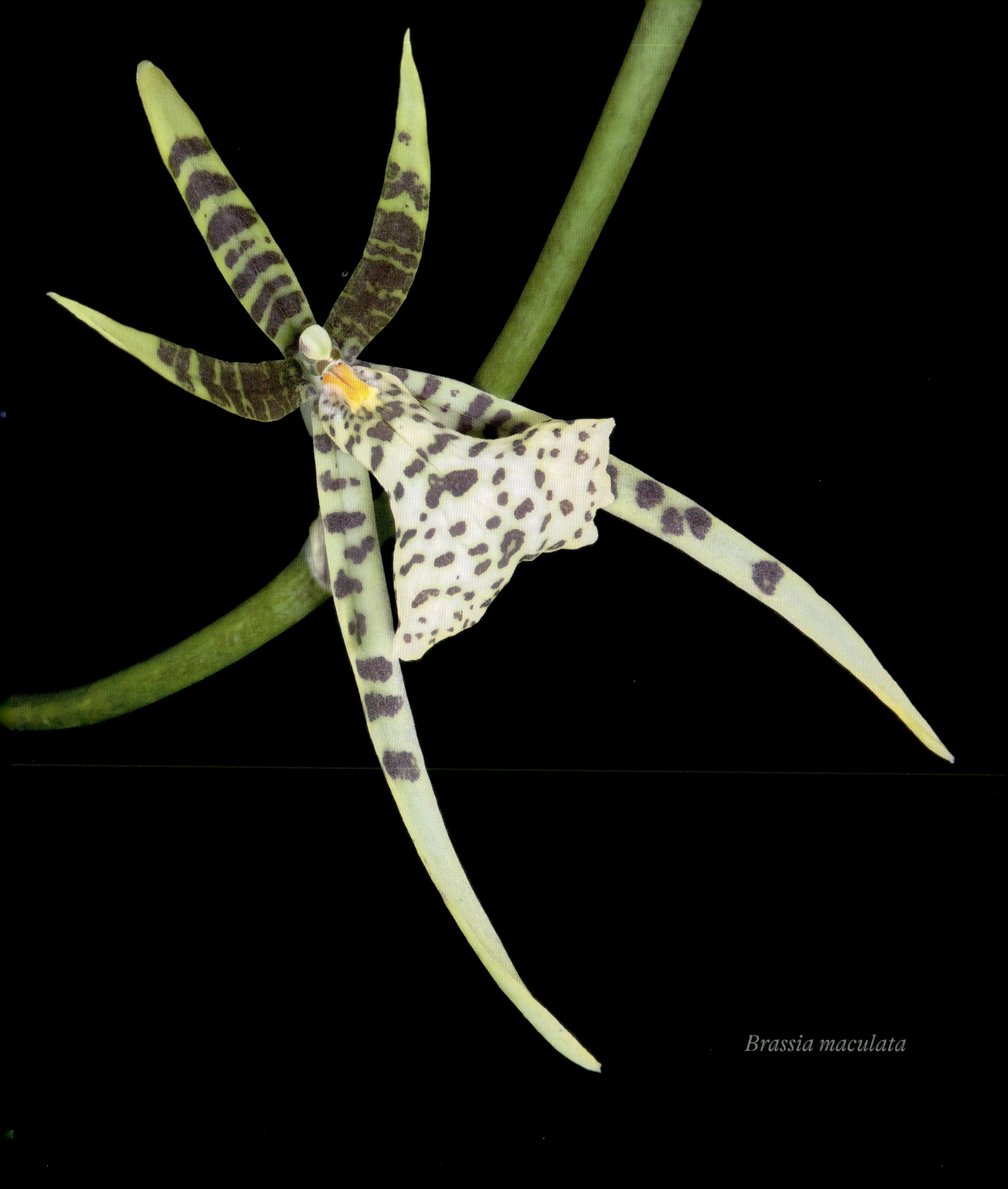

Brassia maculata

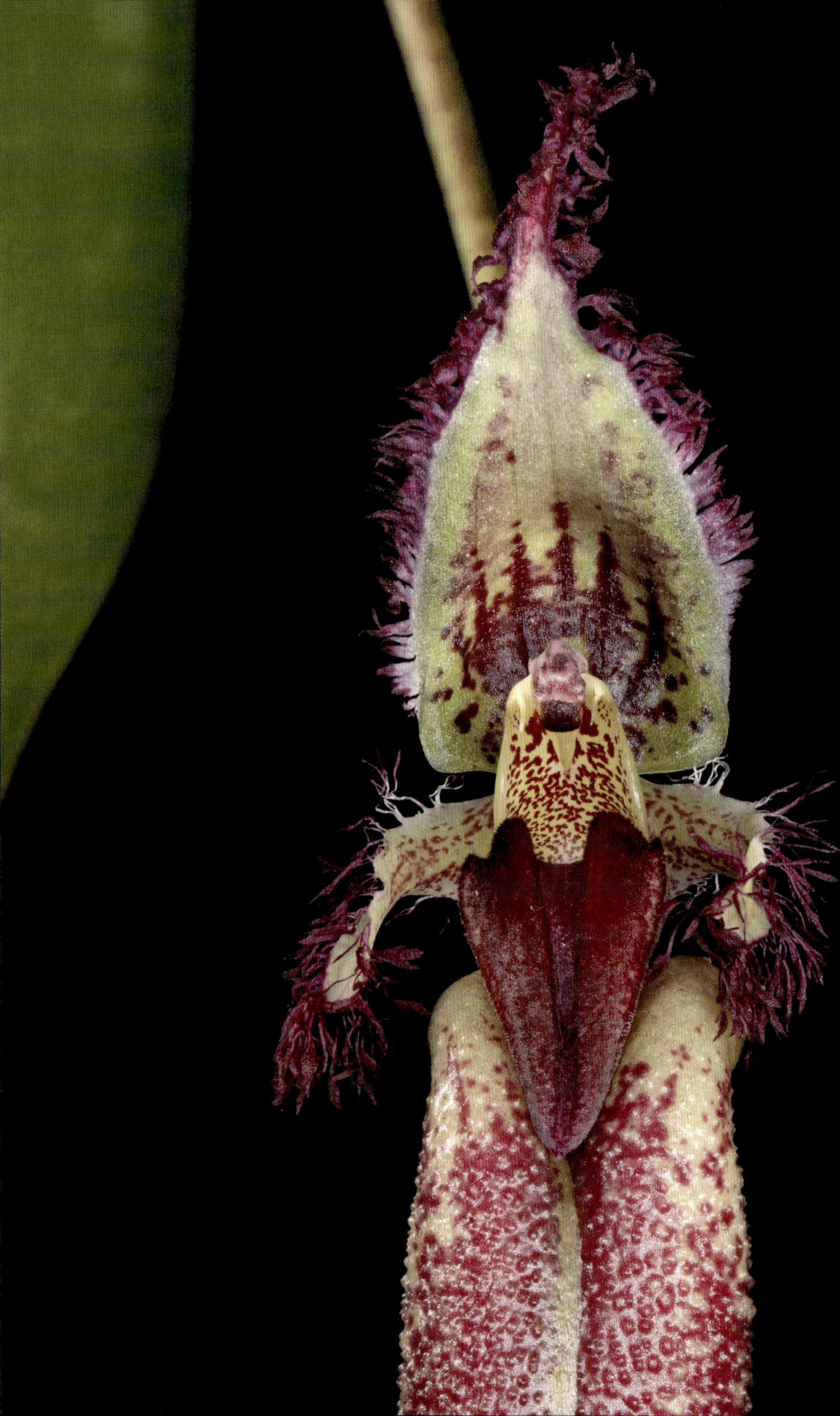

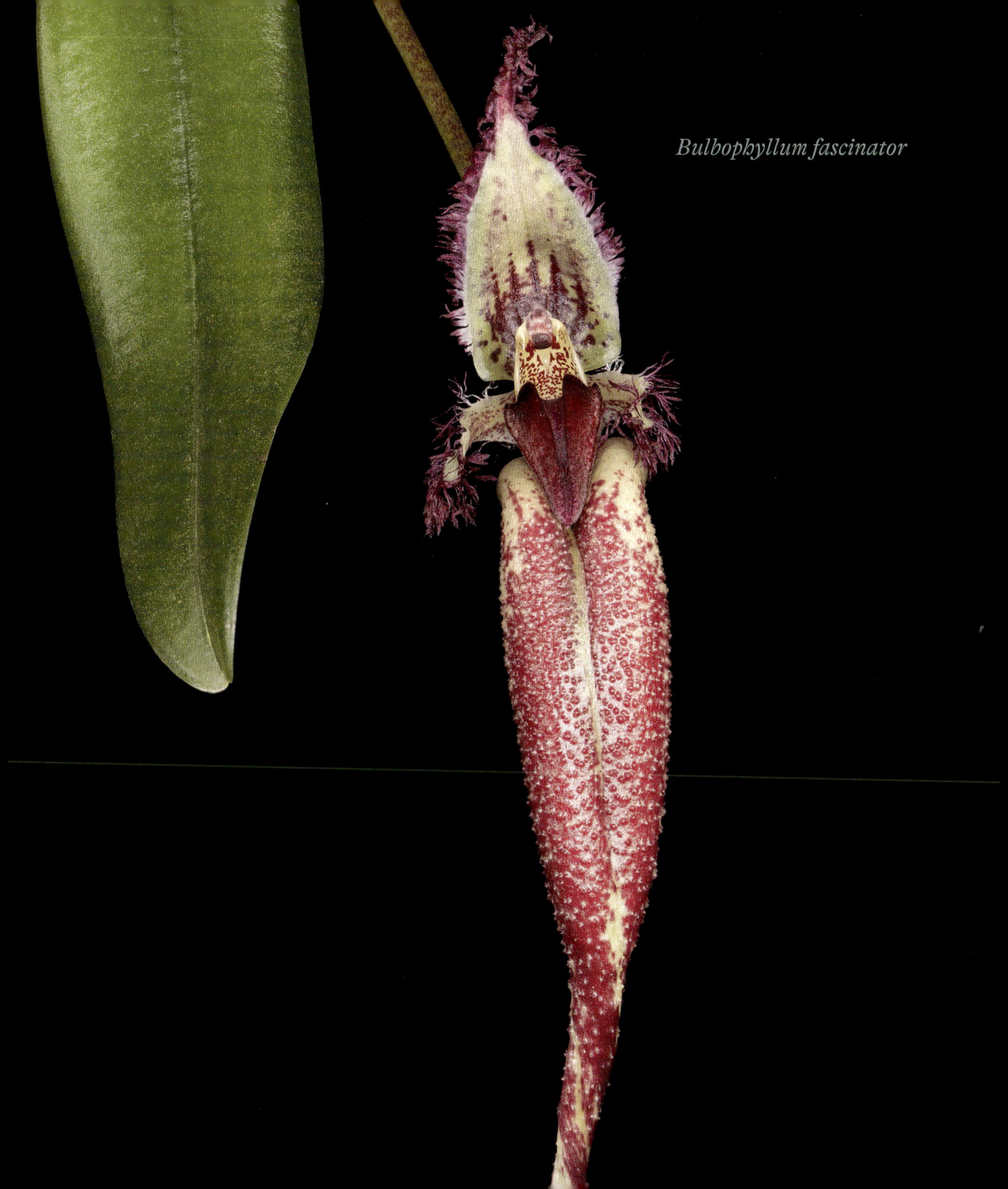

Bulbophyllum fascinator

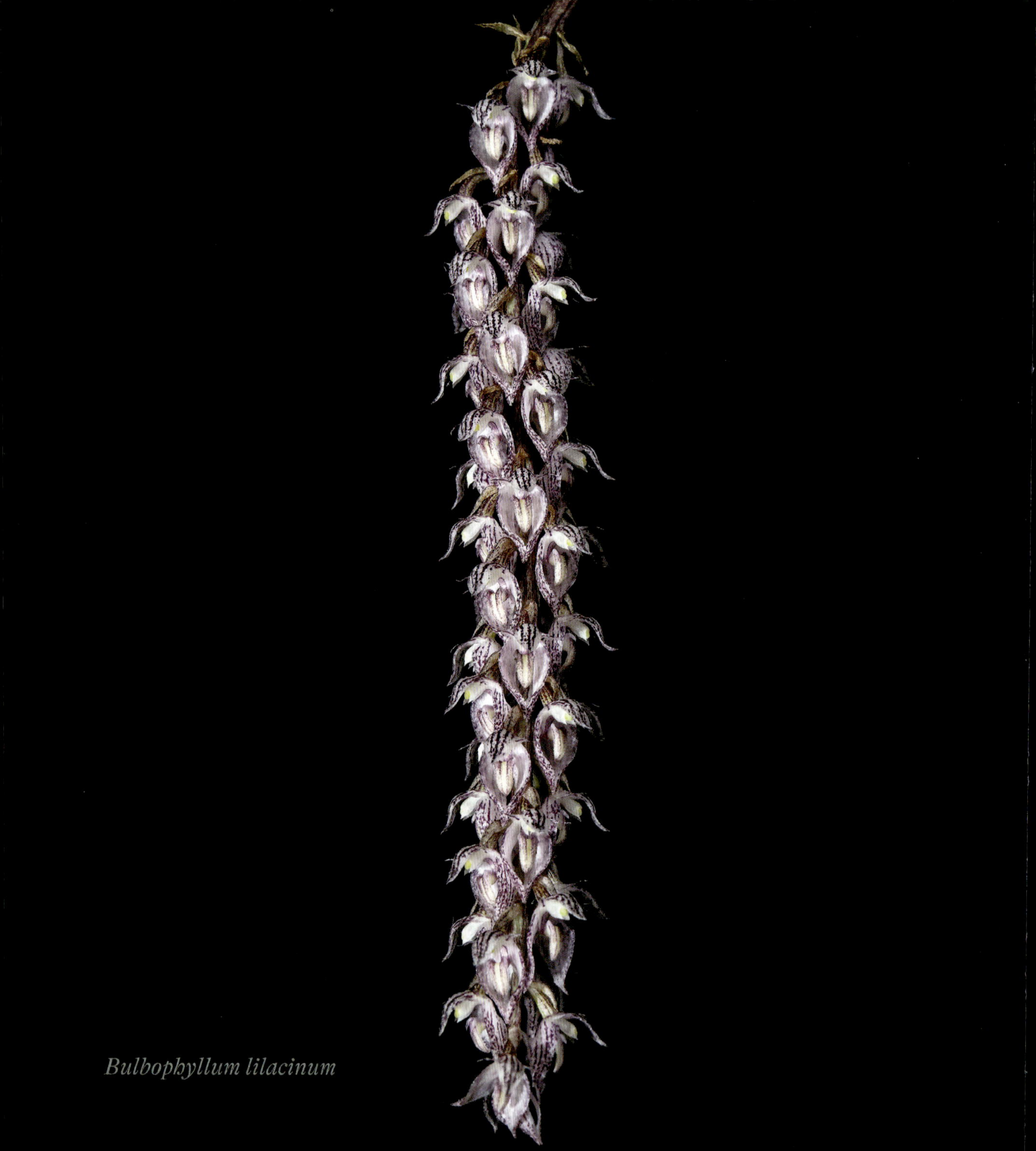

Bulbophyllum lilacinum

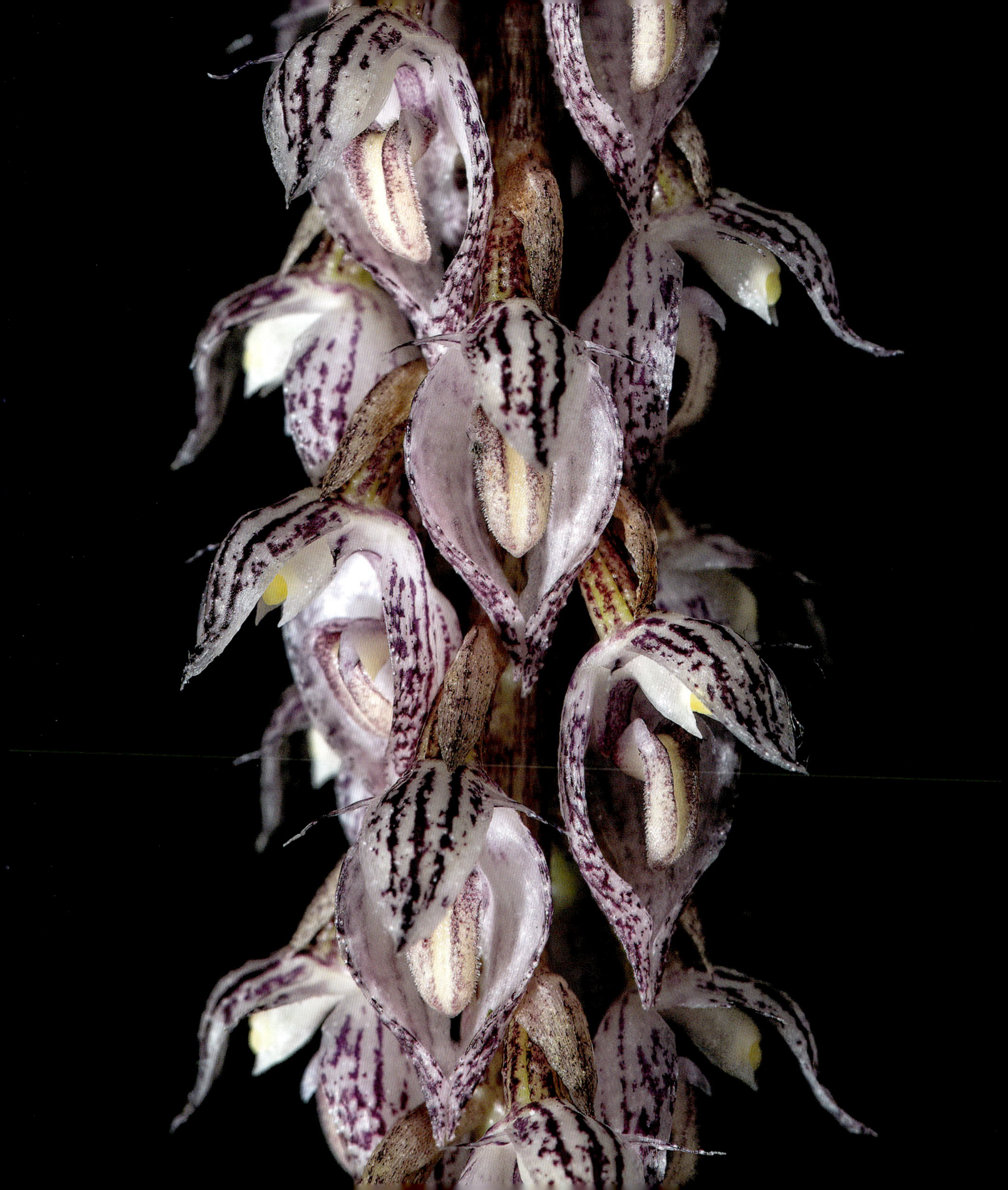

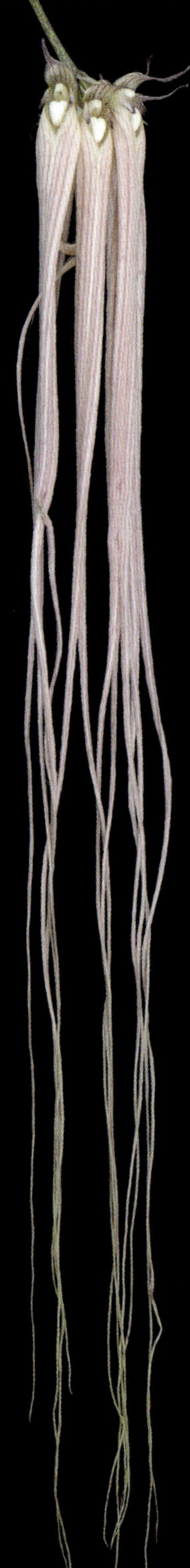

Bulbophyllum longissimum

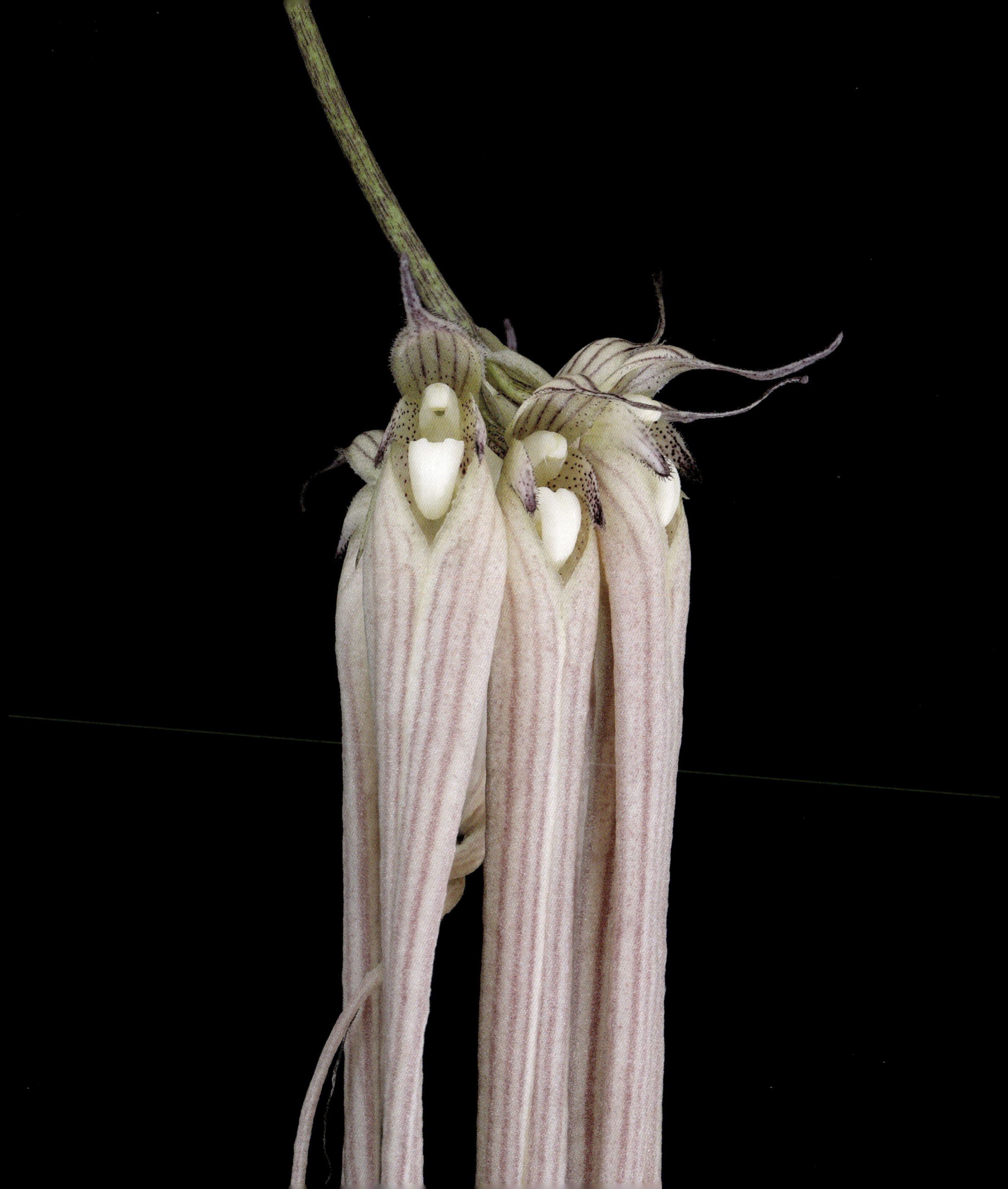

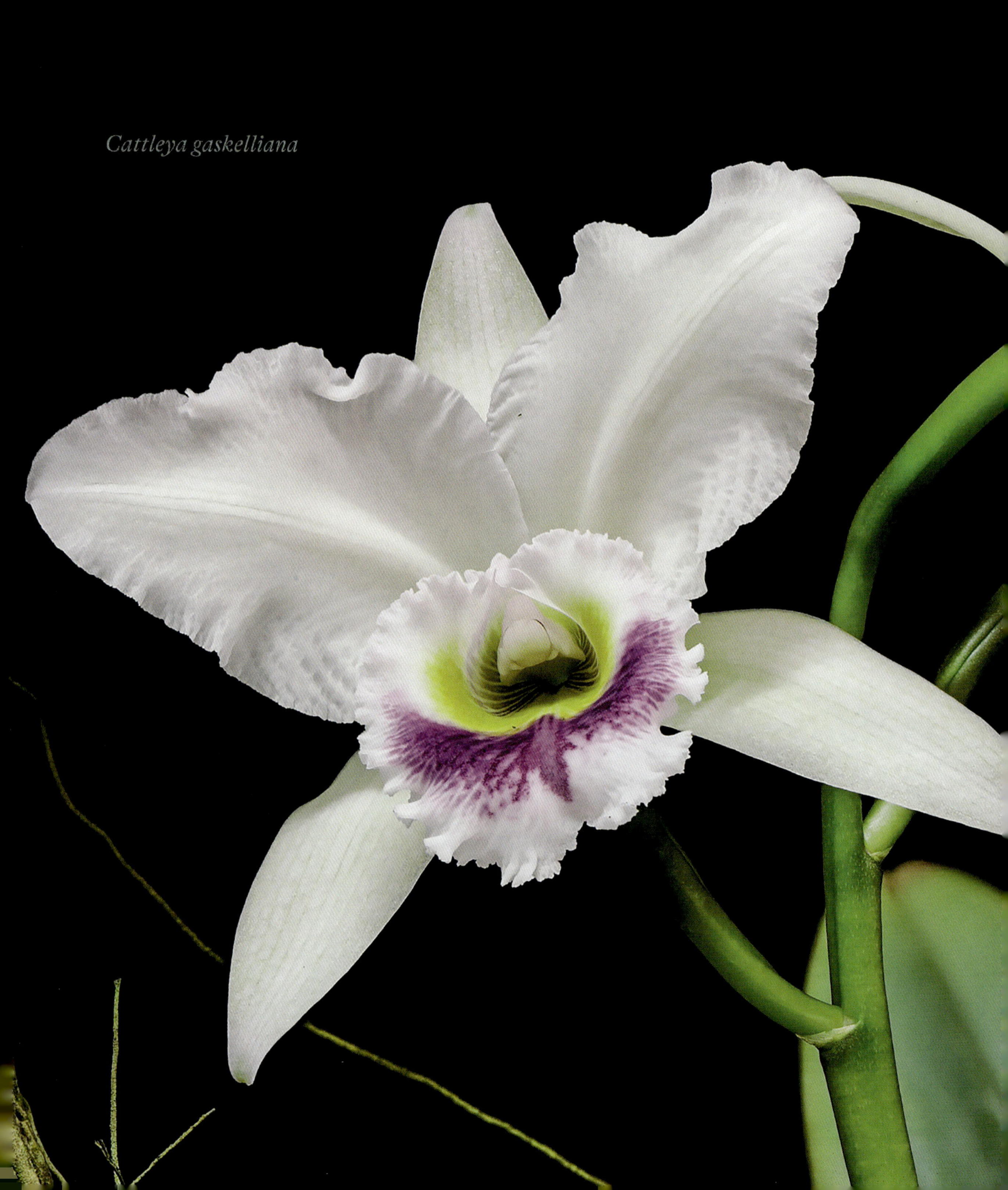

Cattleya gaskelliana

Cattleya lawrenceana

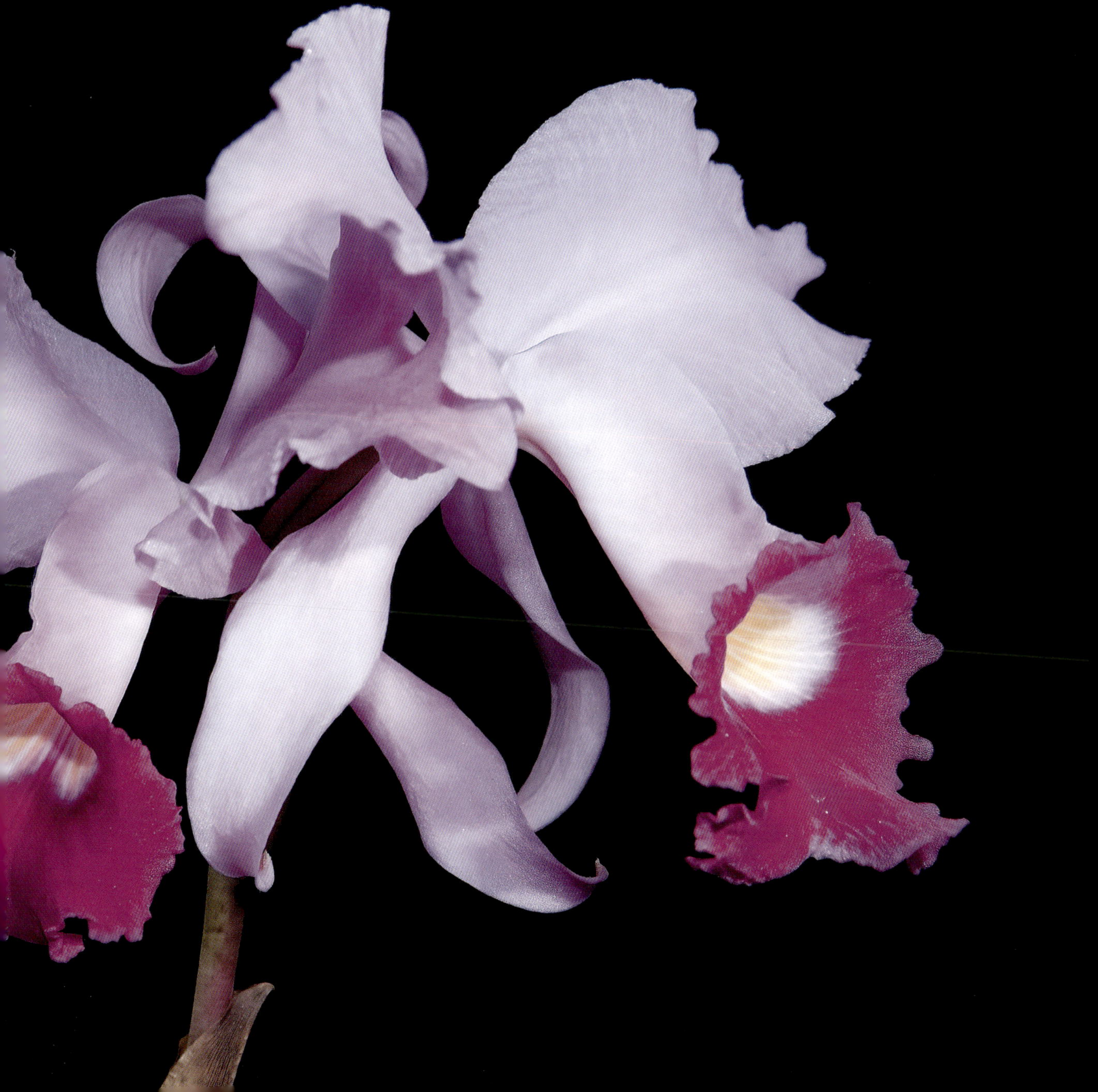

Ceratostylis retisquama

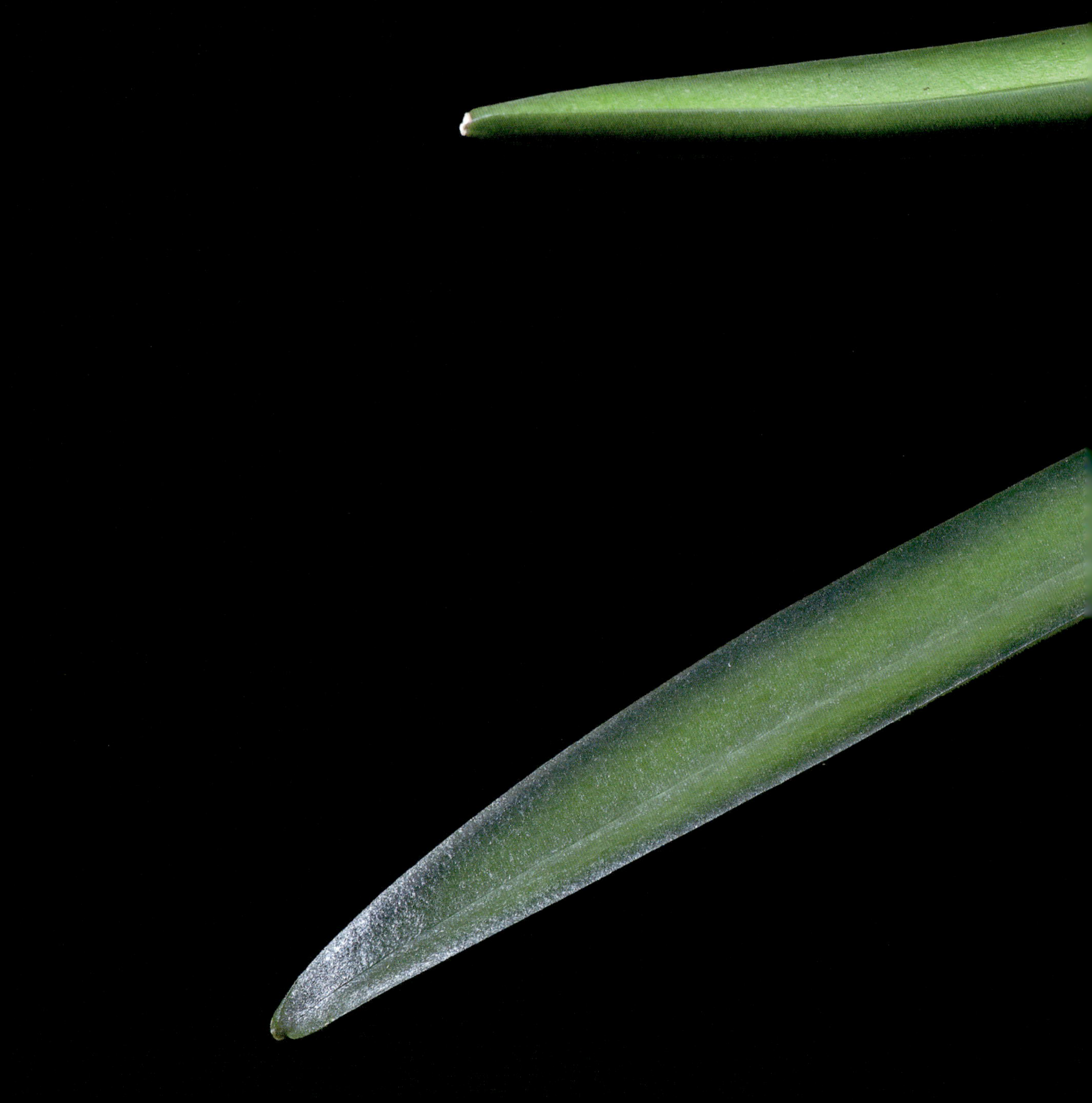

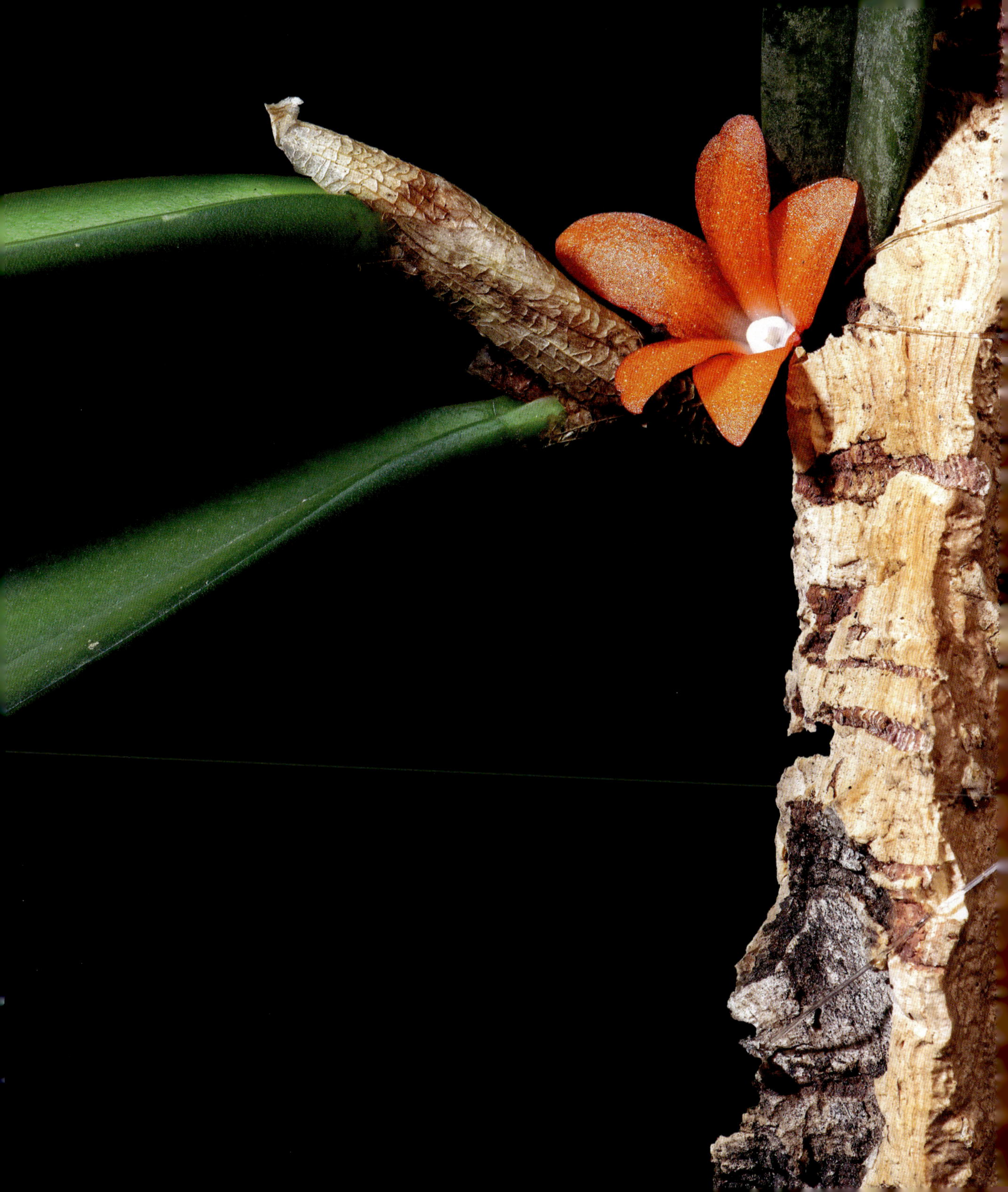

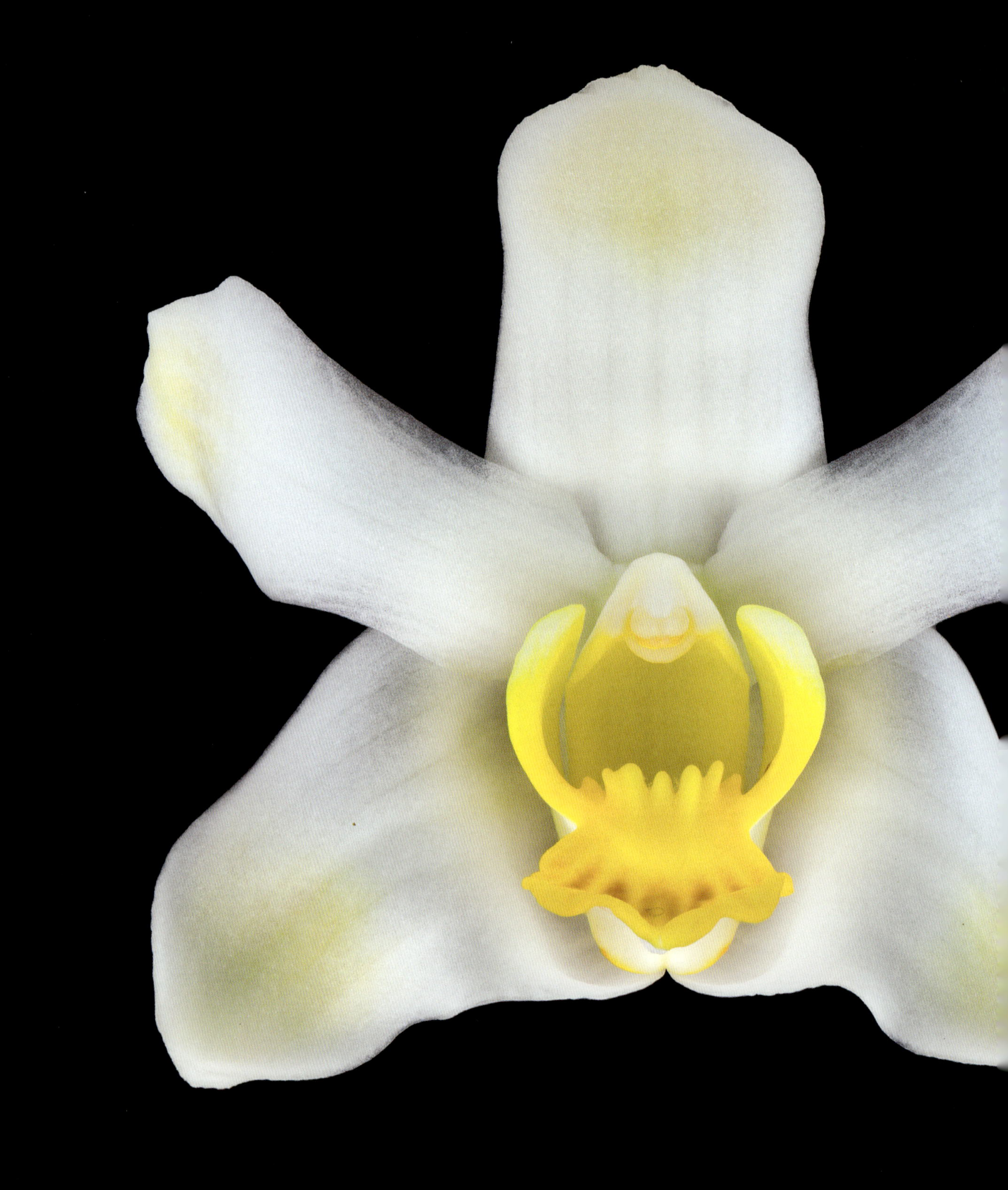

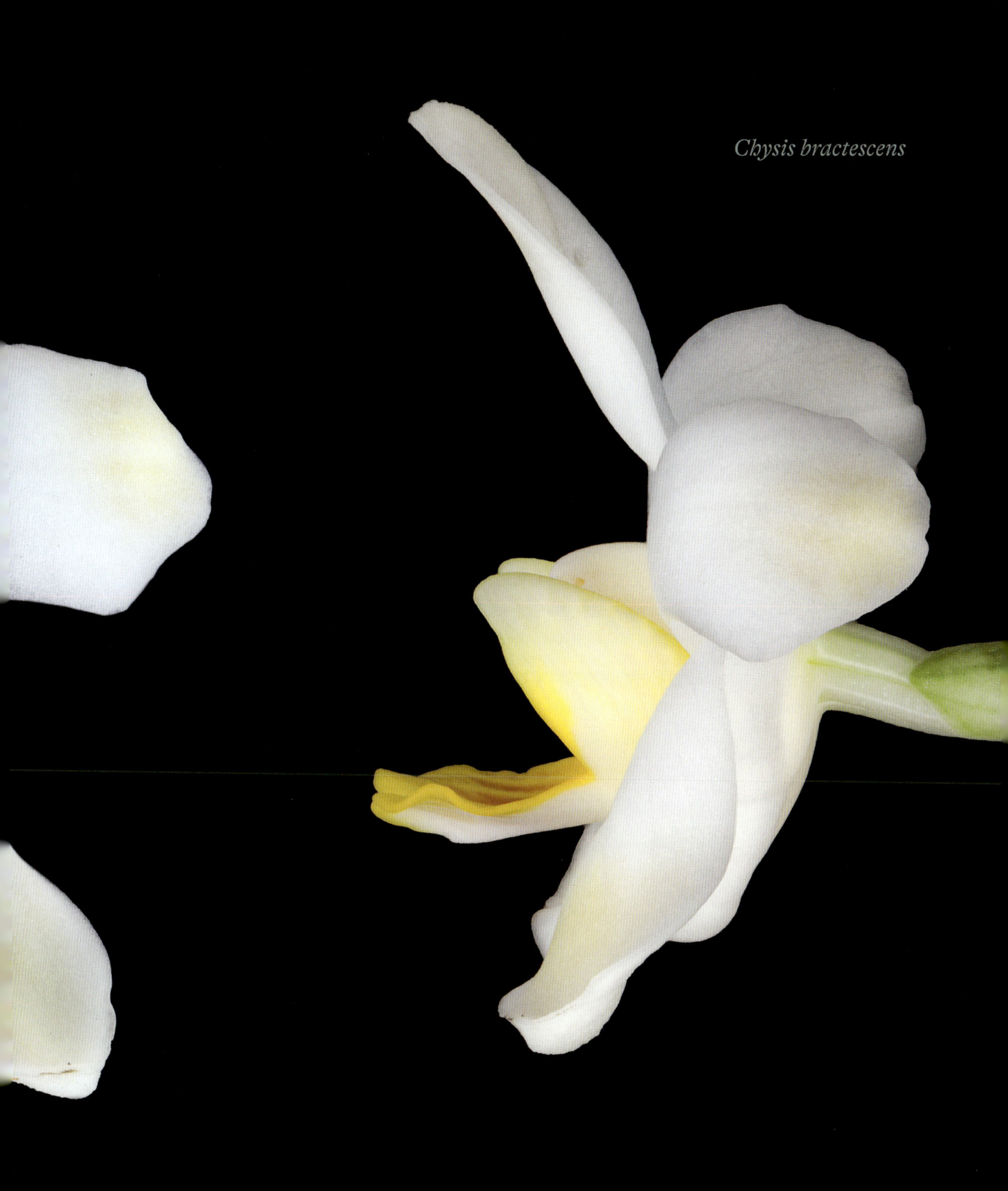

Chysis bractescens

Coelogyne pandurata

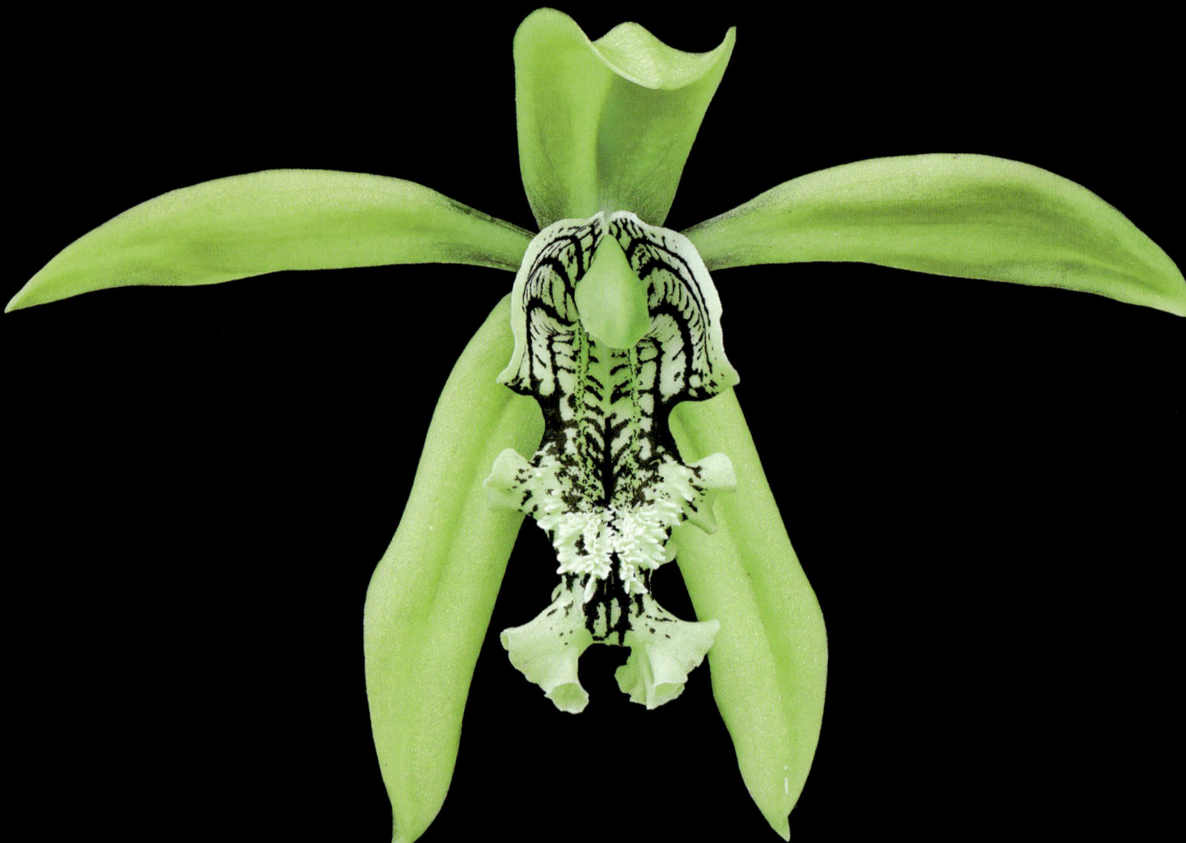

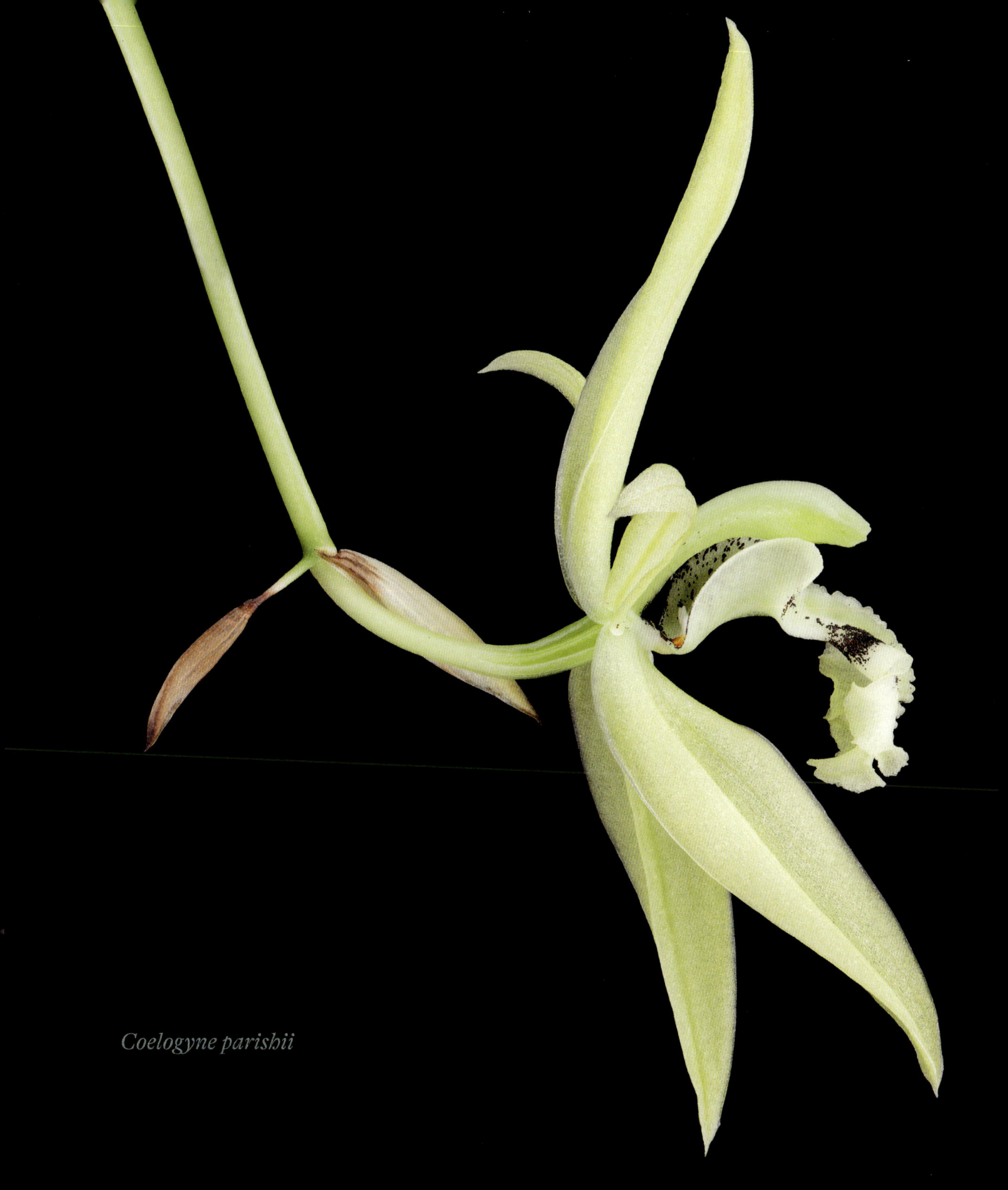

Coelogyne parishii

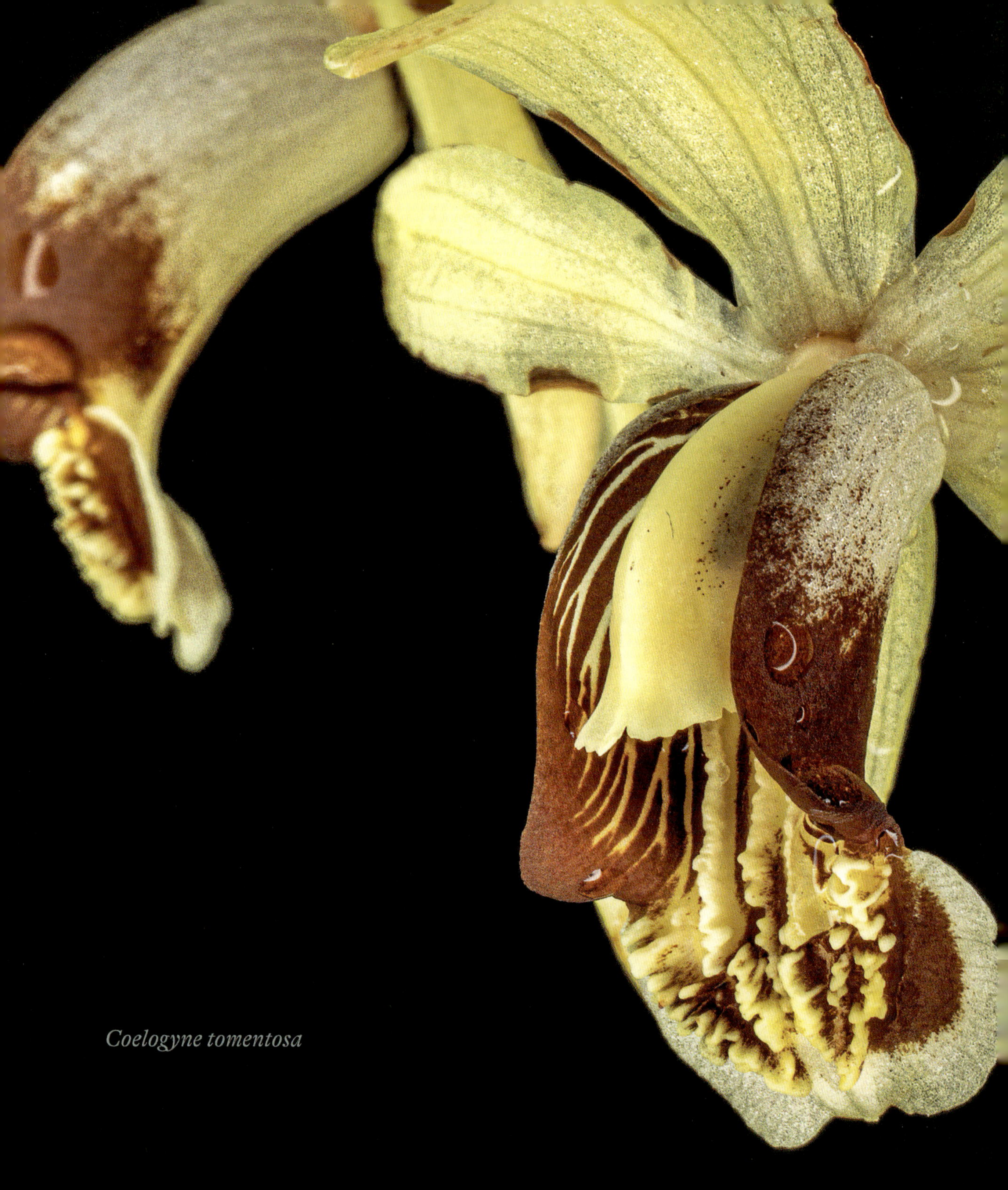

Coelogyne tomentosa

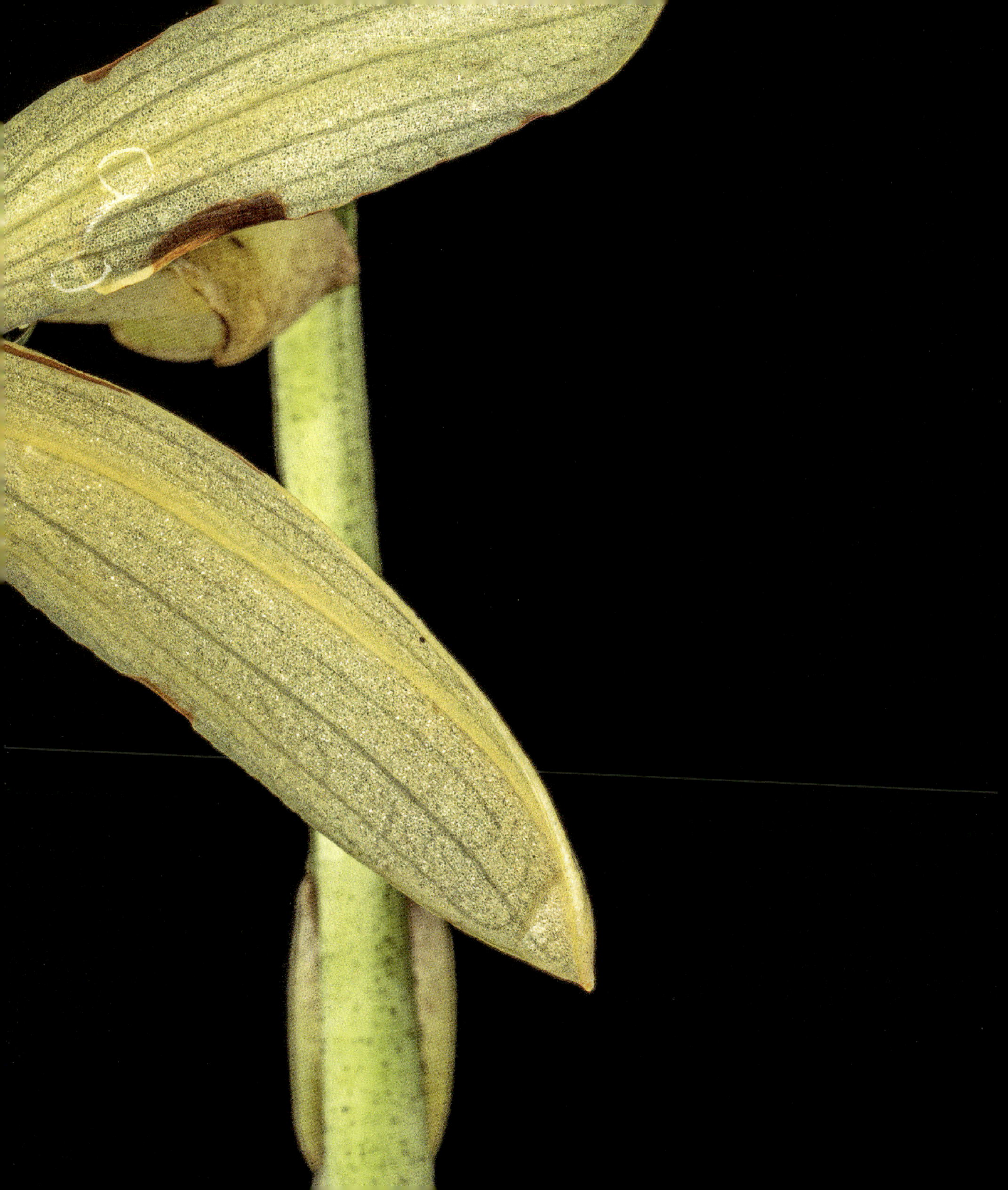

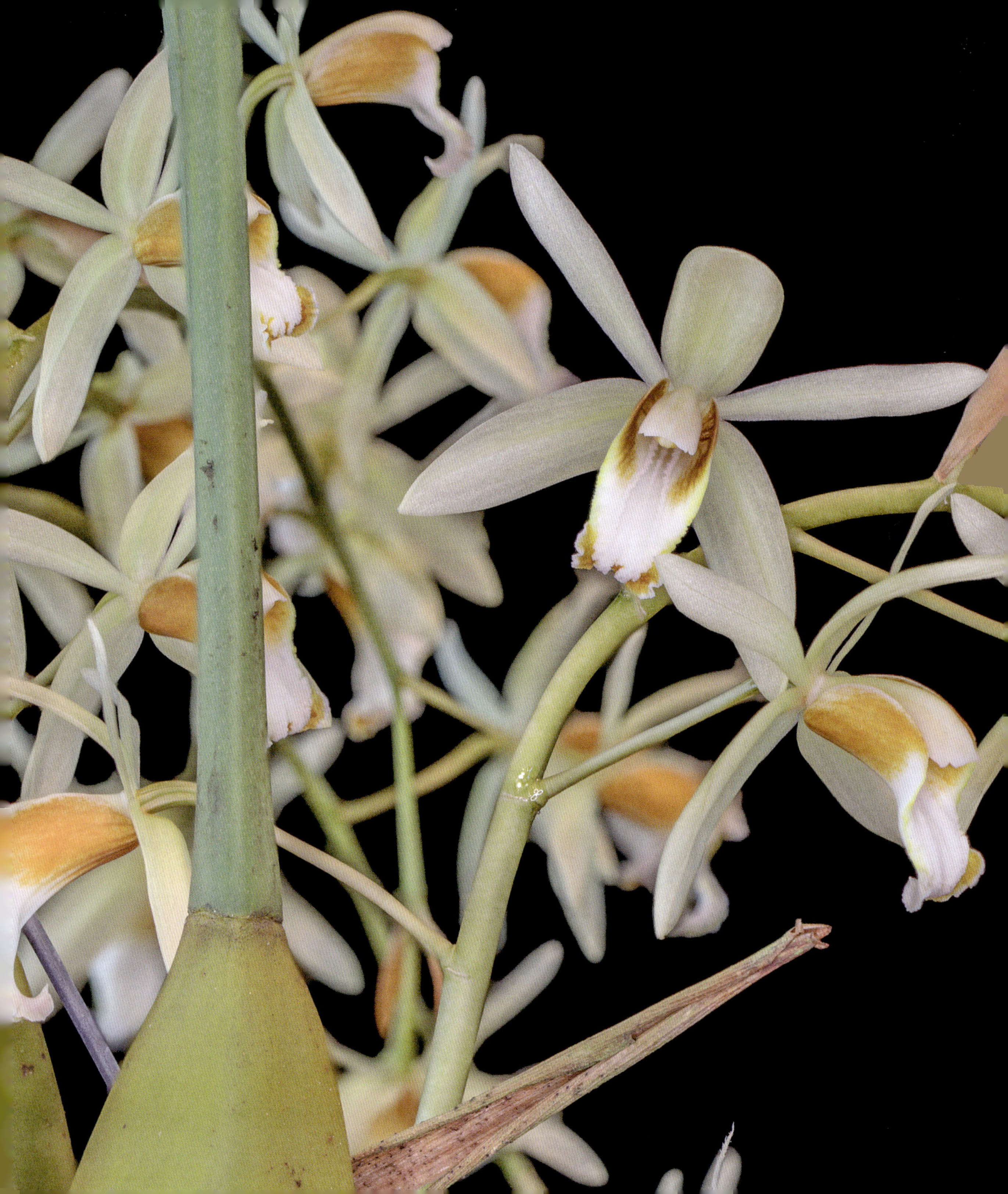

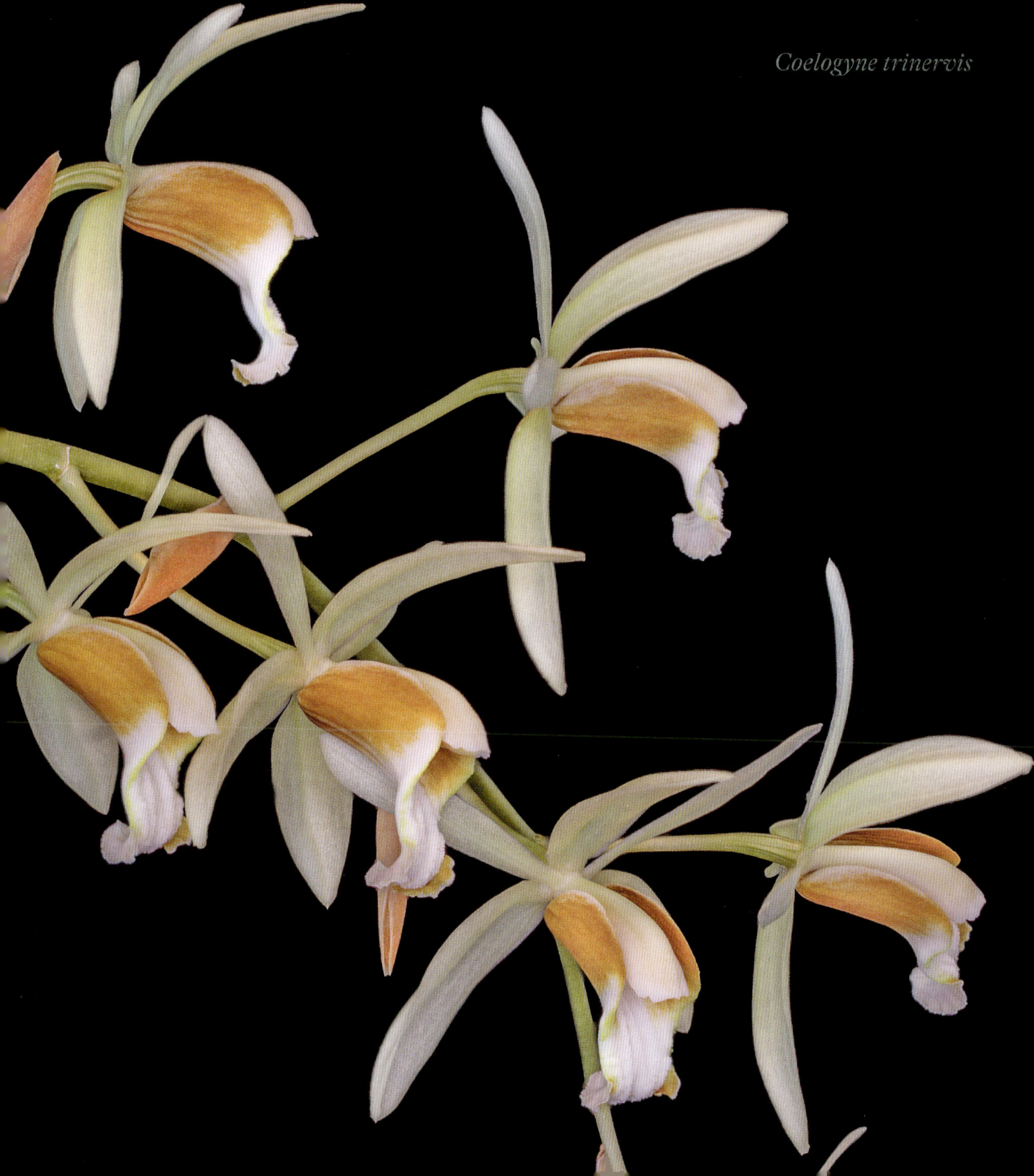

Coelogyne trinervis

Coryanthes macrantha

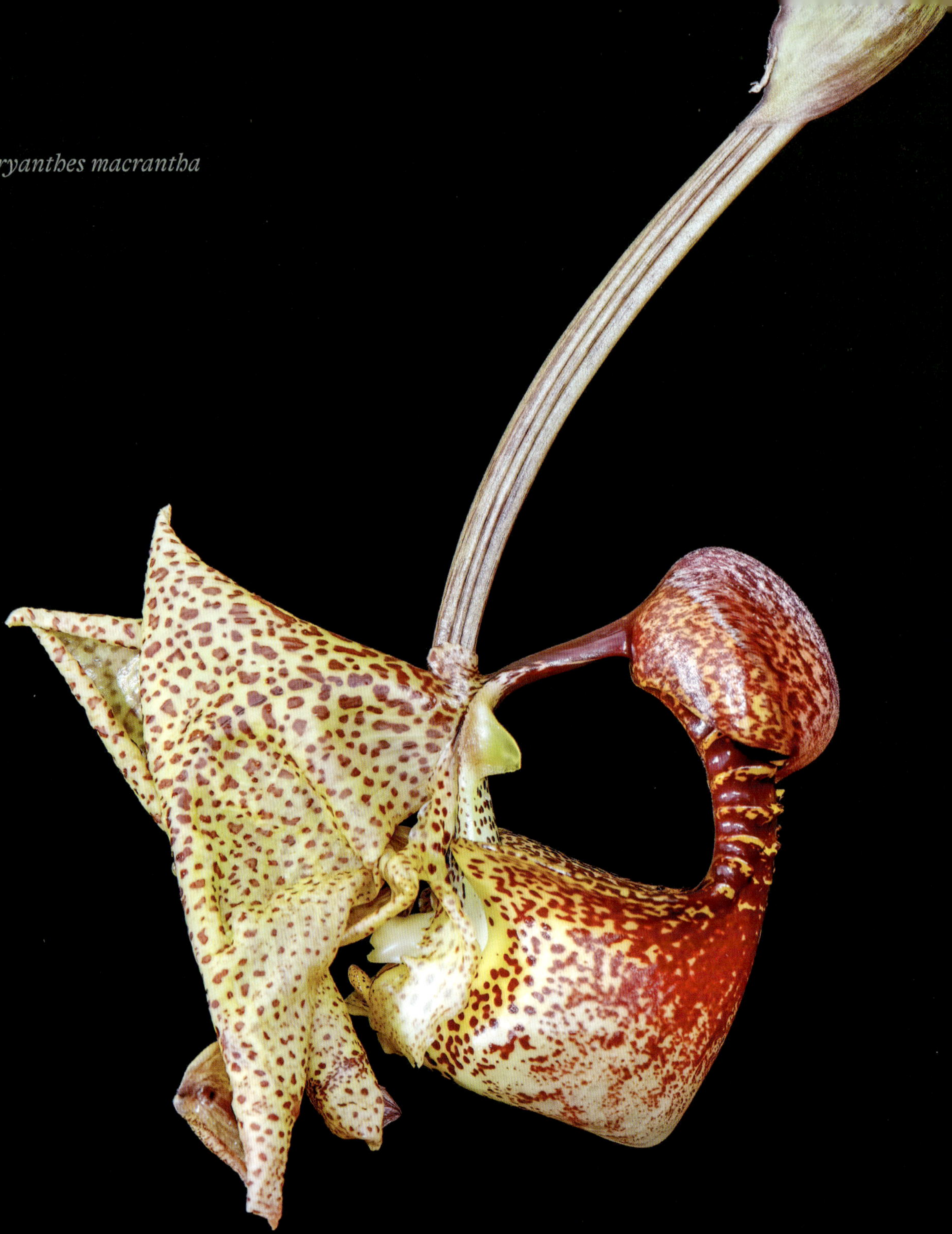

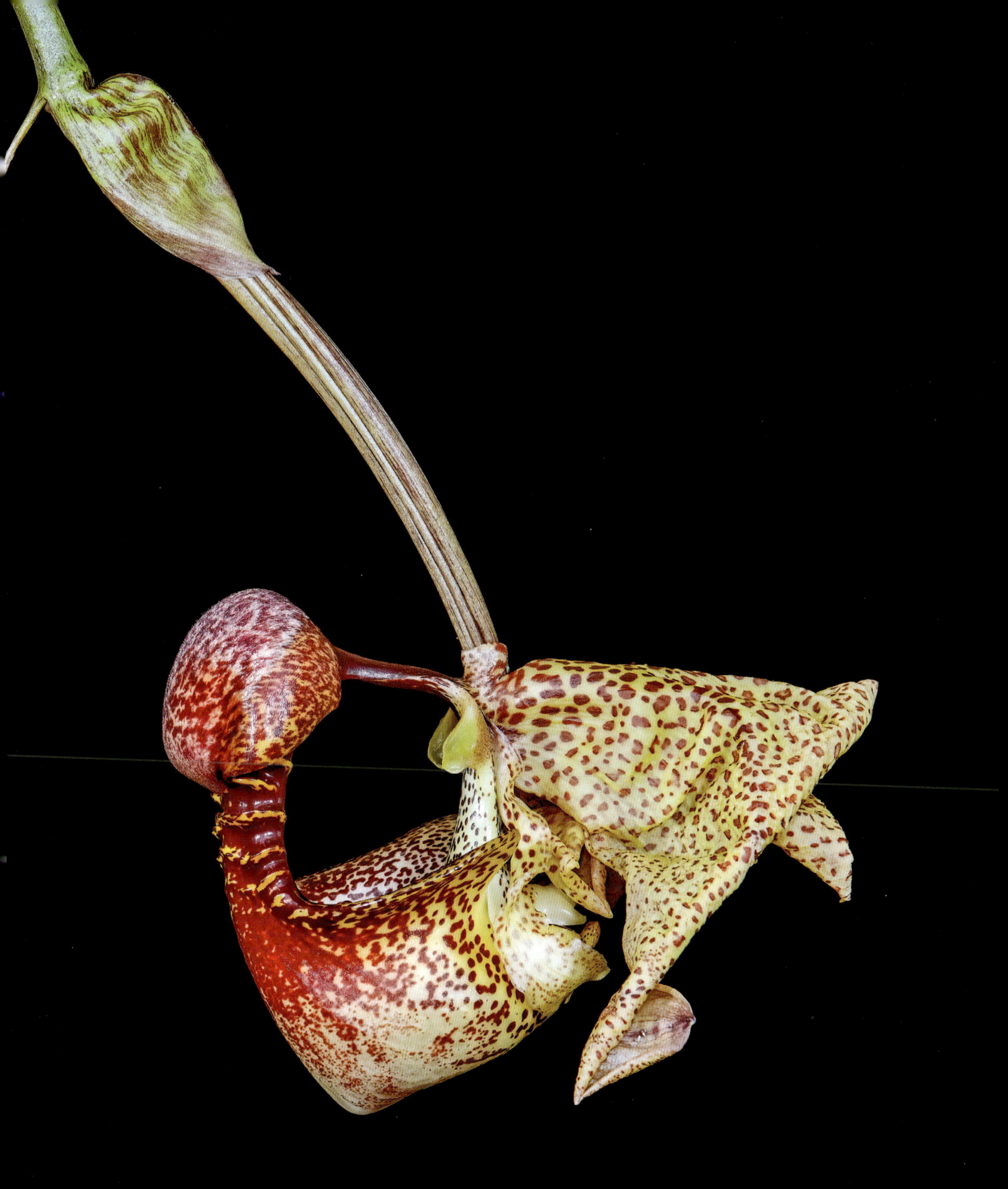

Coryanthes picturata

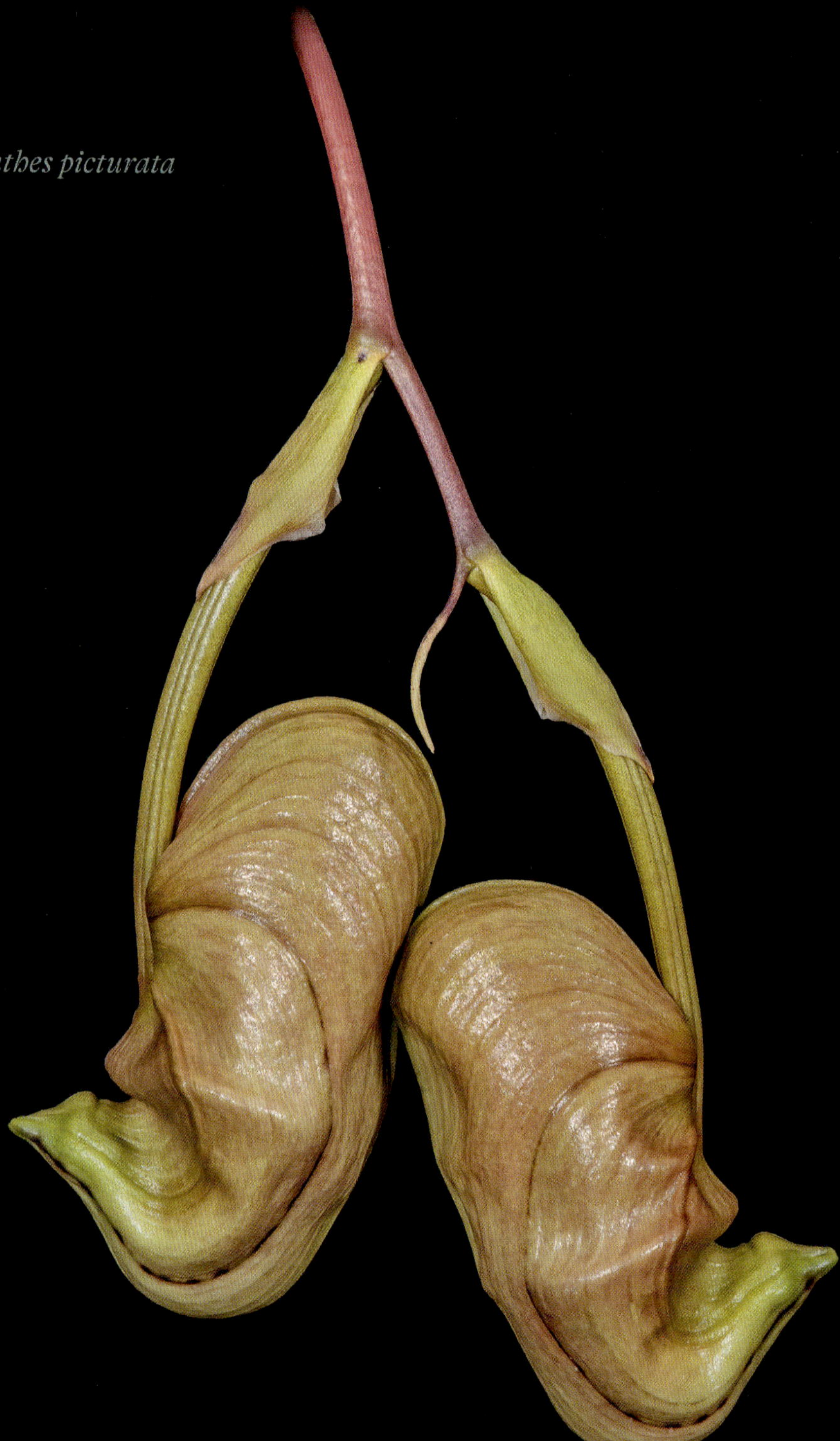

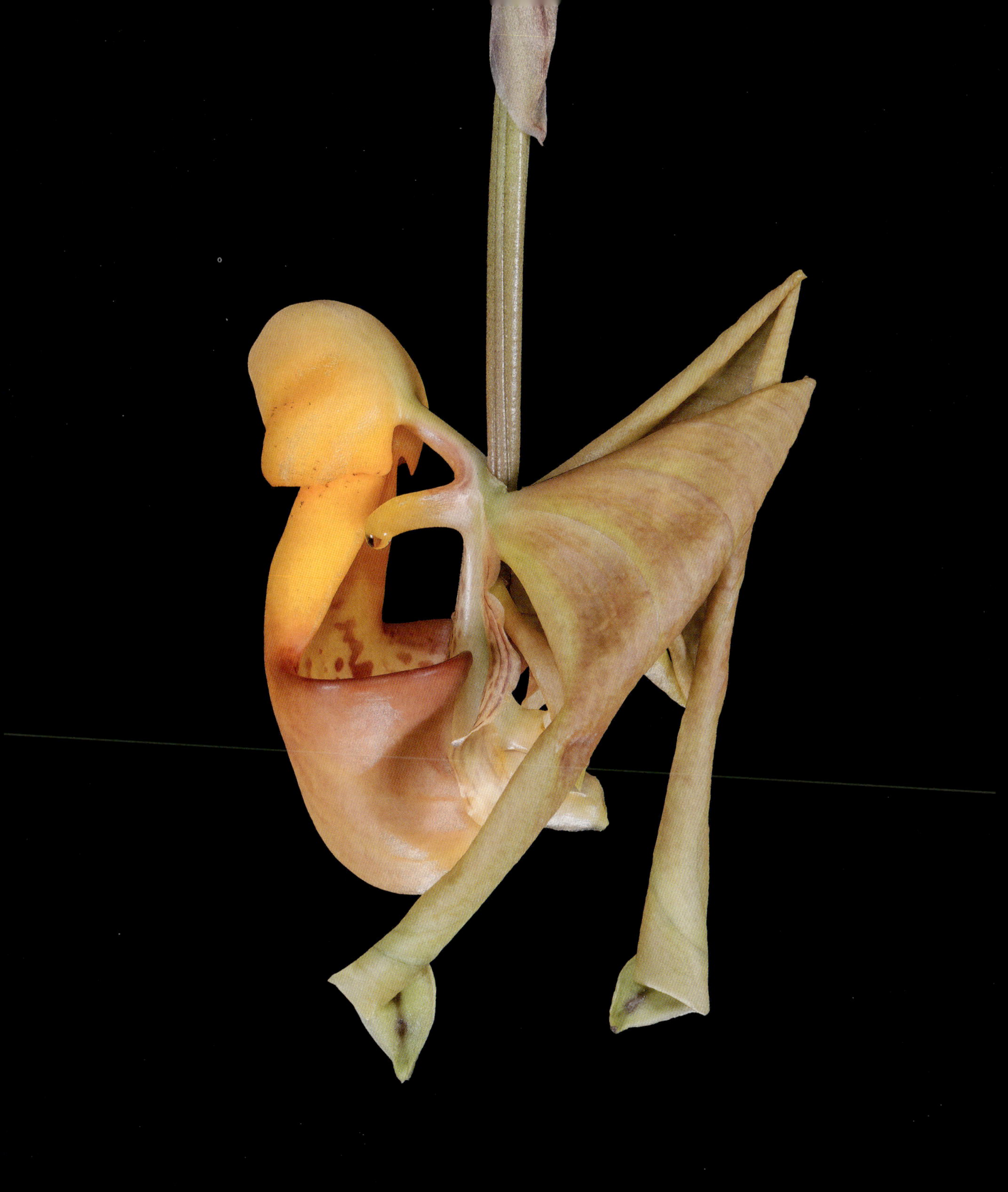

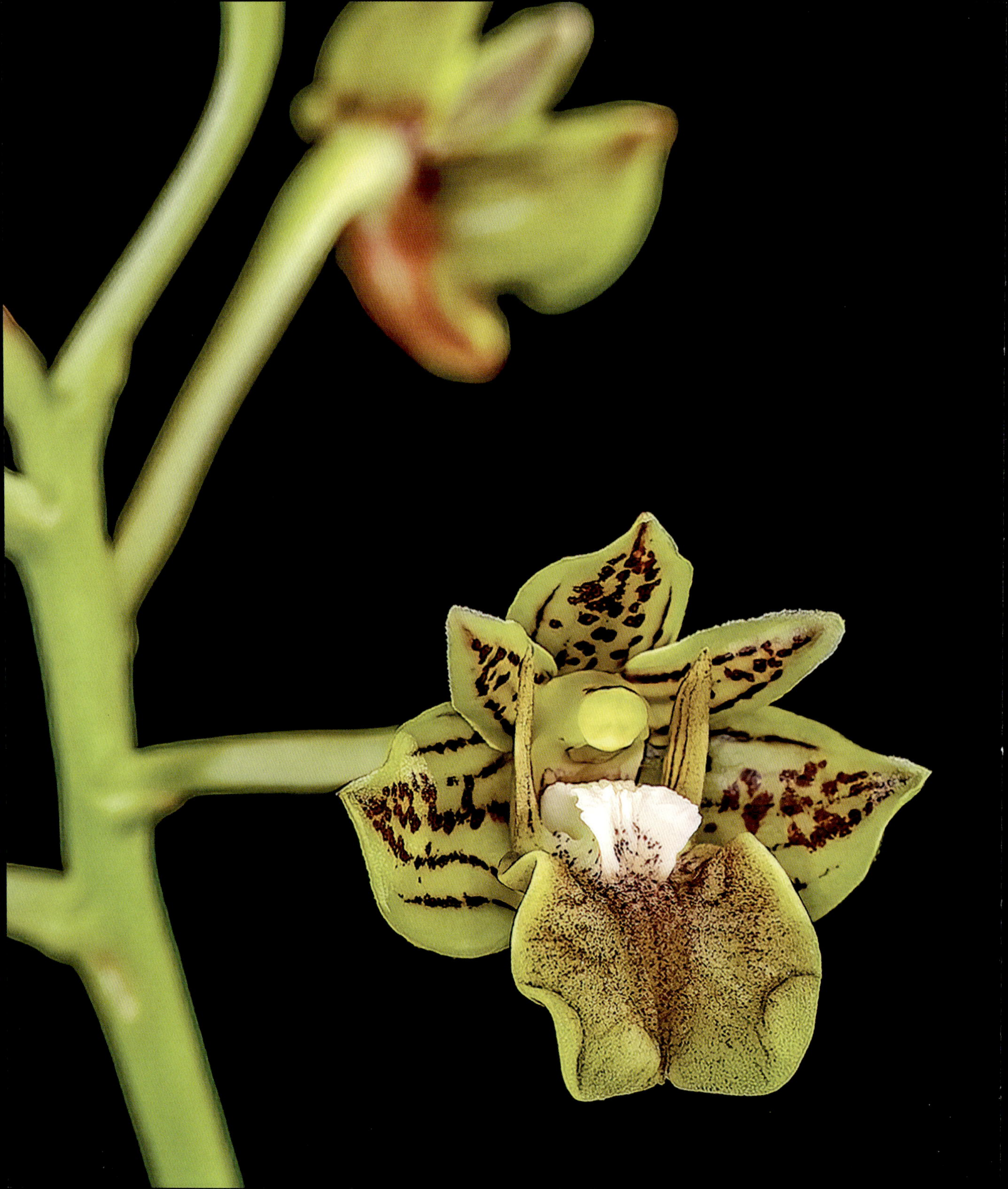

Dendrobium bifalce

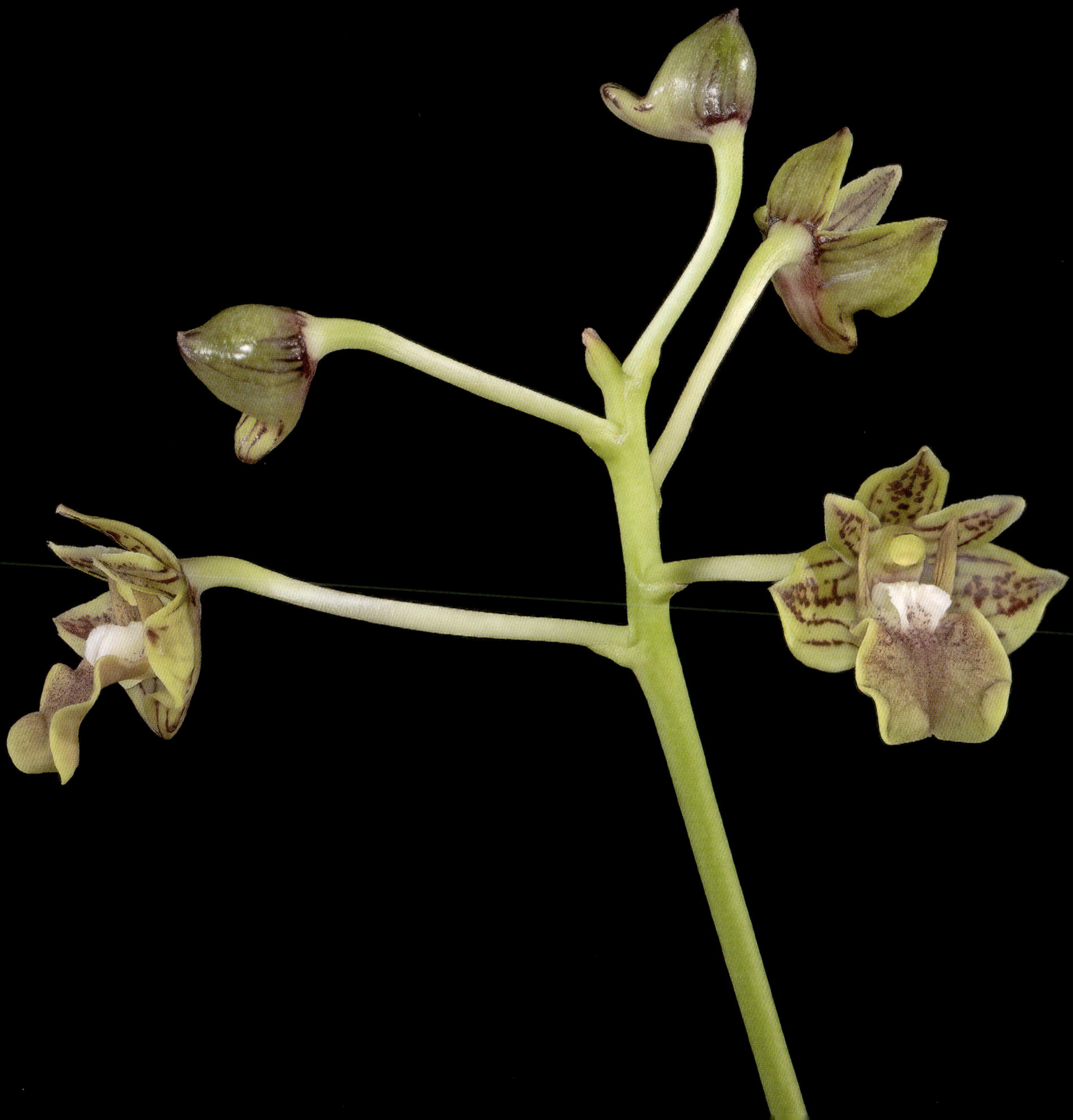

Dendrobium goldschmidtianum

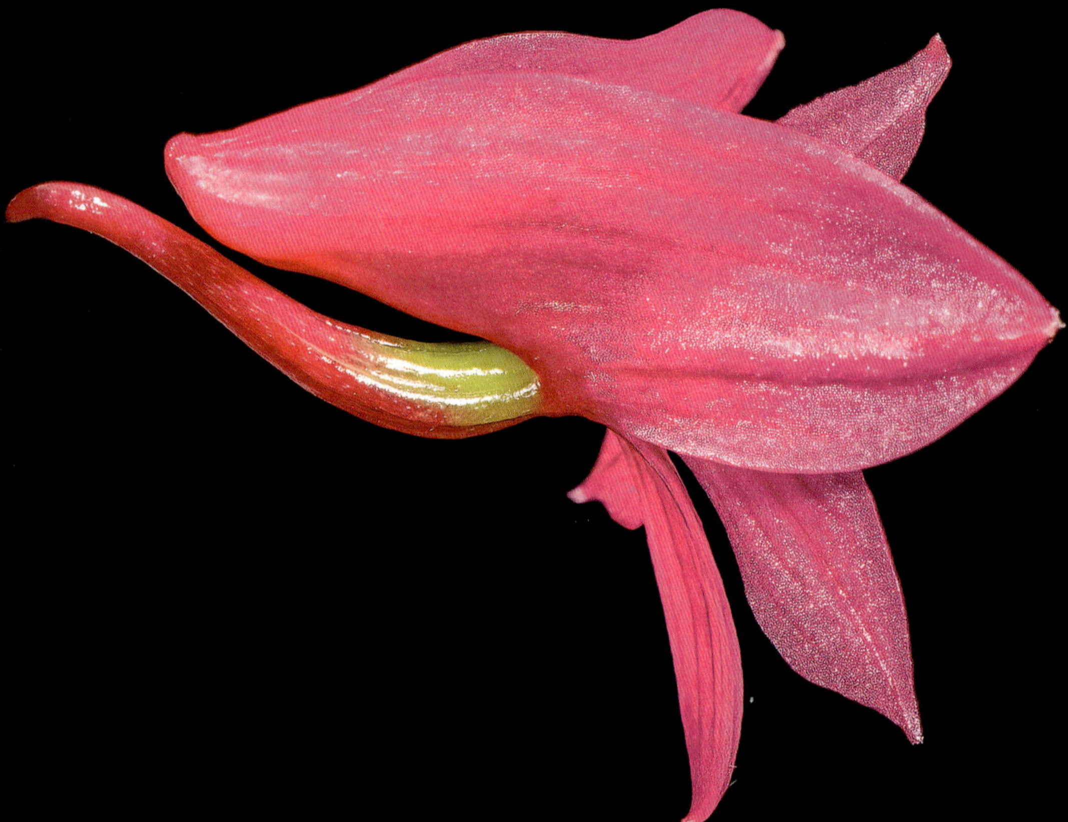

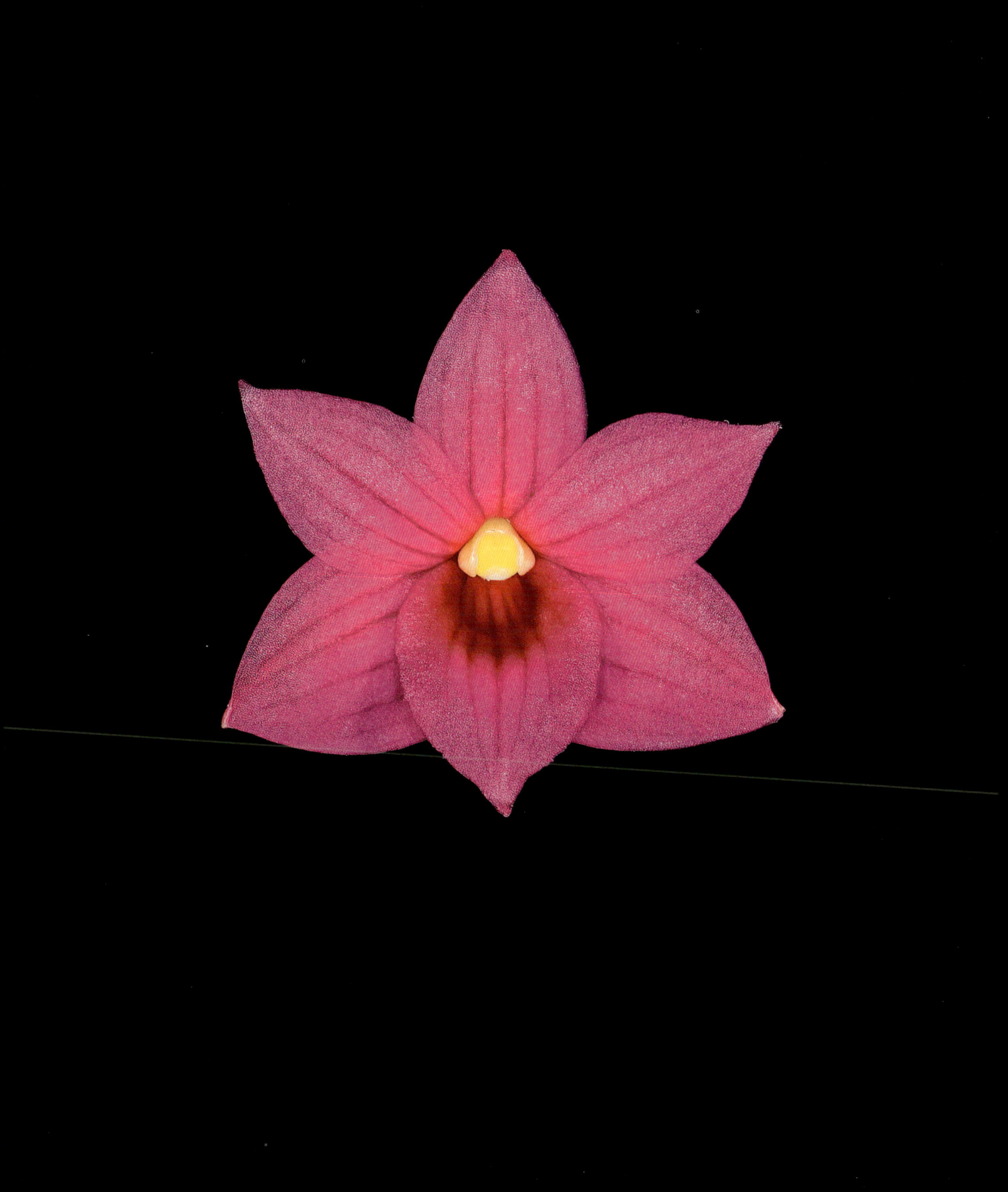

Dendrobium pachyphyllum

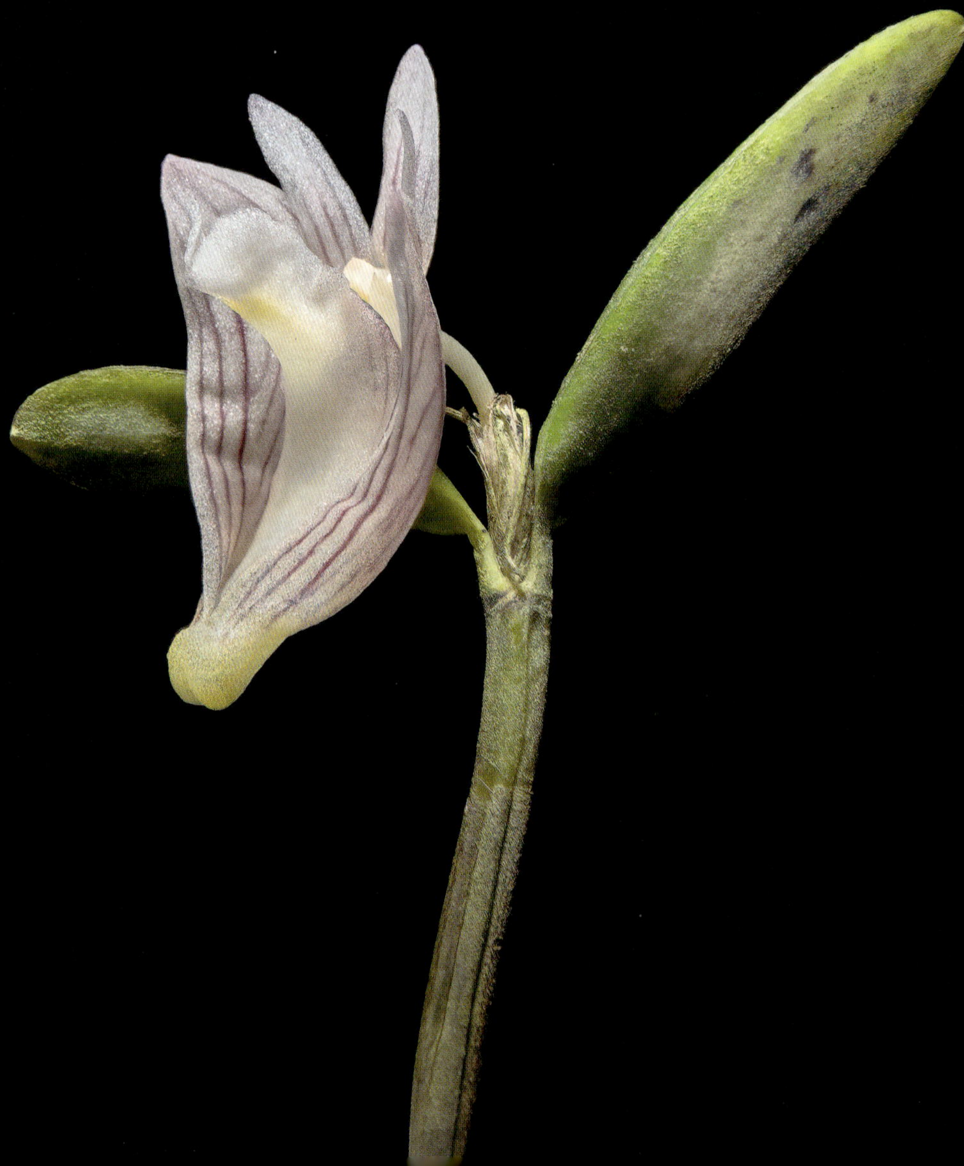

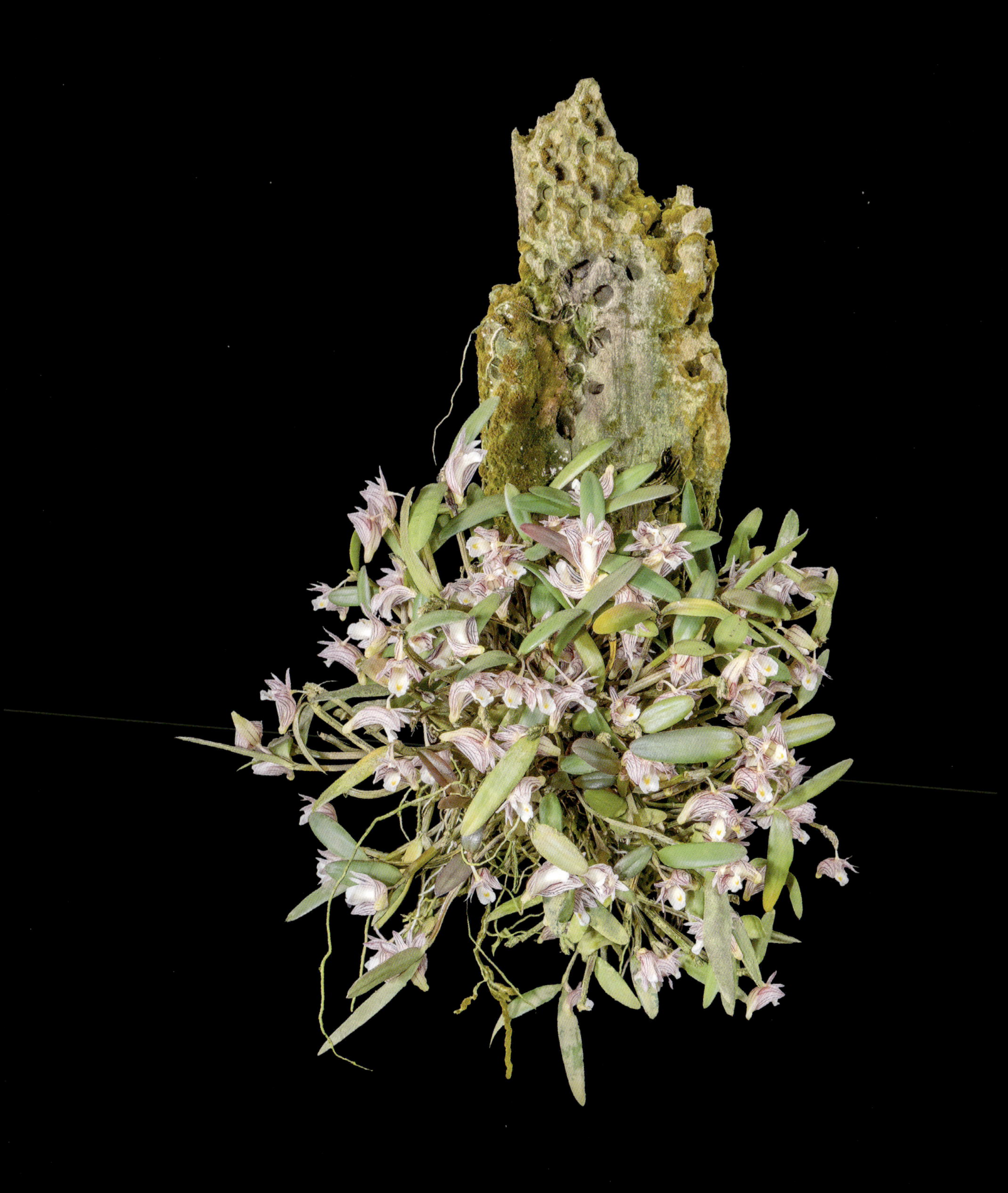

Dendrobium secundum

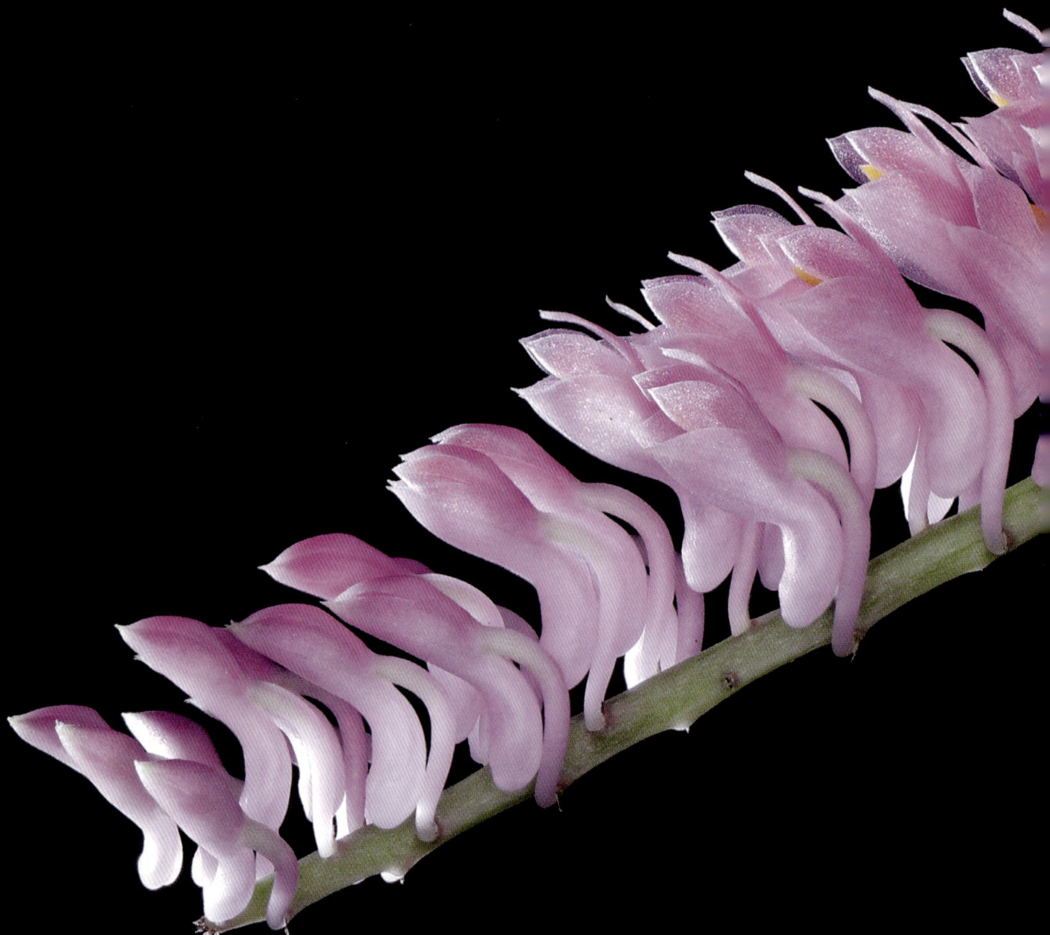

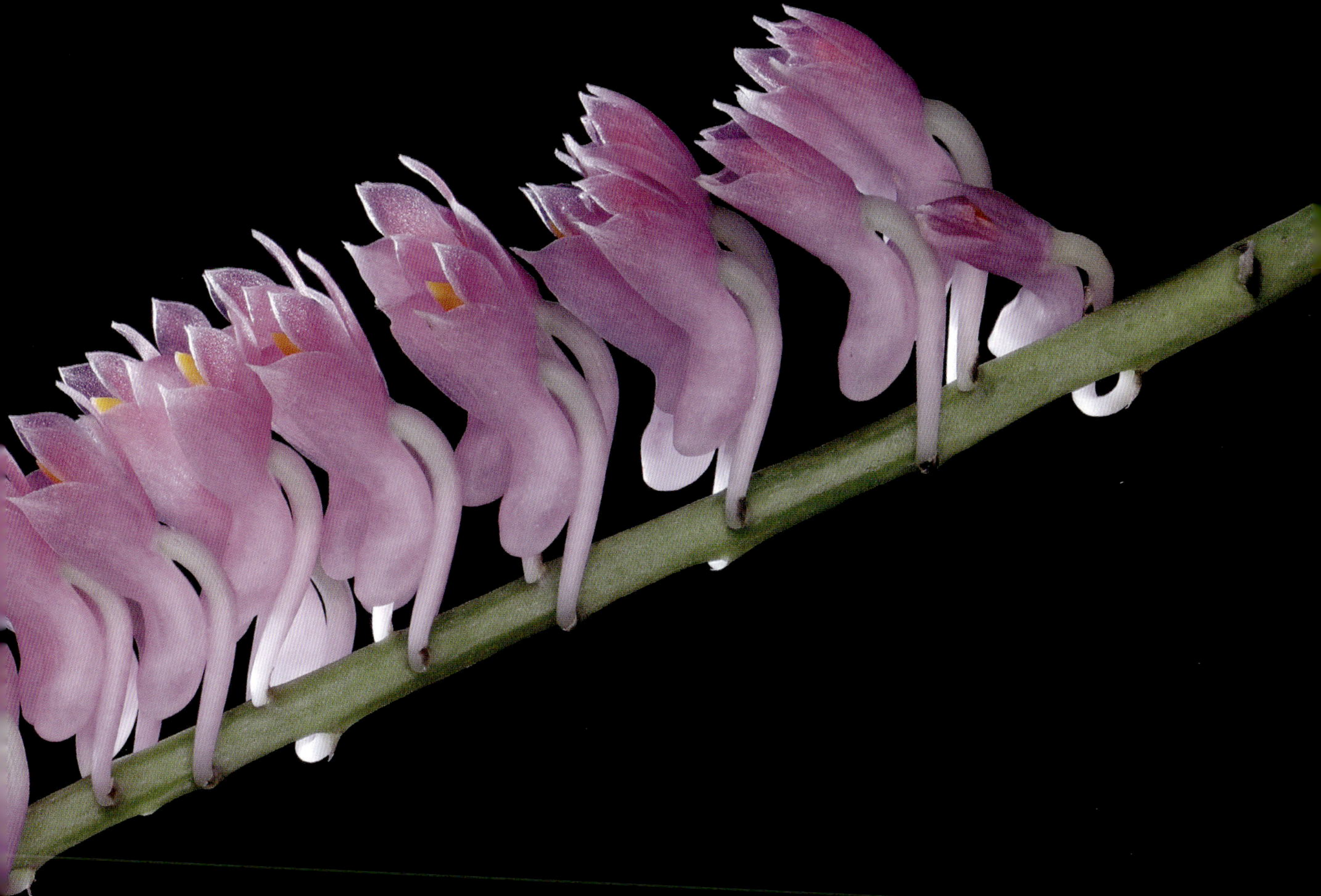

Dendrobium spectabile

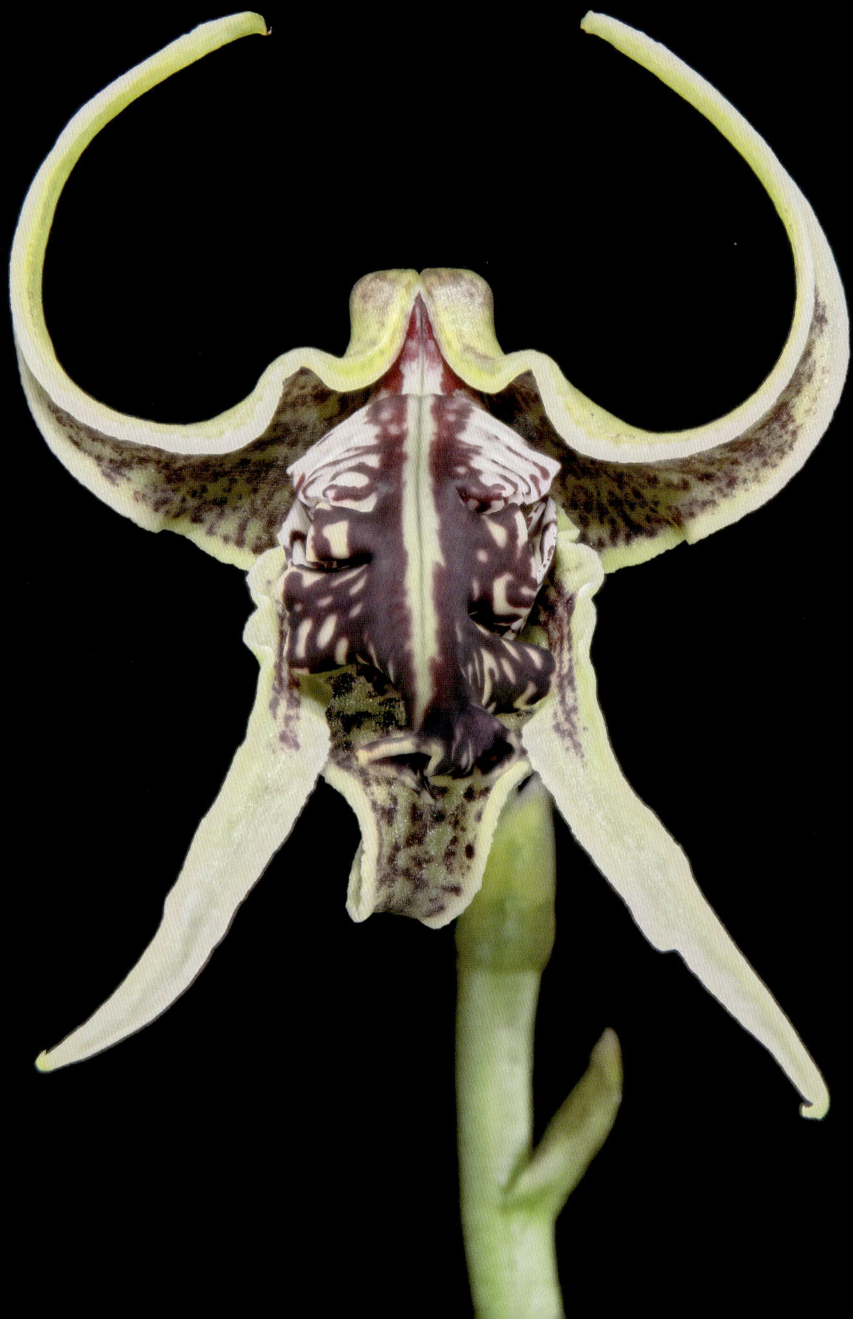

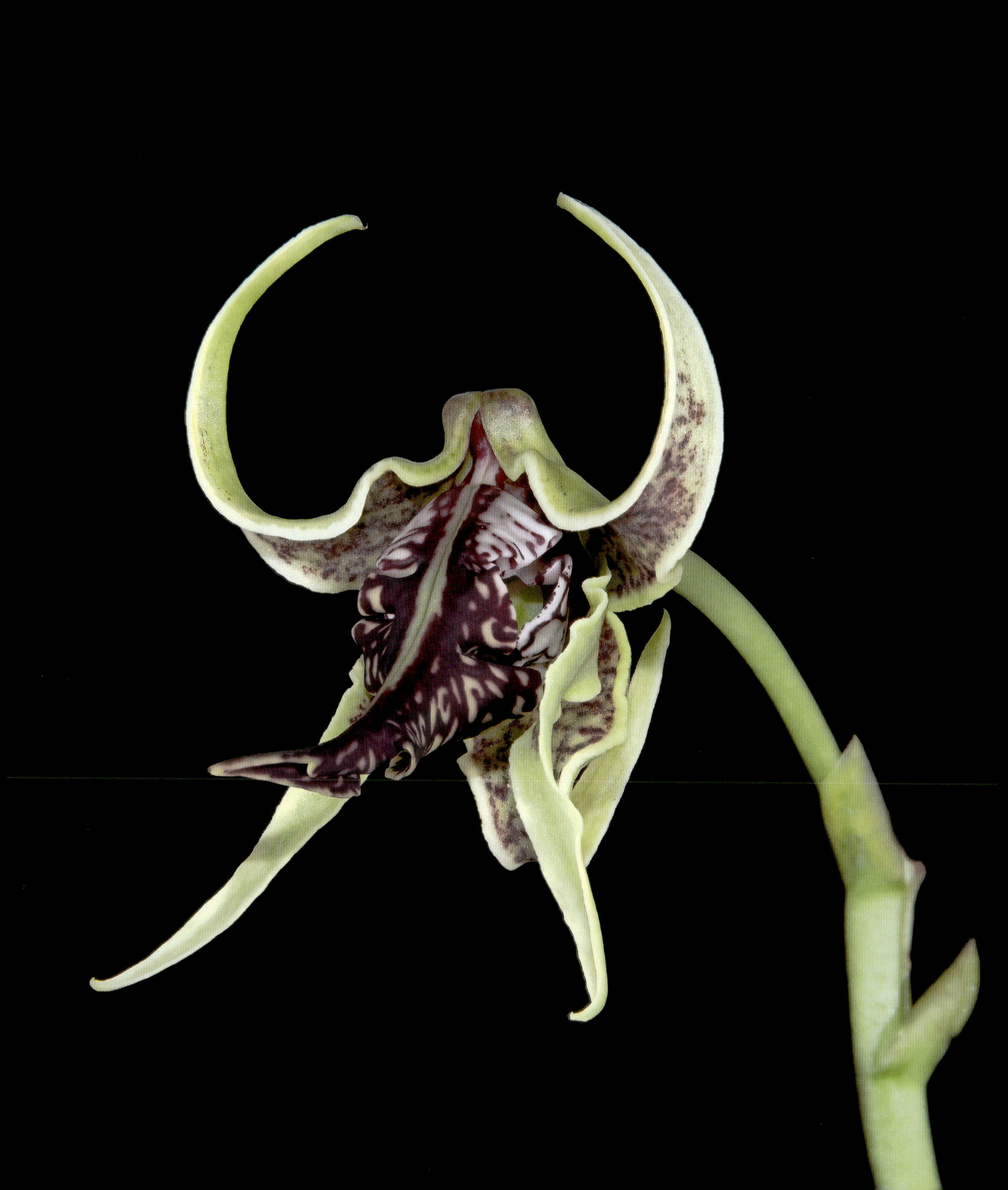

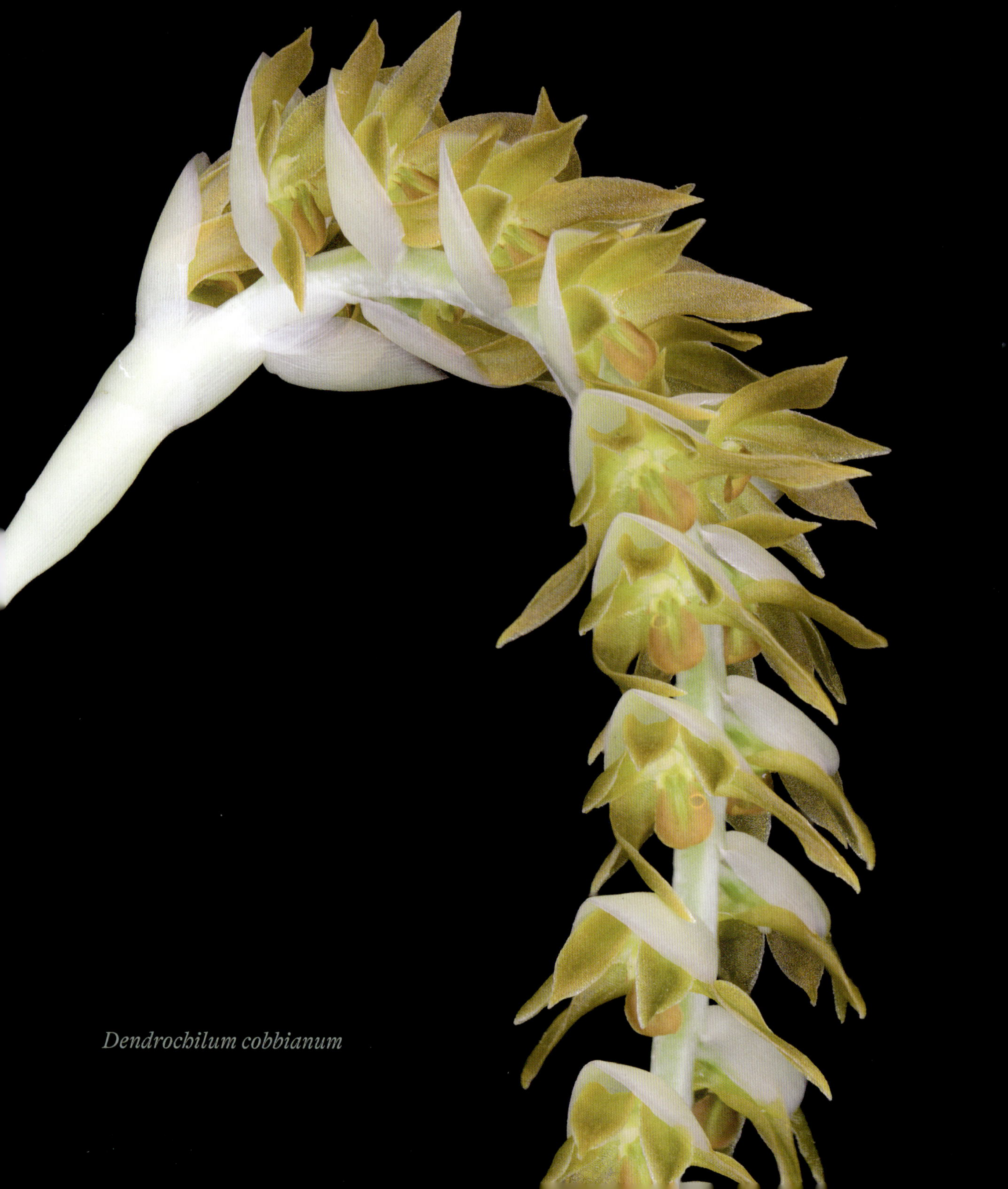

Dendrochilum cobbianum

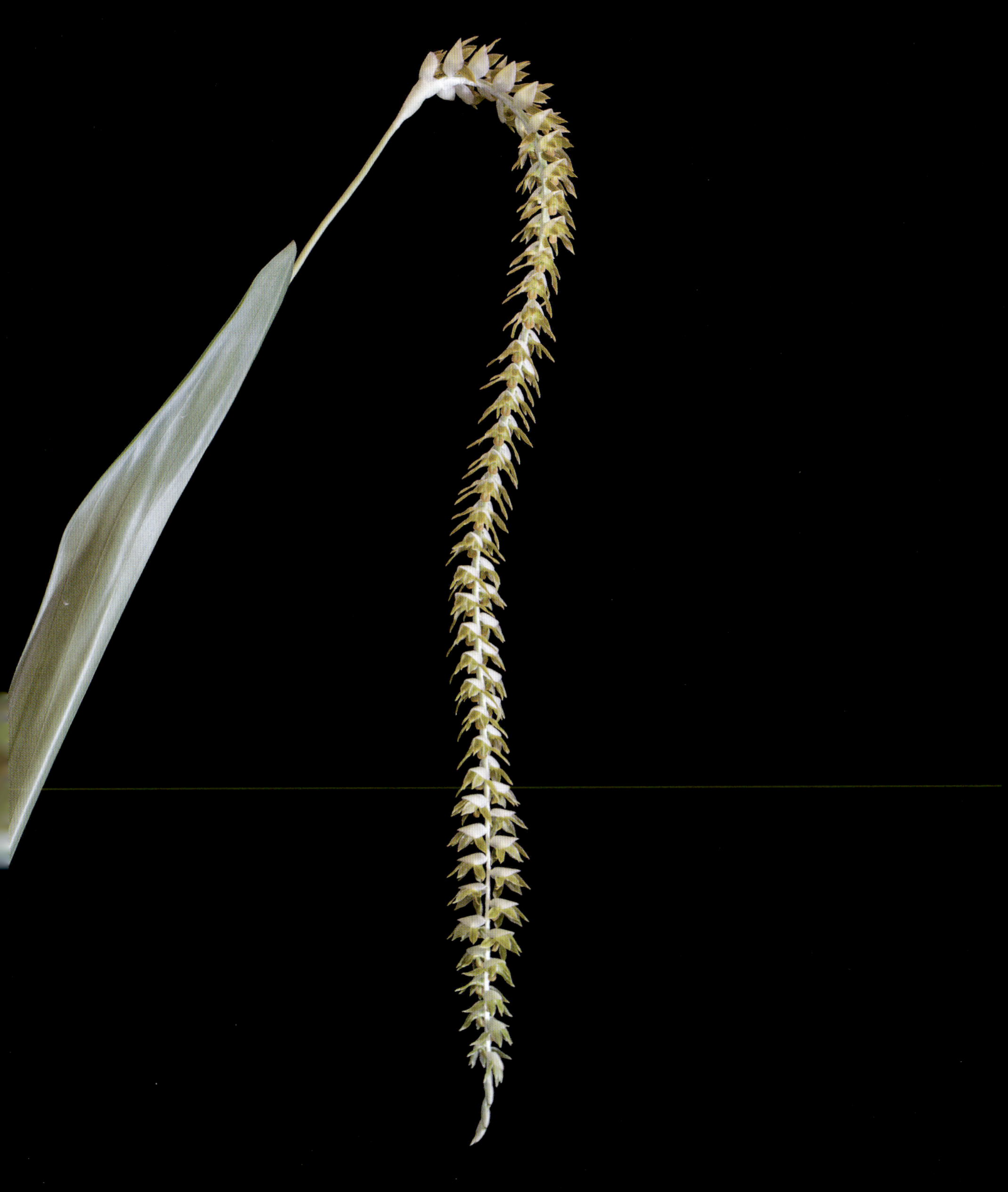

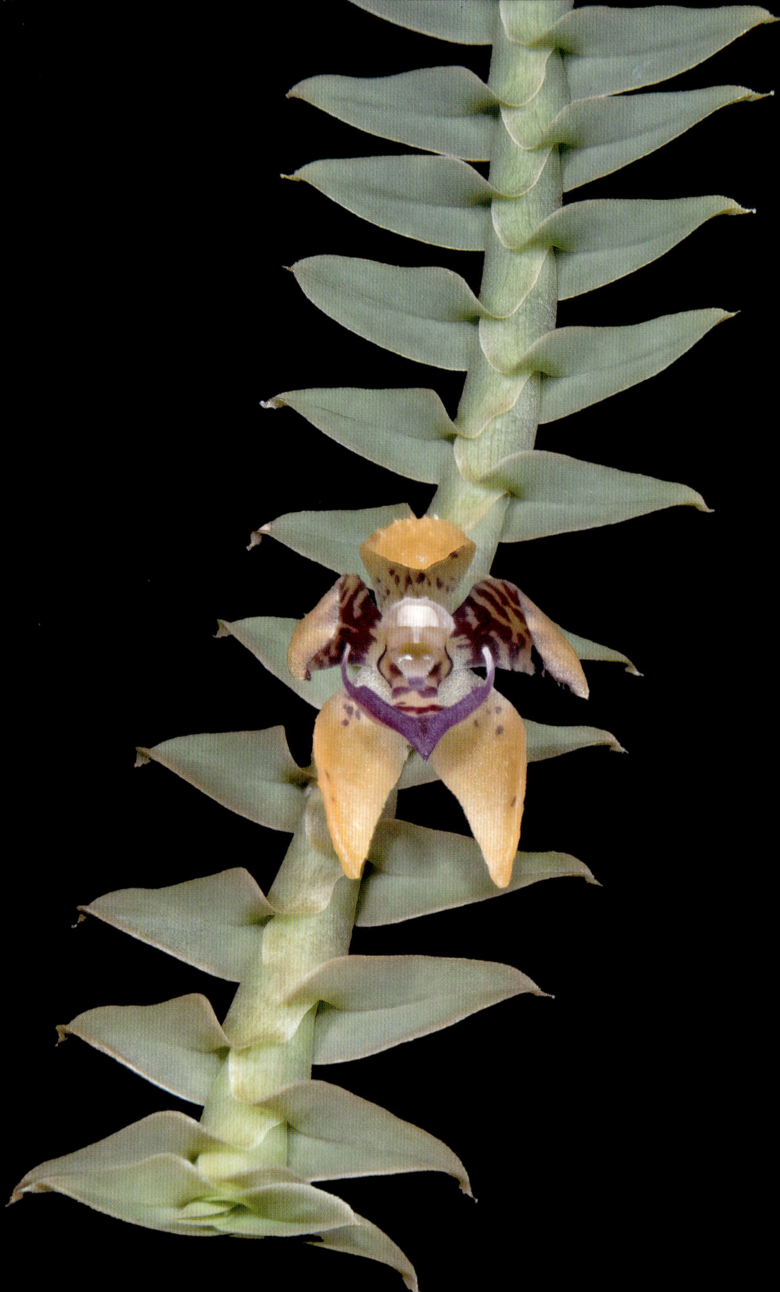

Dichaea muricatoides

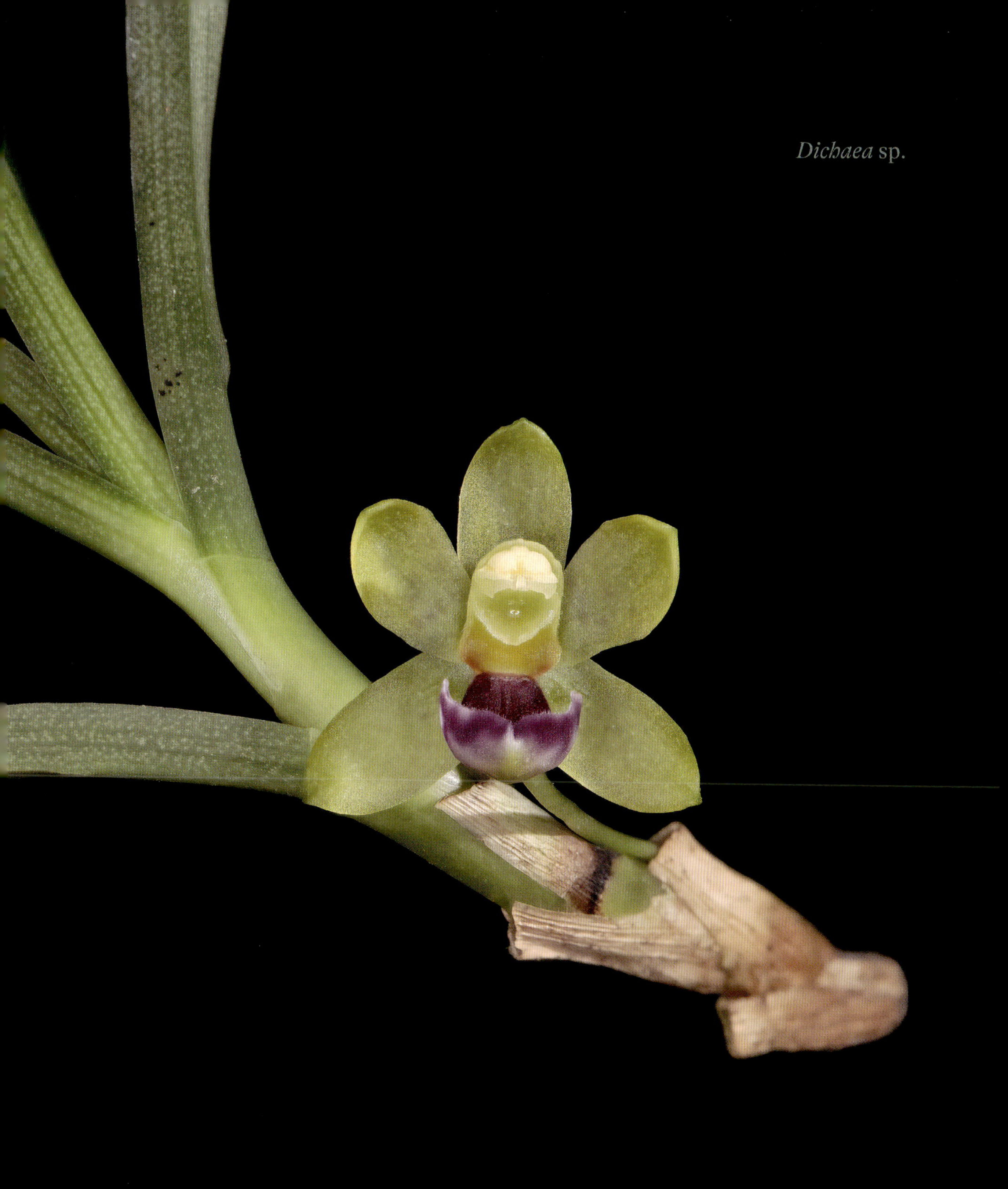

Dichaea sp.

Dinema polybulbon

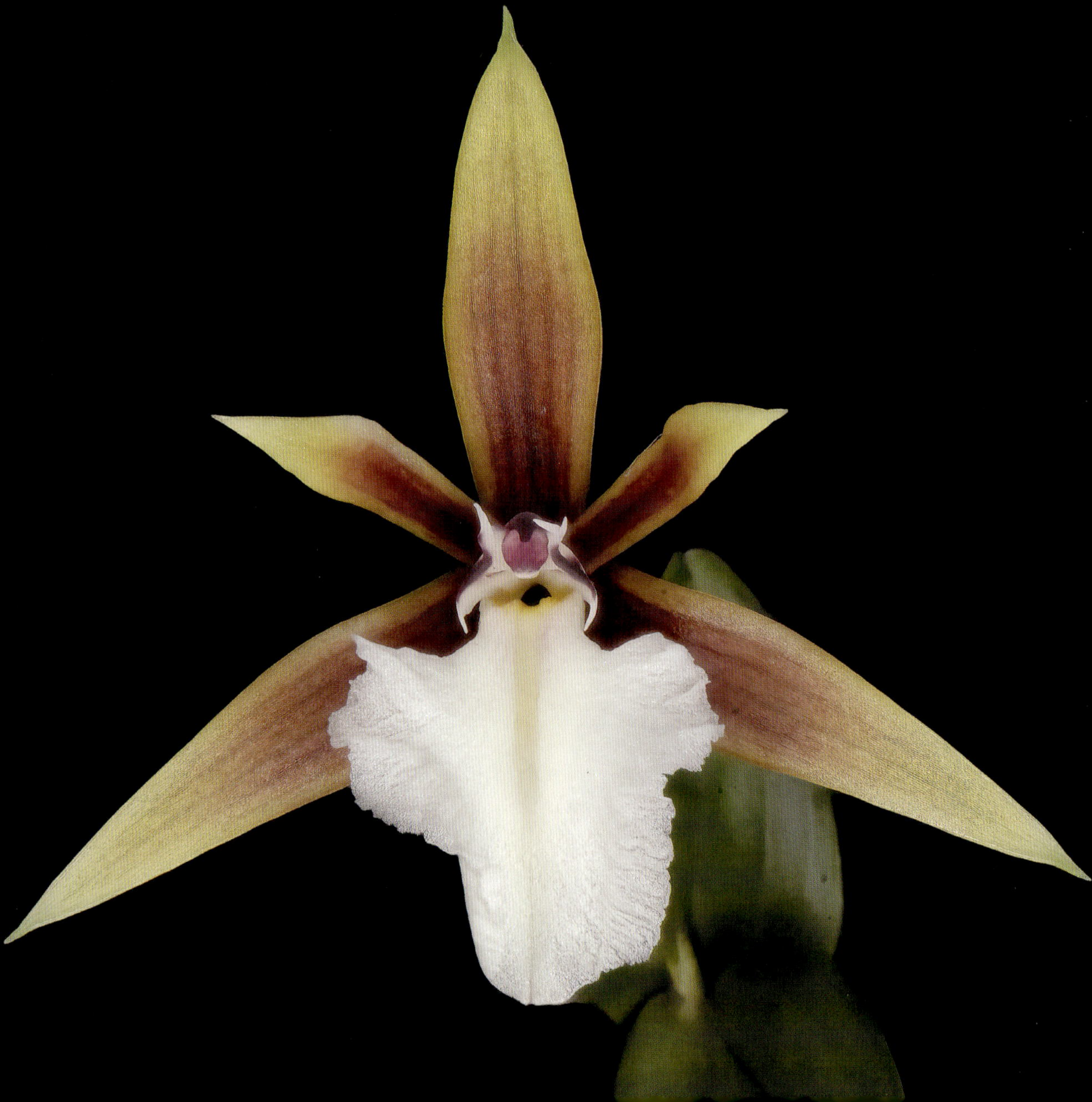

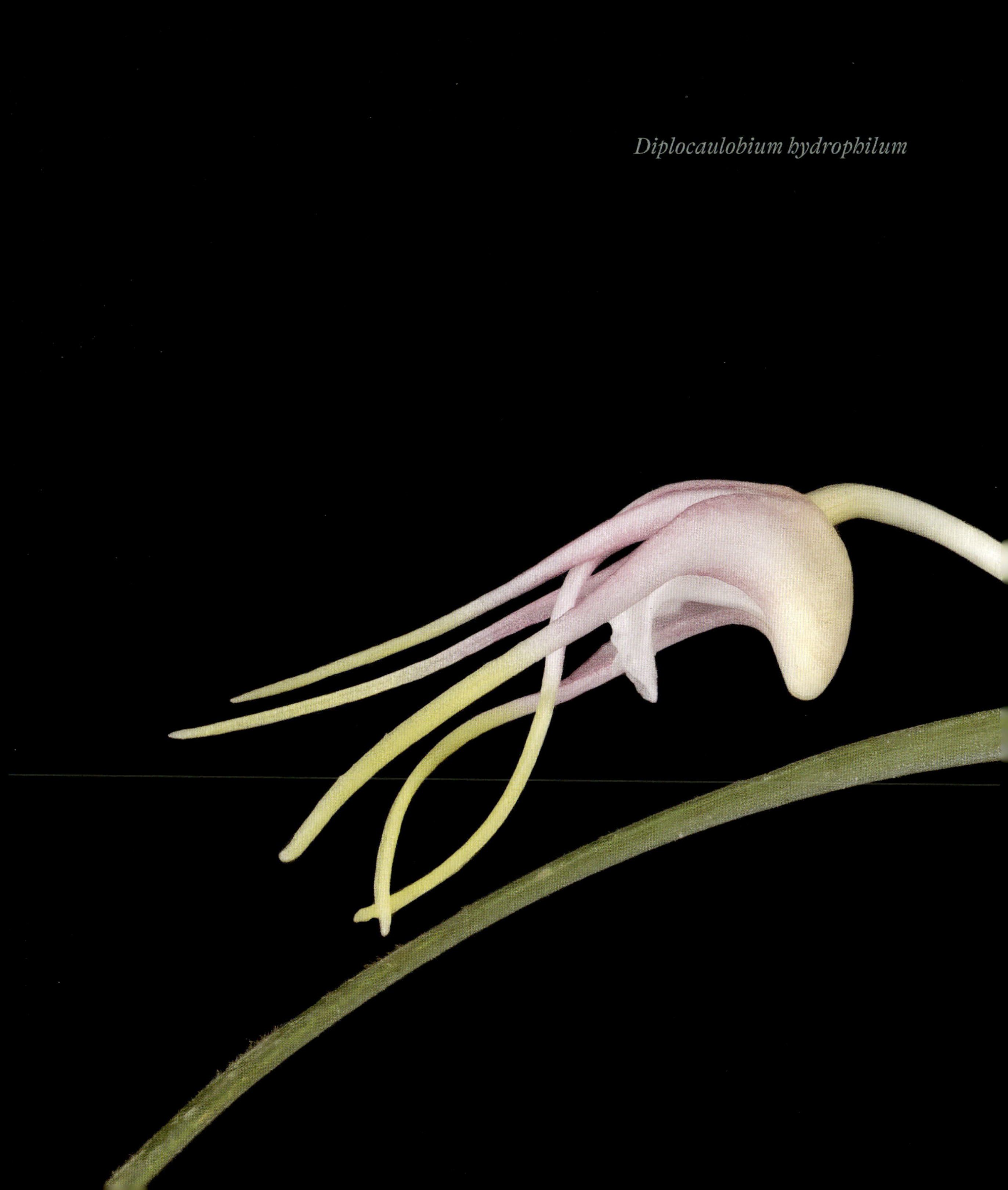

Diplocaulobium hydrophilum

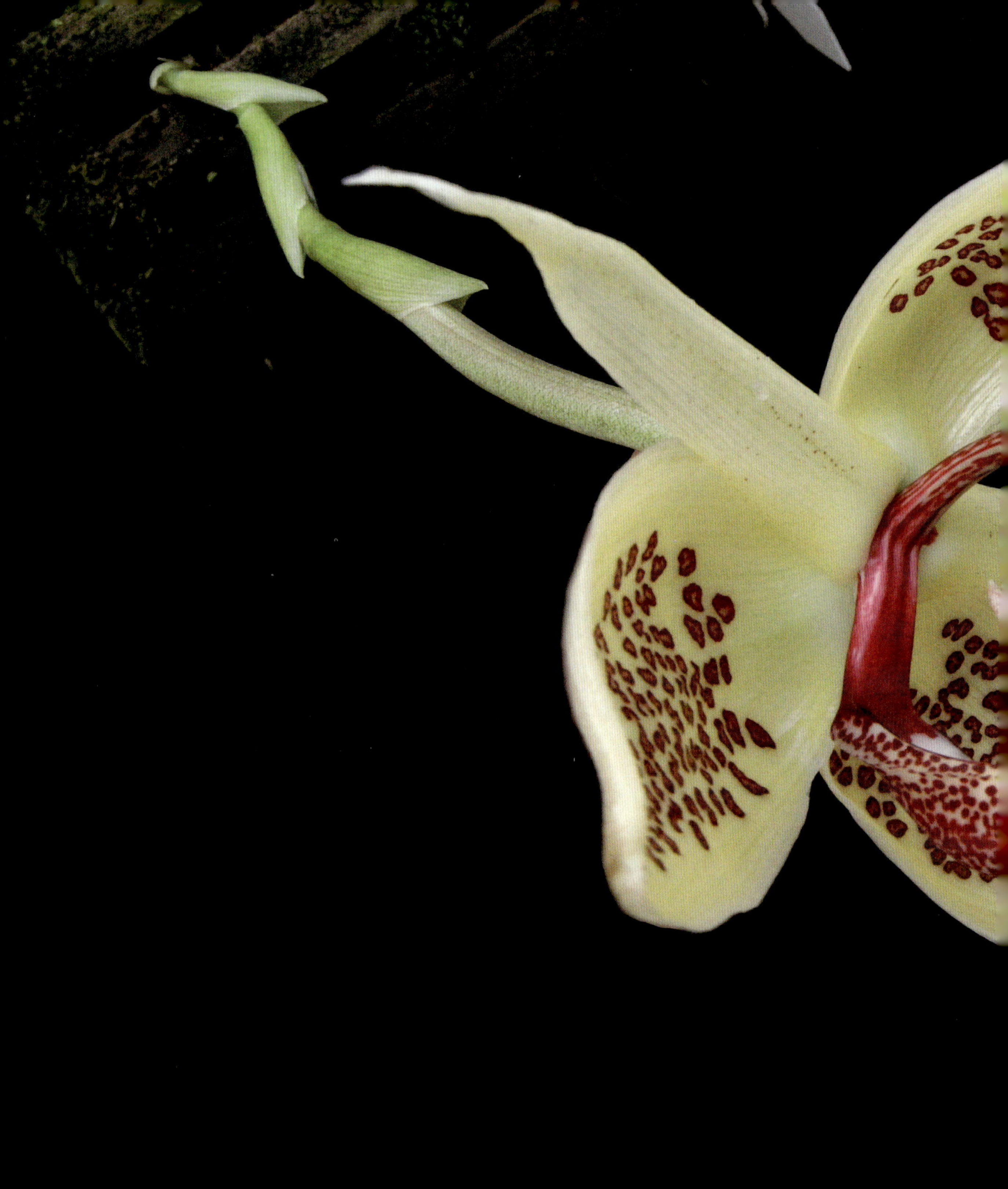

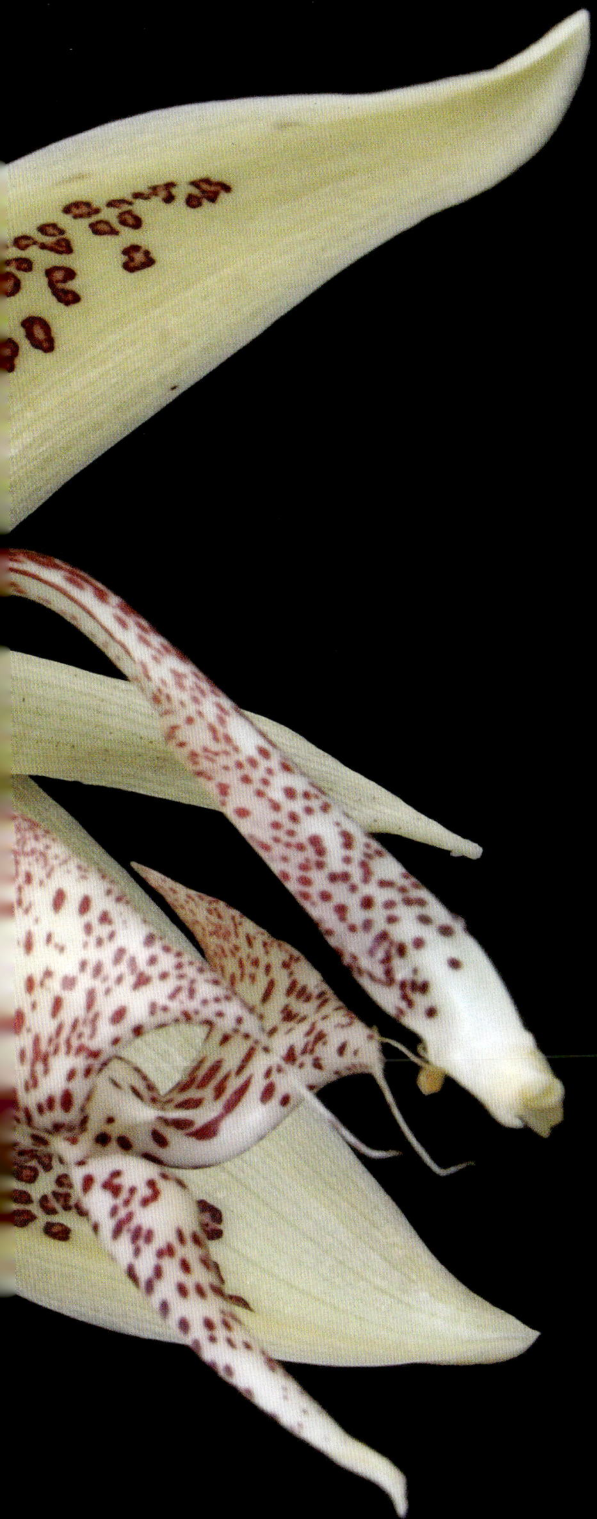

Embreea rodigasiana

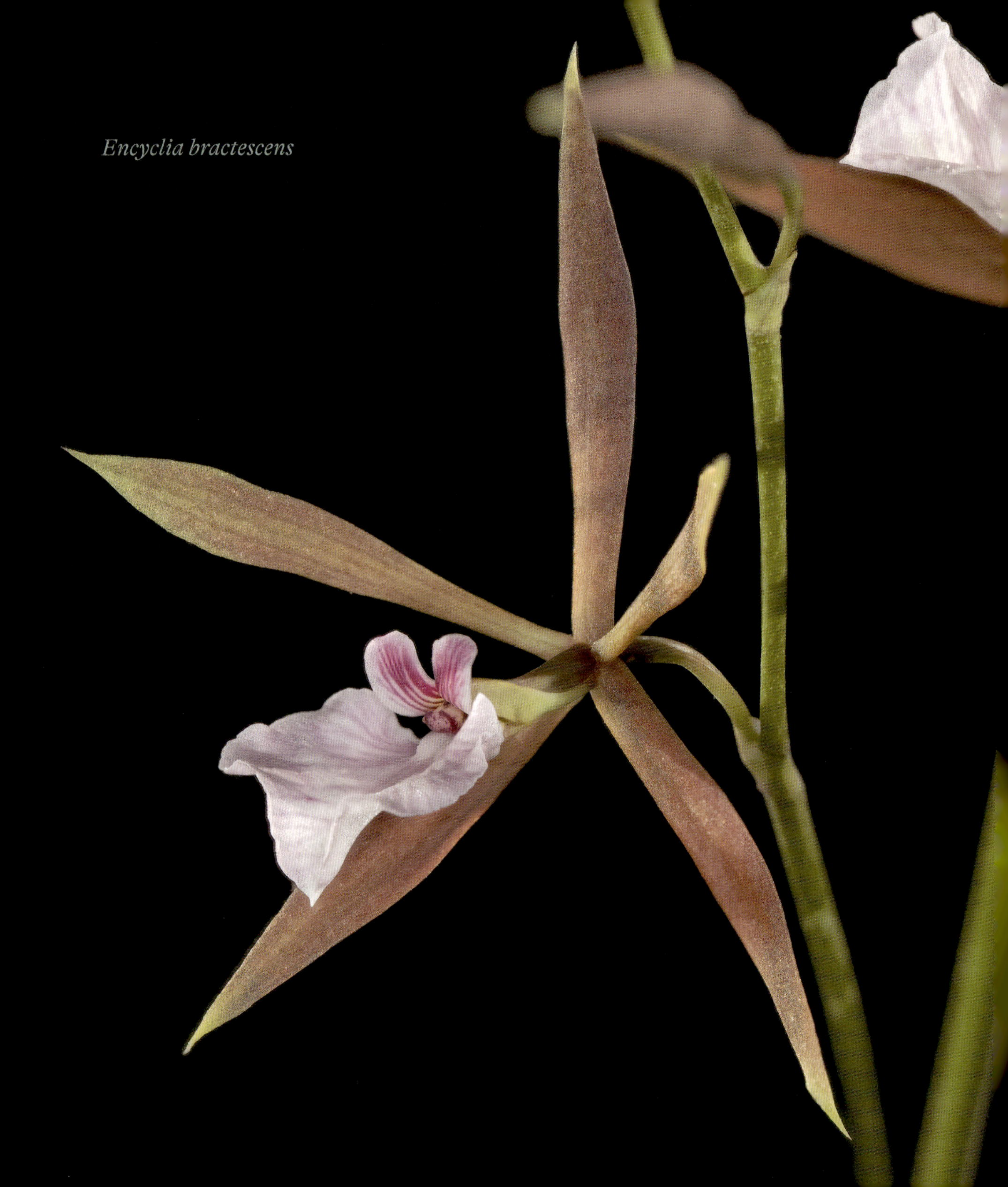

Encyclia bractescens

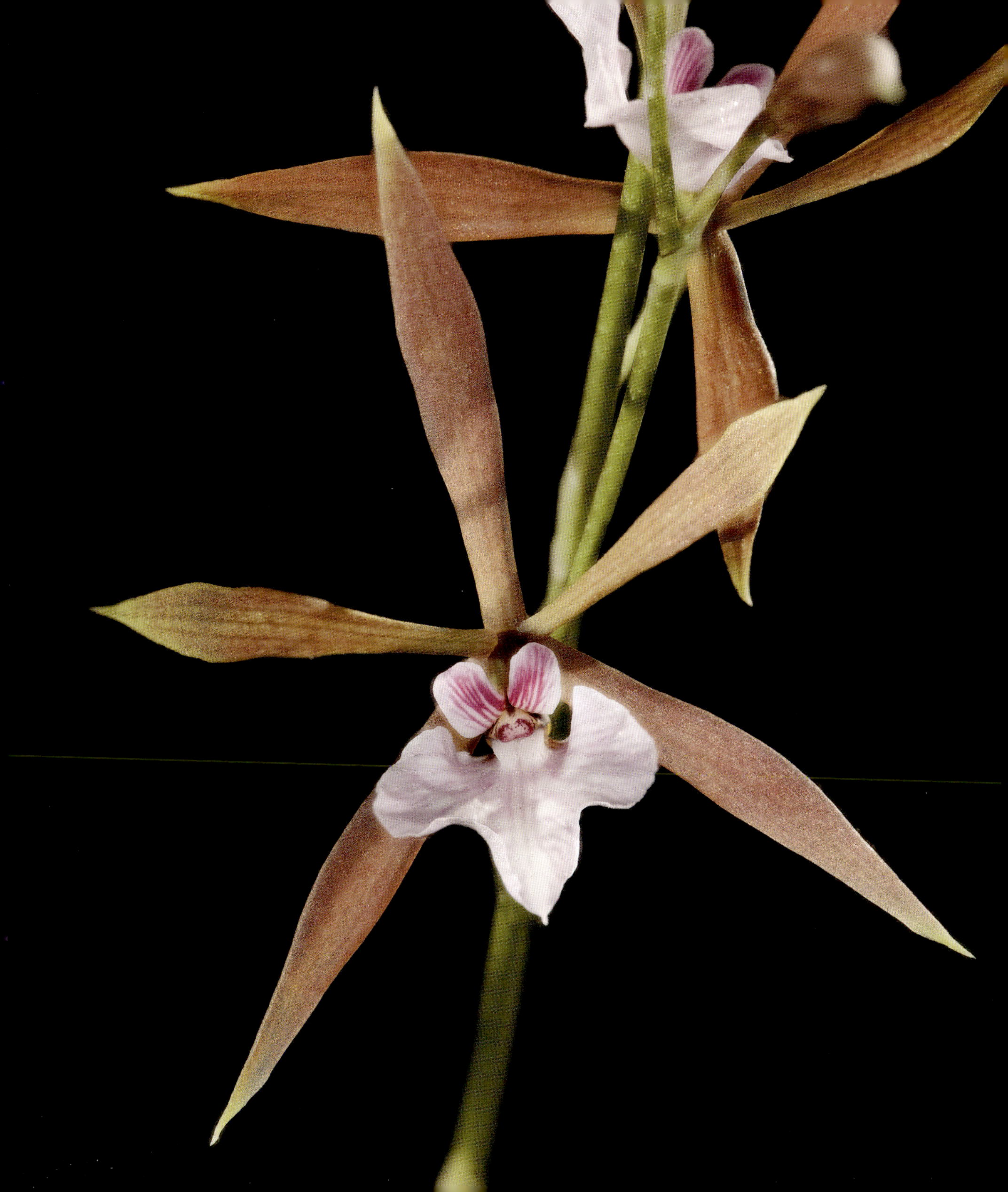

Encyclia howardii

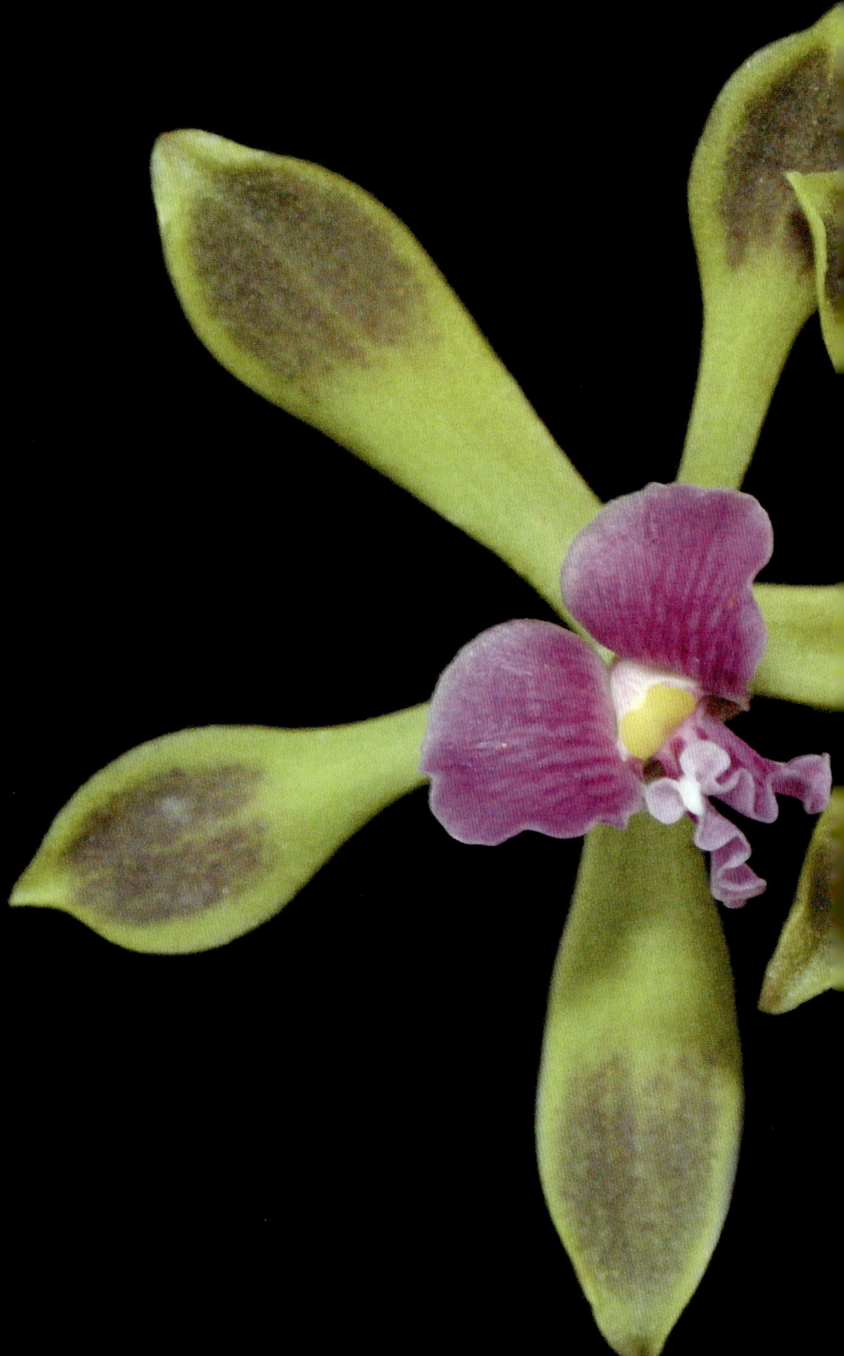

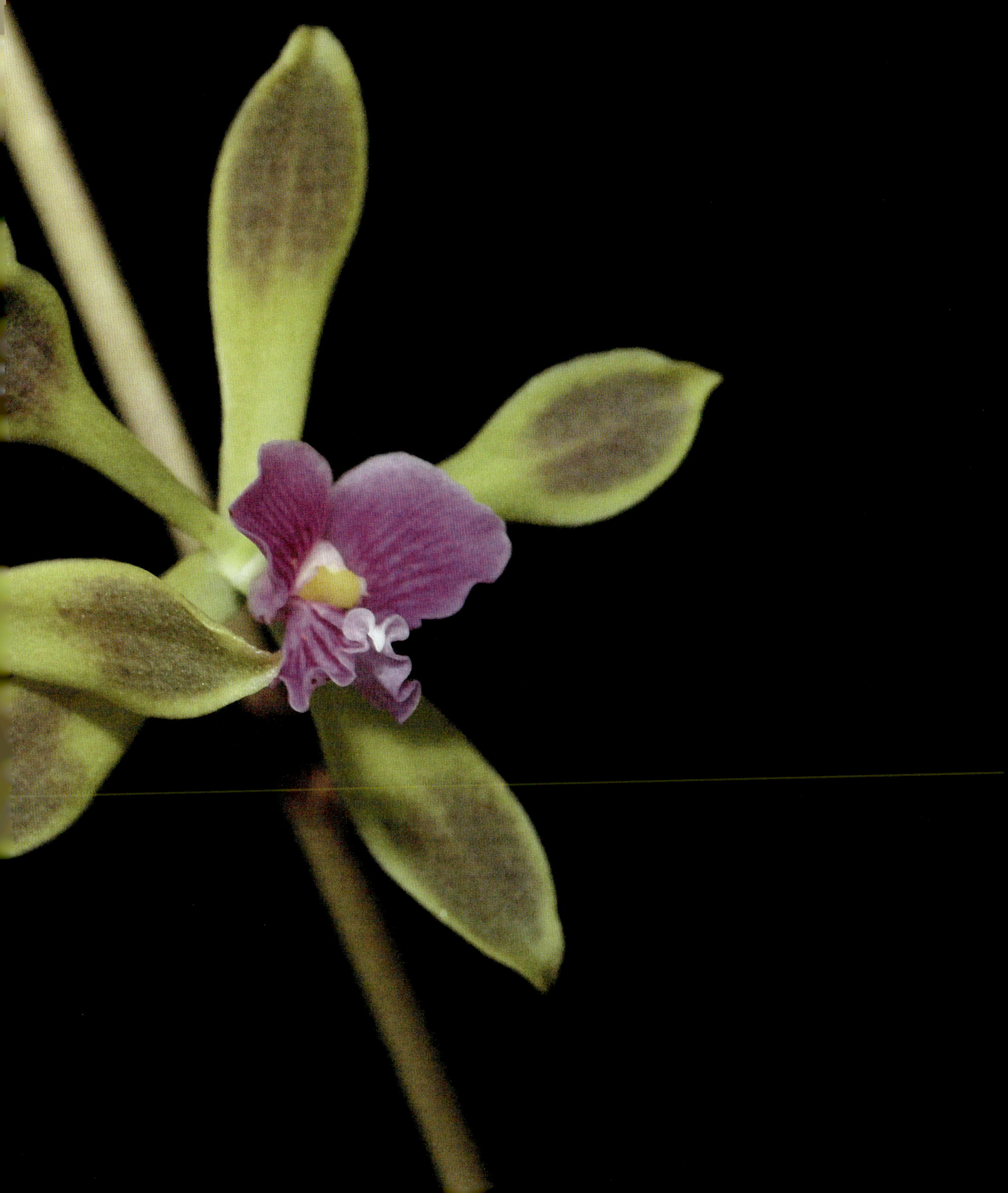

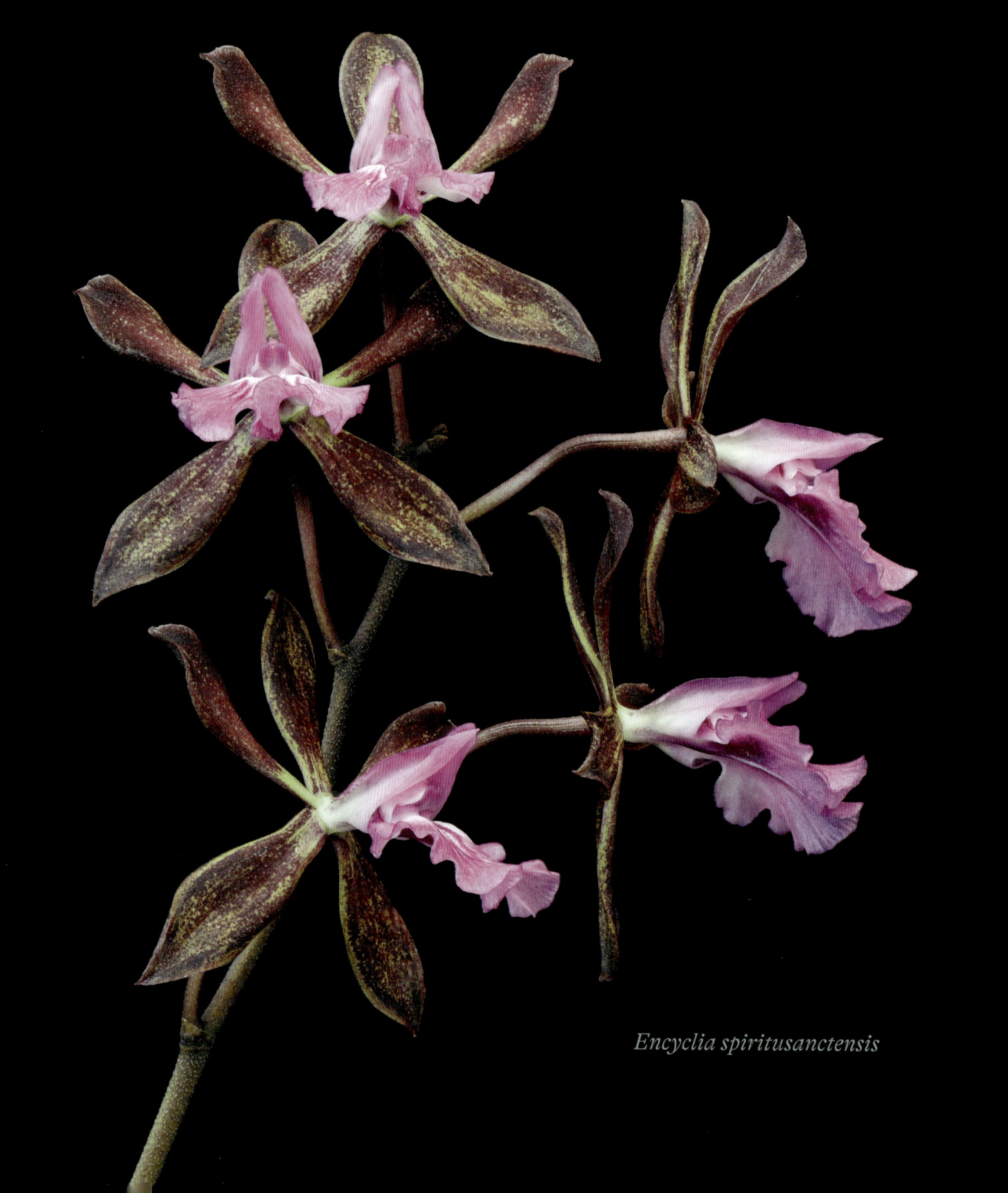

Encyclia spiritusanctensis

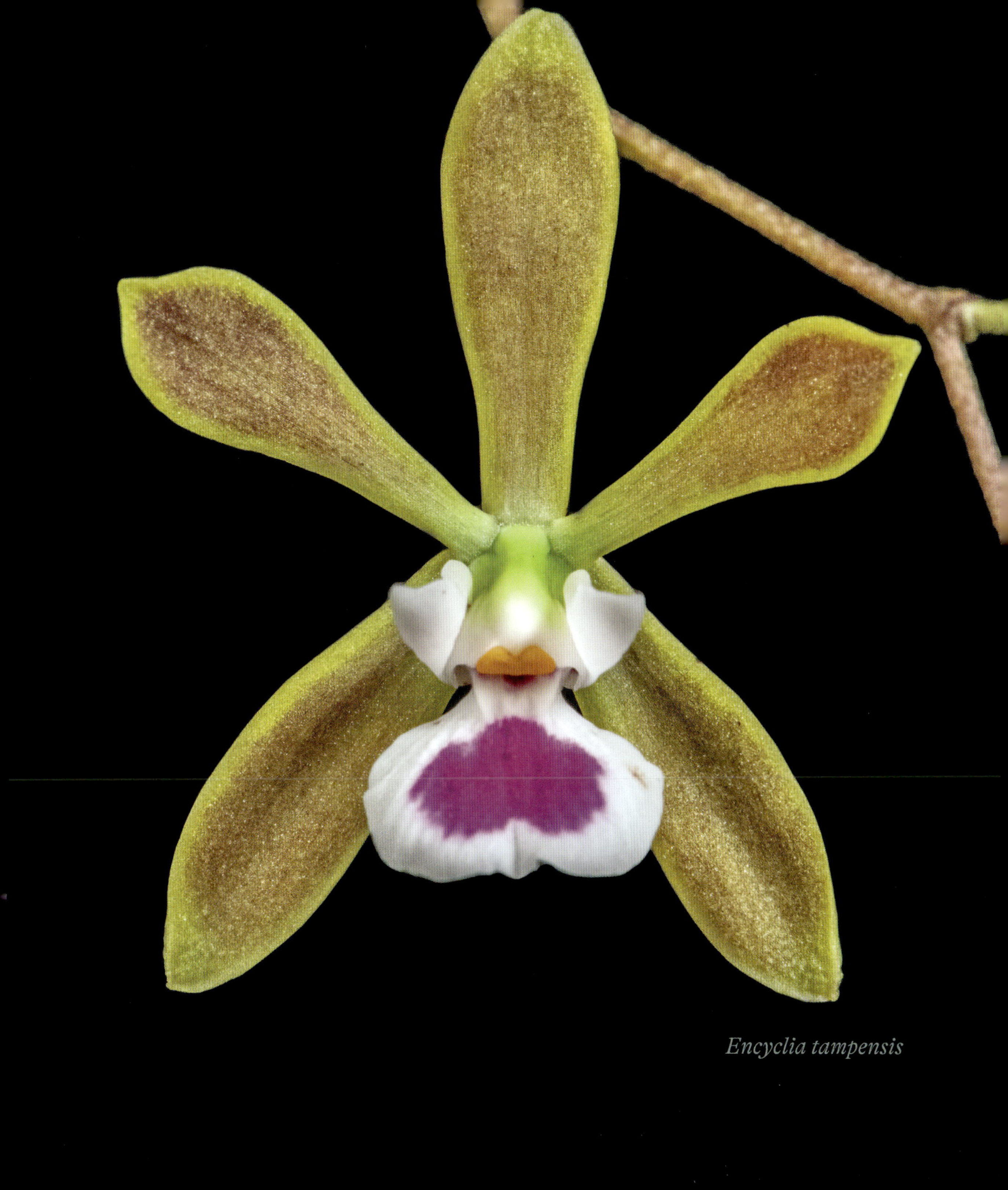

Encyclia tampensis

Epidendrum flexuosum

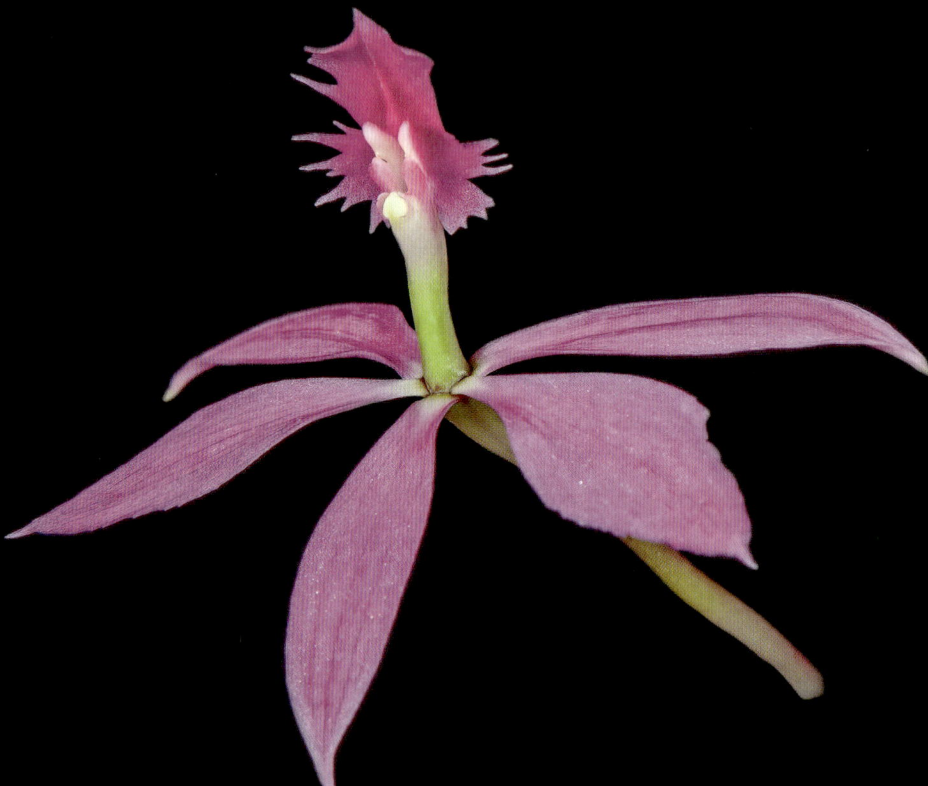

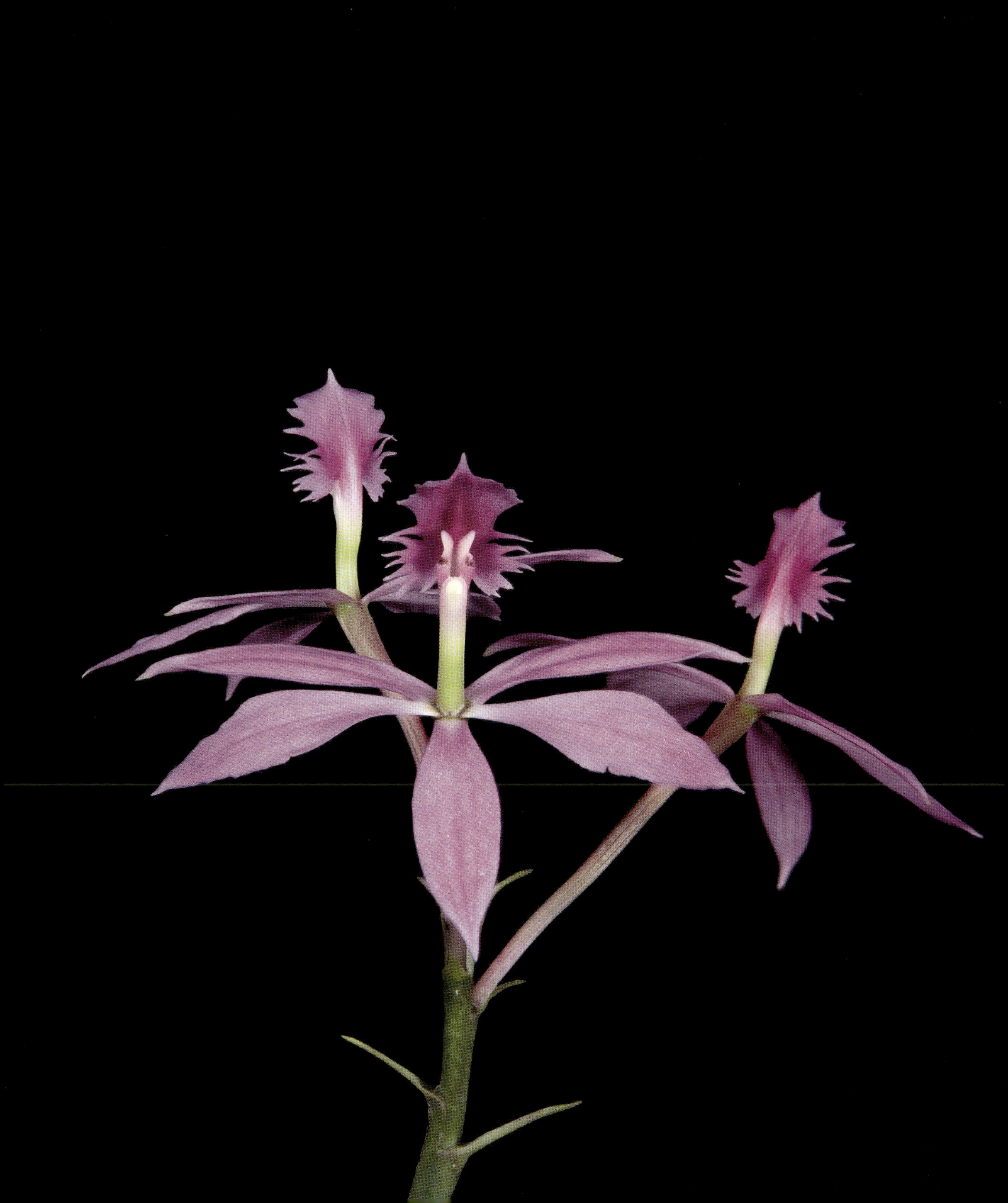

Epidendrum galeottianum

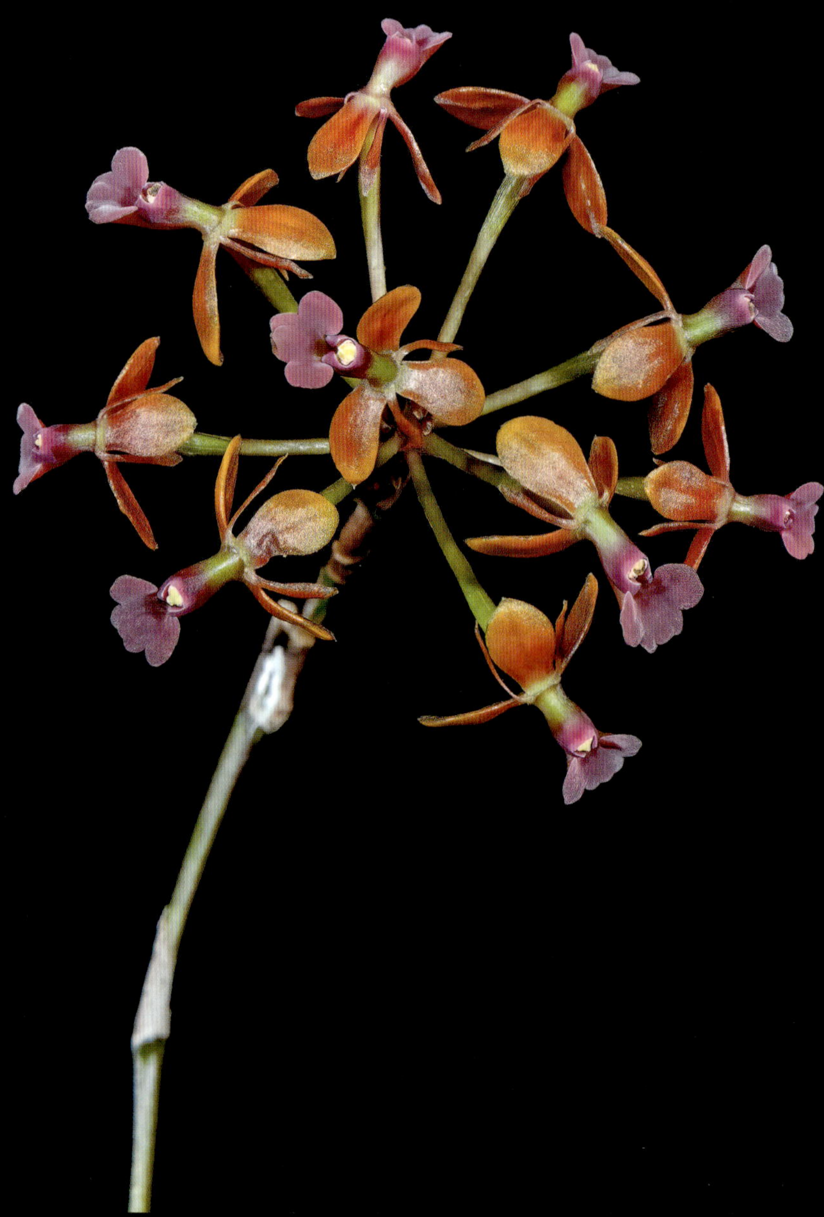

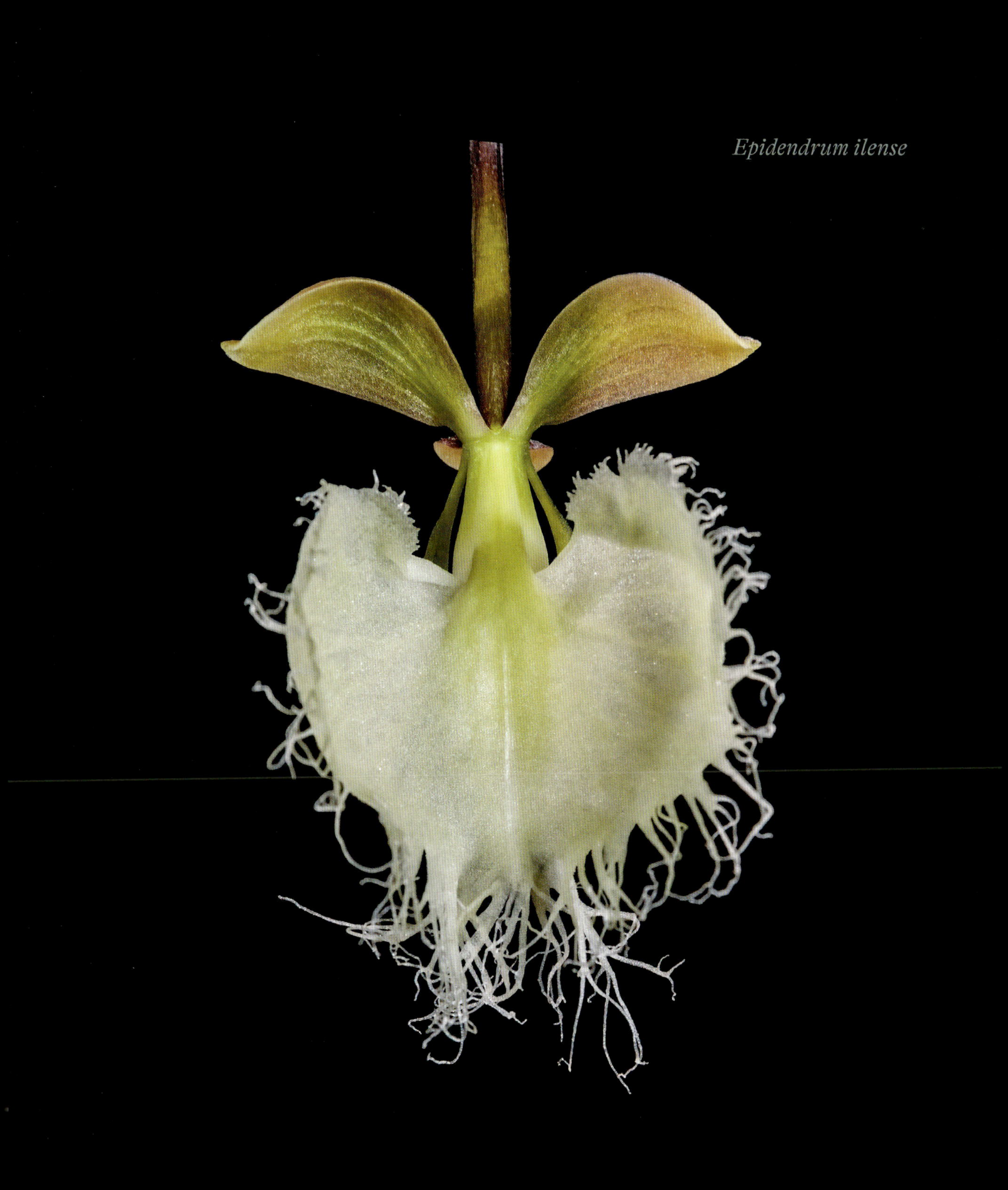

Epidendrum ilense

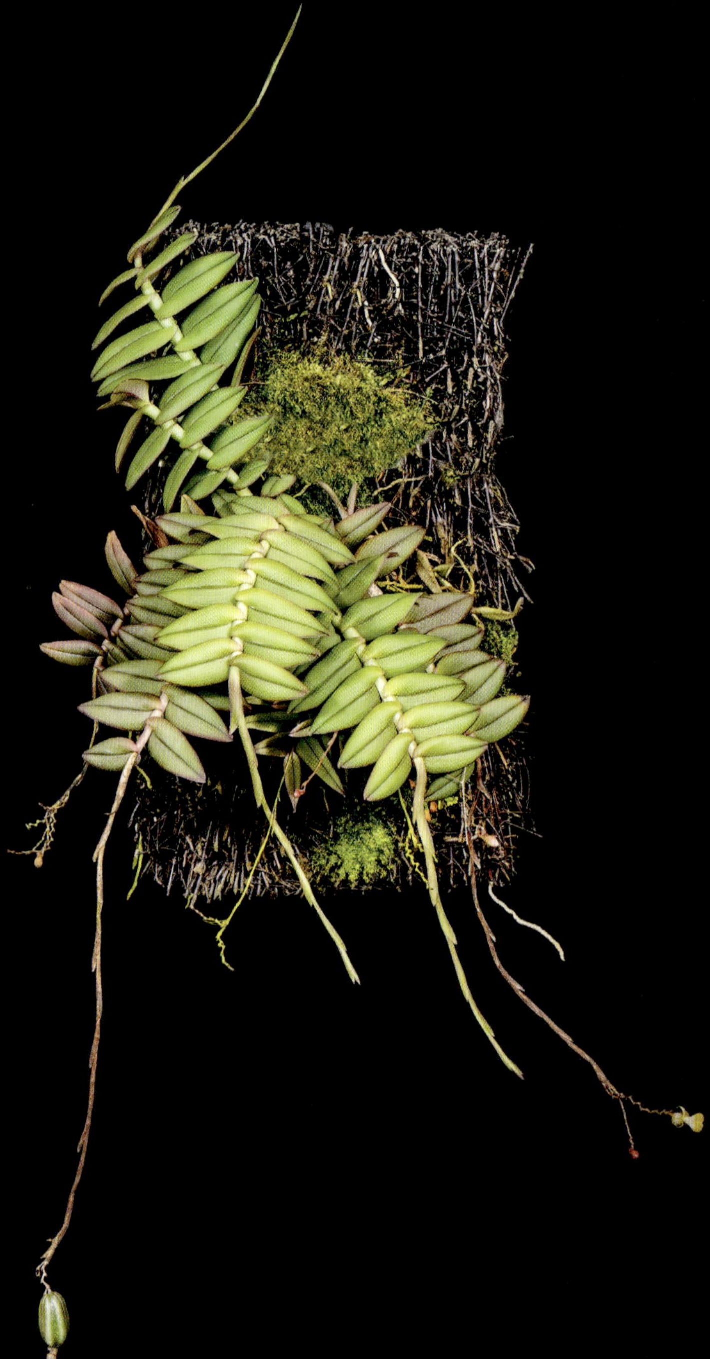

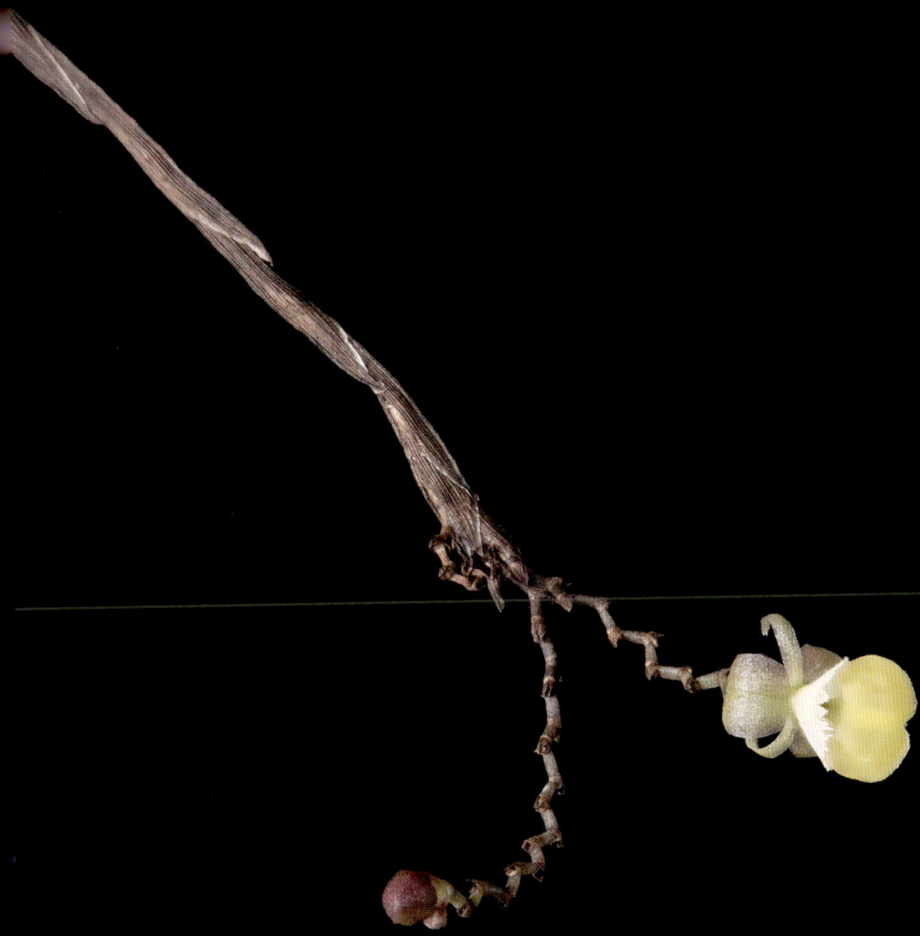

Epidendrum macroclinium

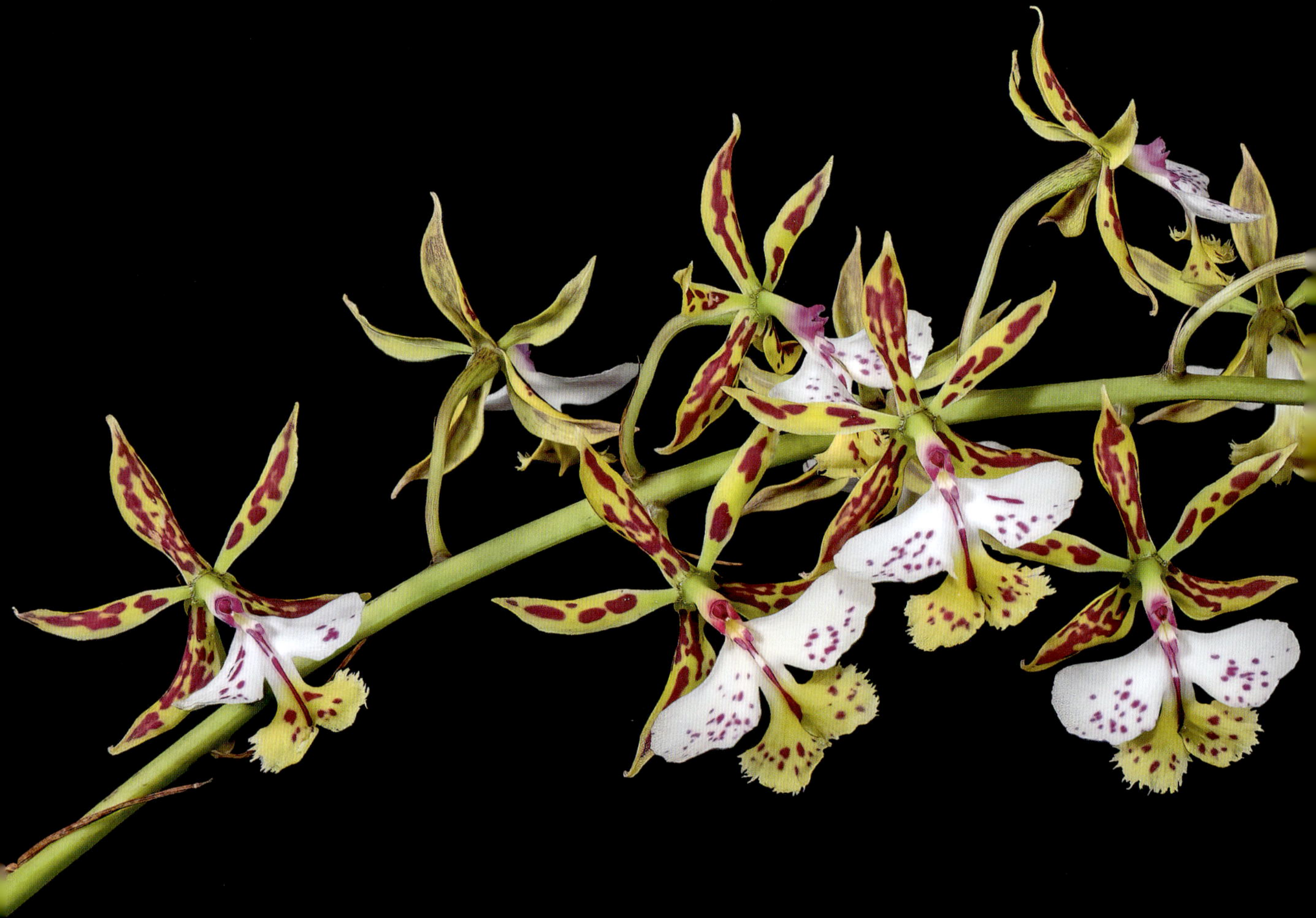

Epidendrum stamfordianum

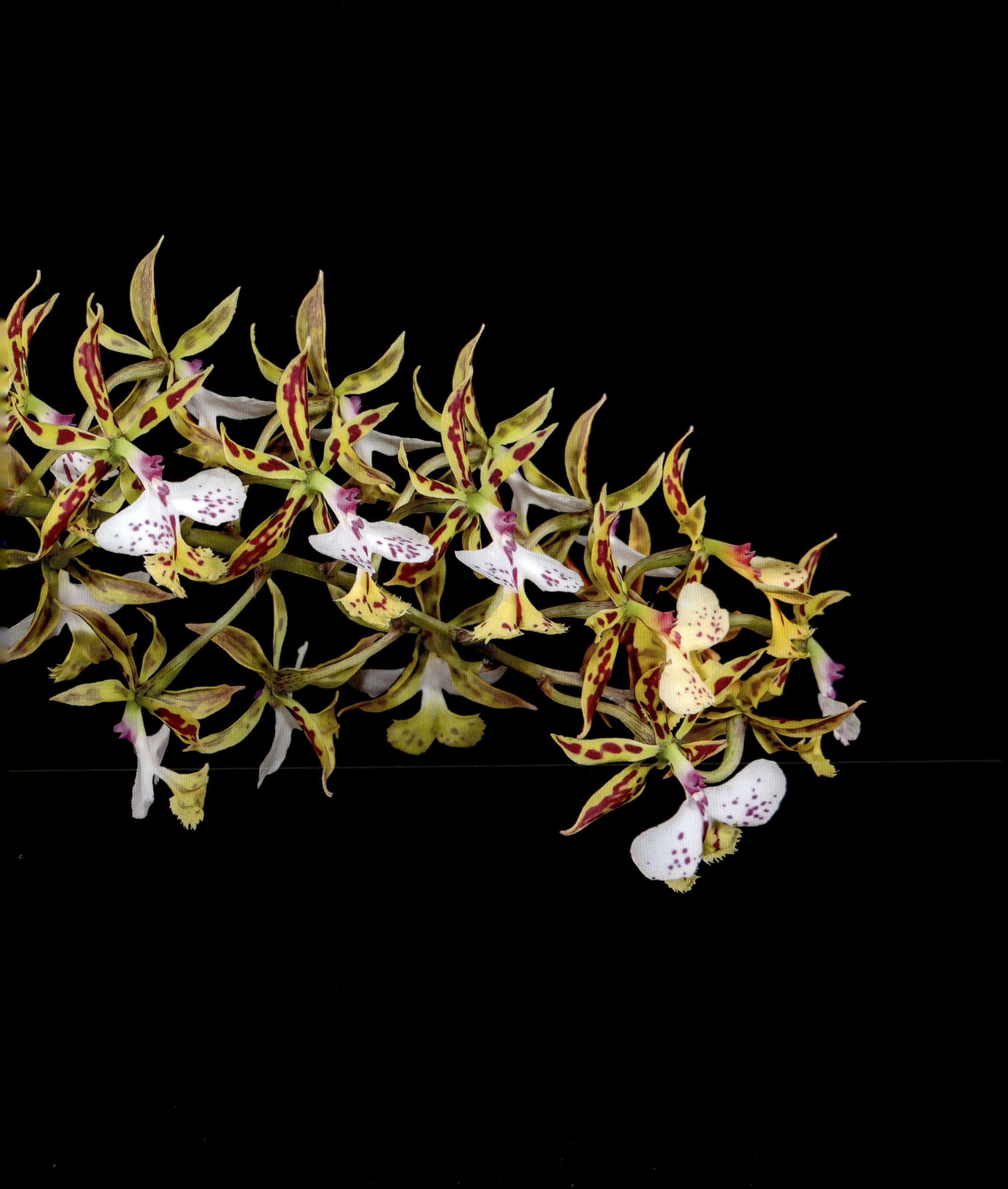

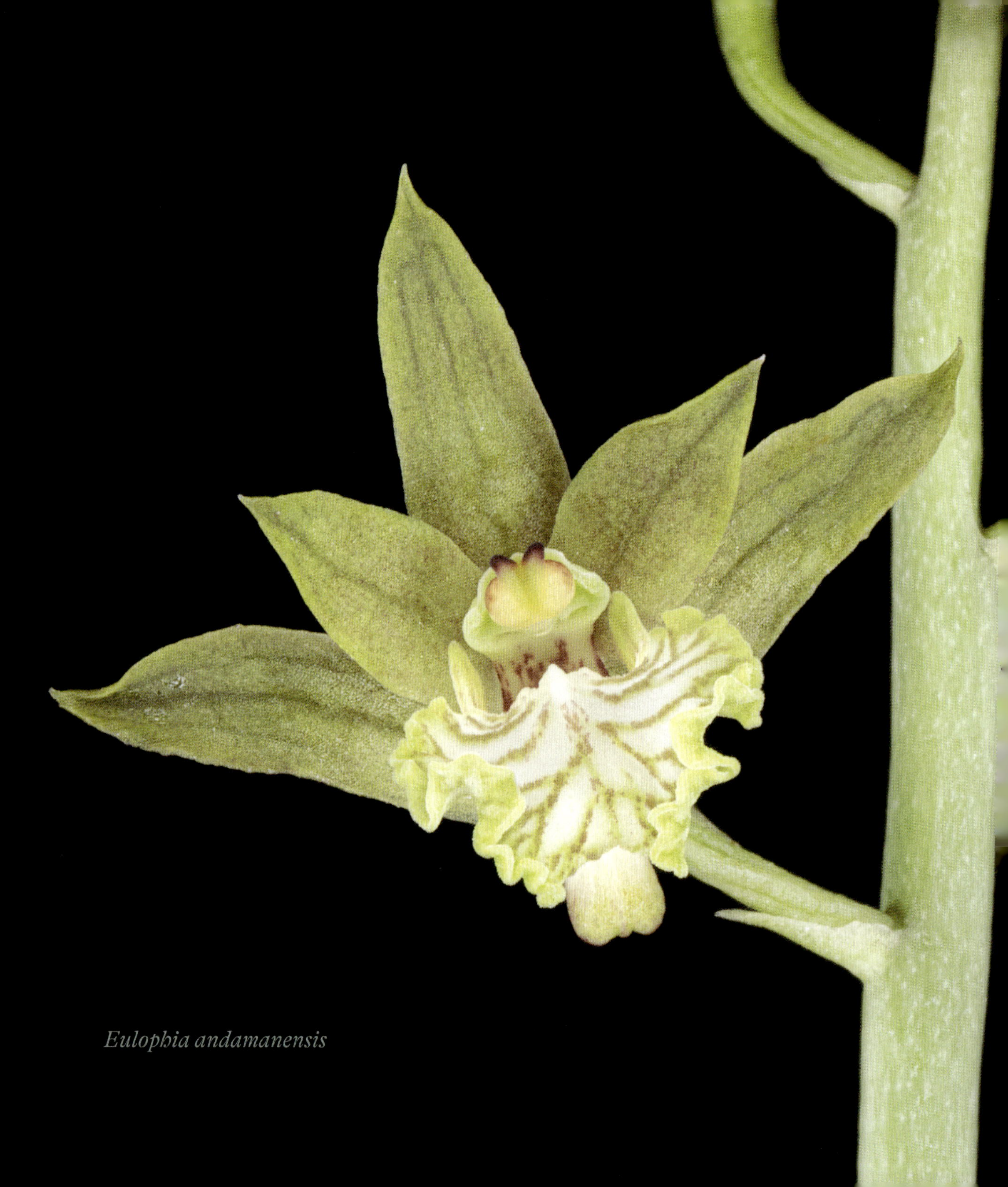

Eulophia andamanensis

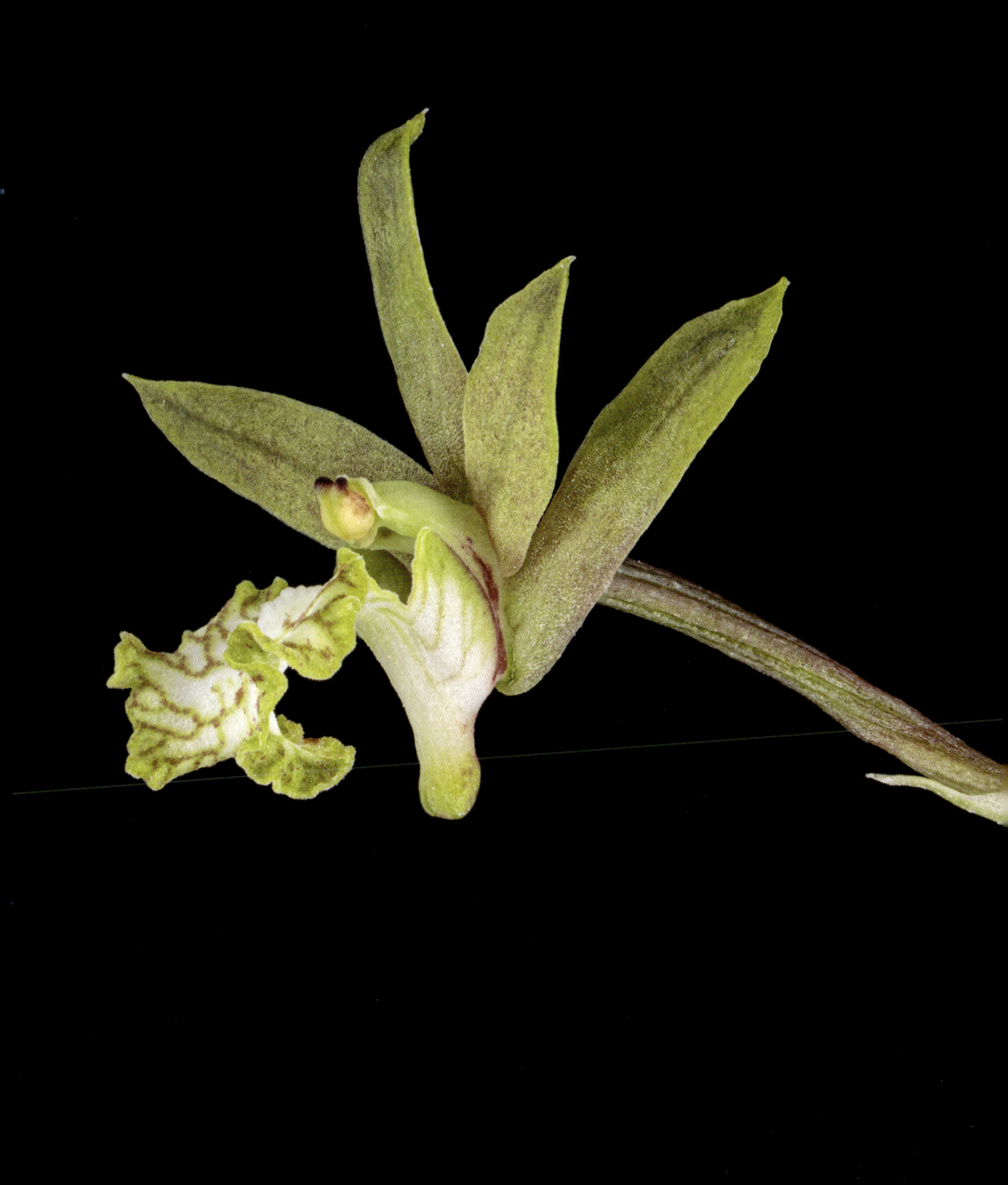

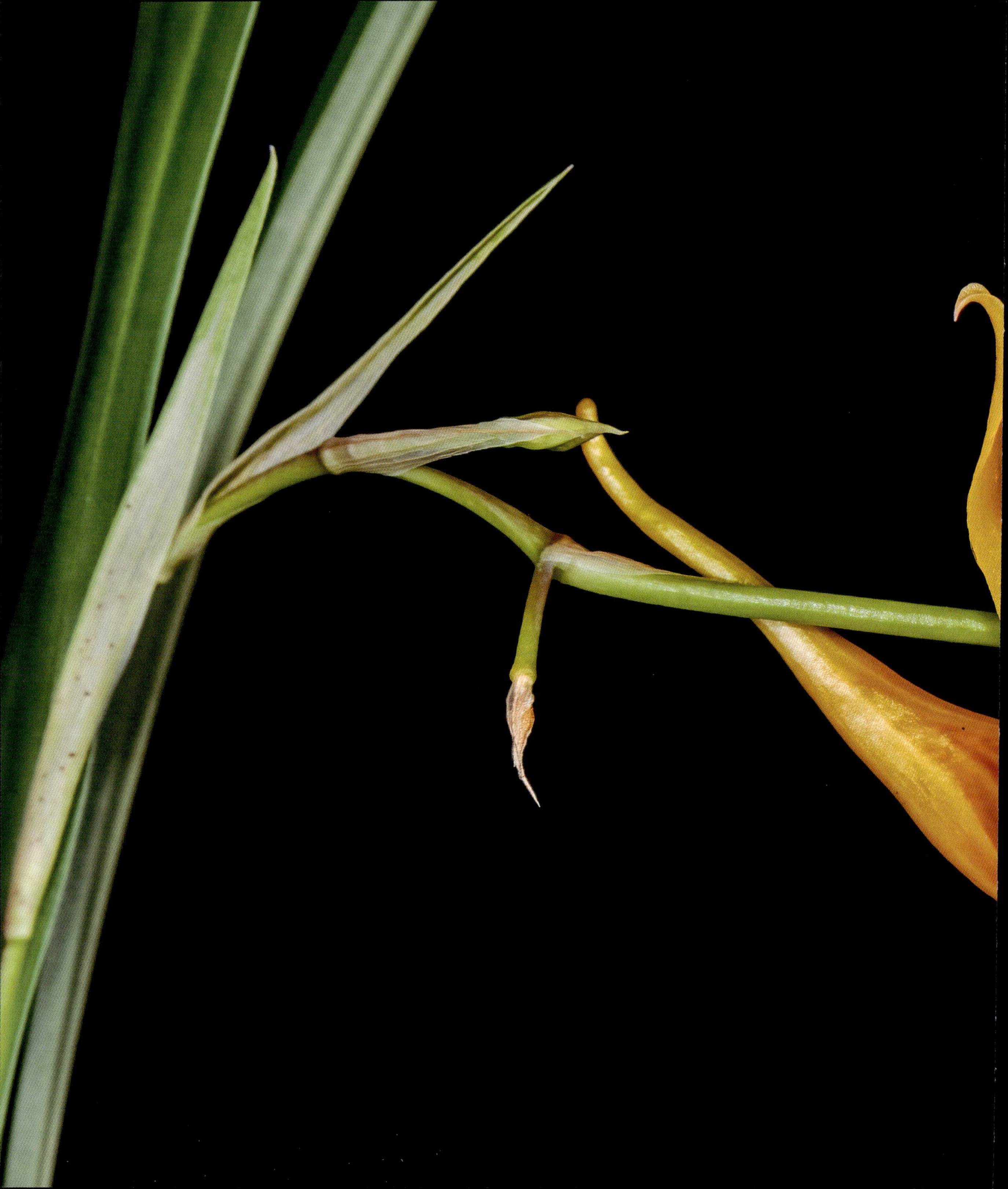

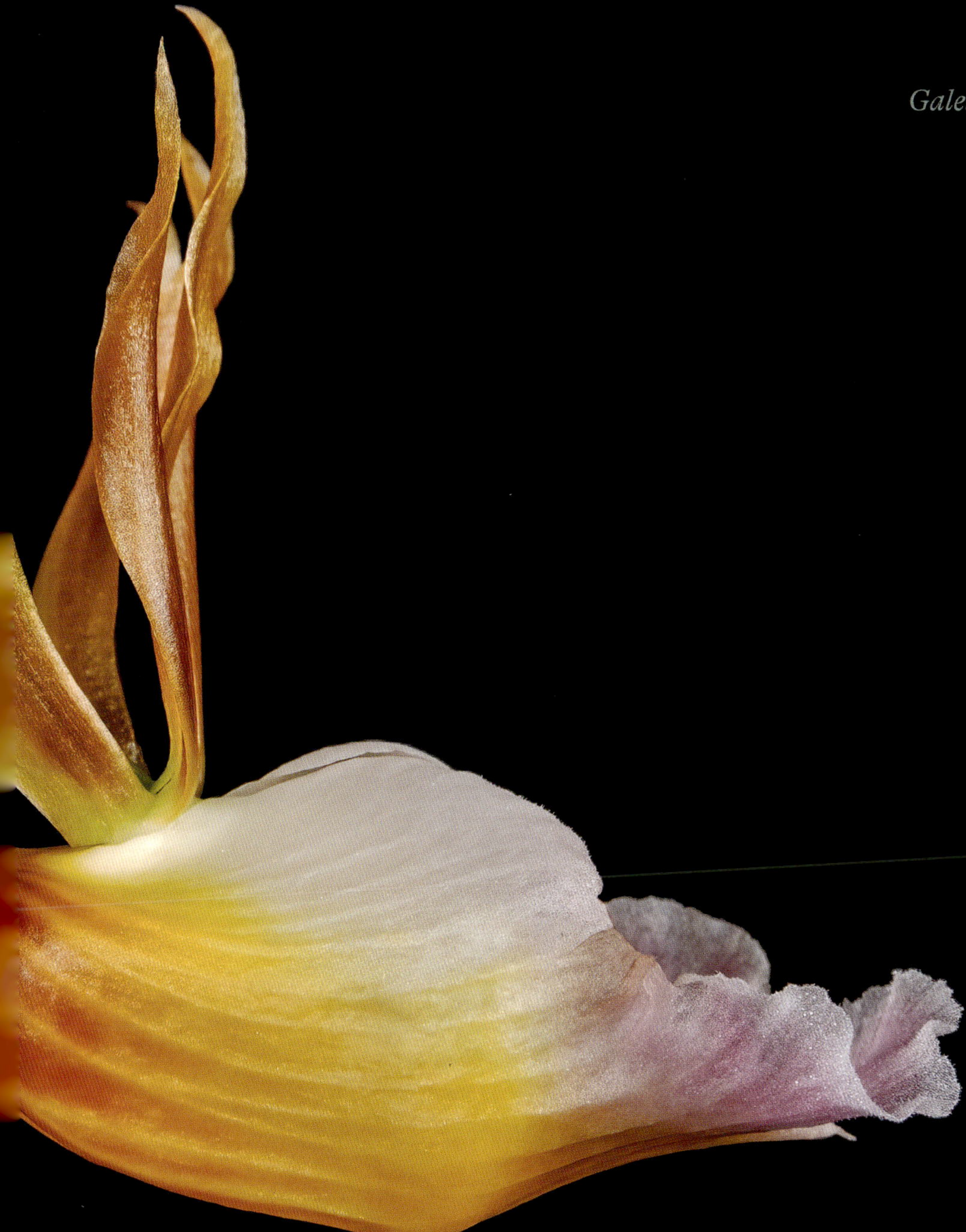

Galeandra arundinis

Gomesa croesus

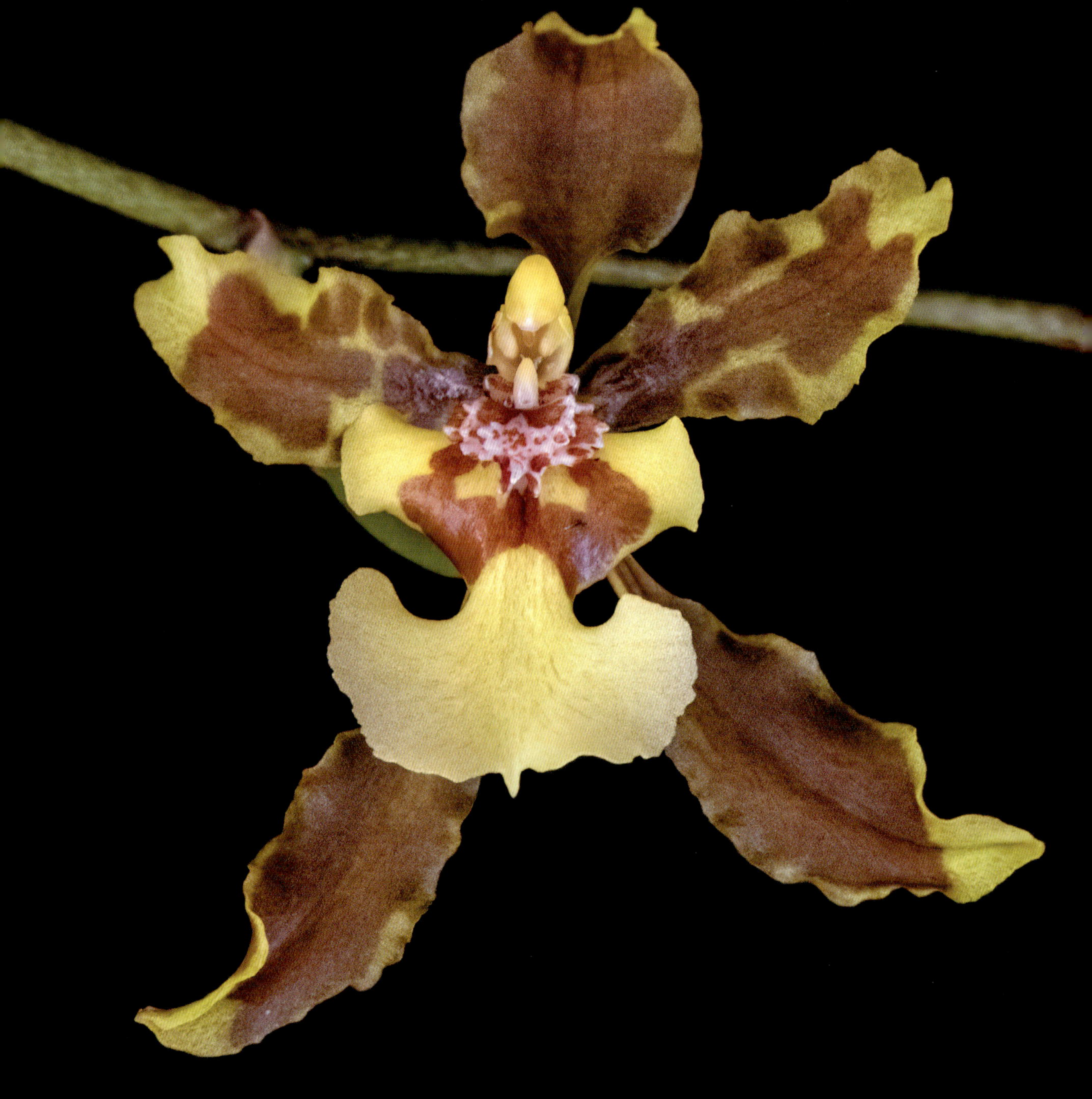

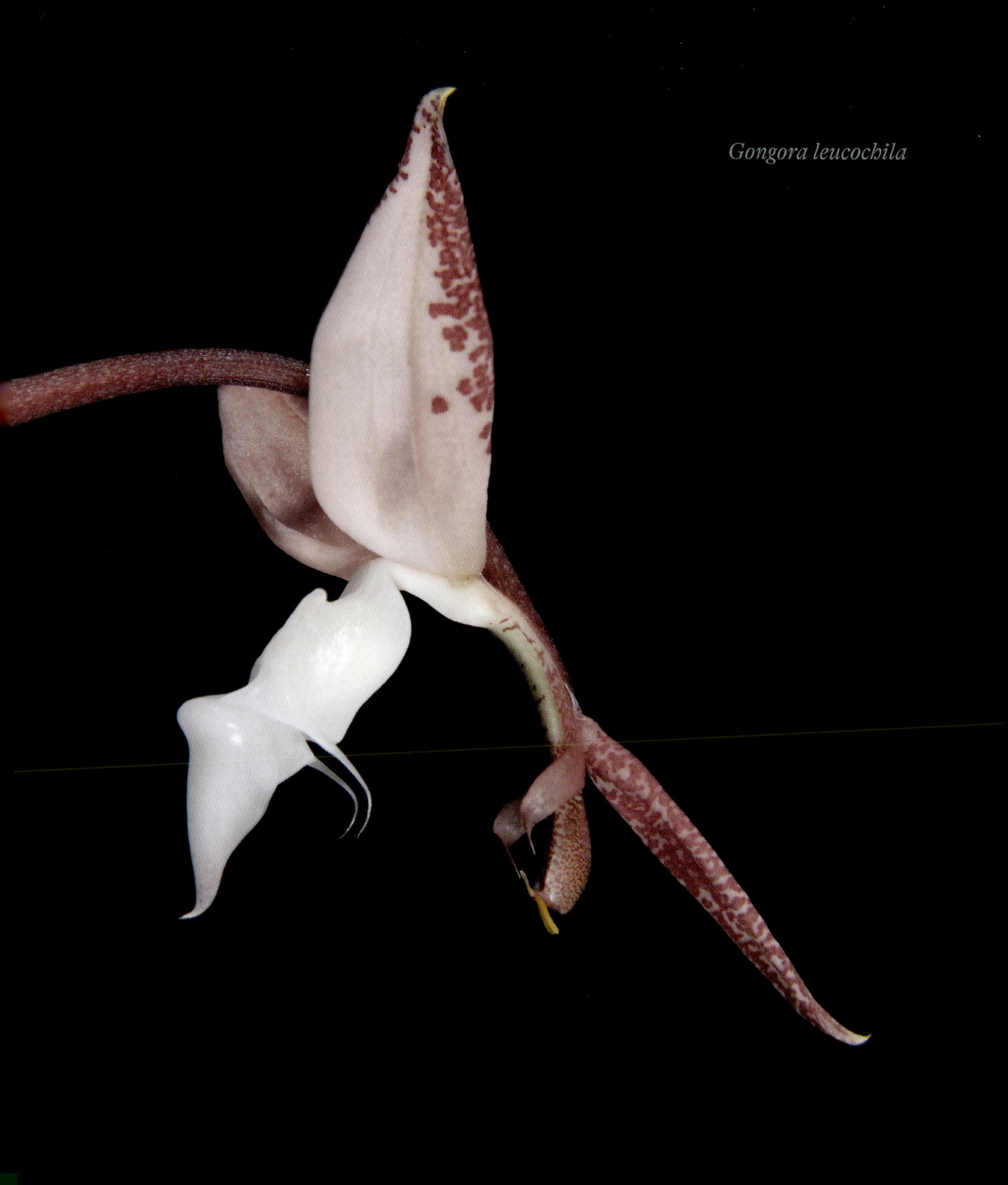

Gongora leucochila

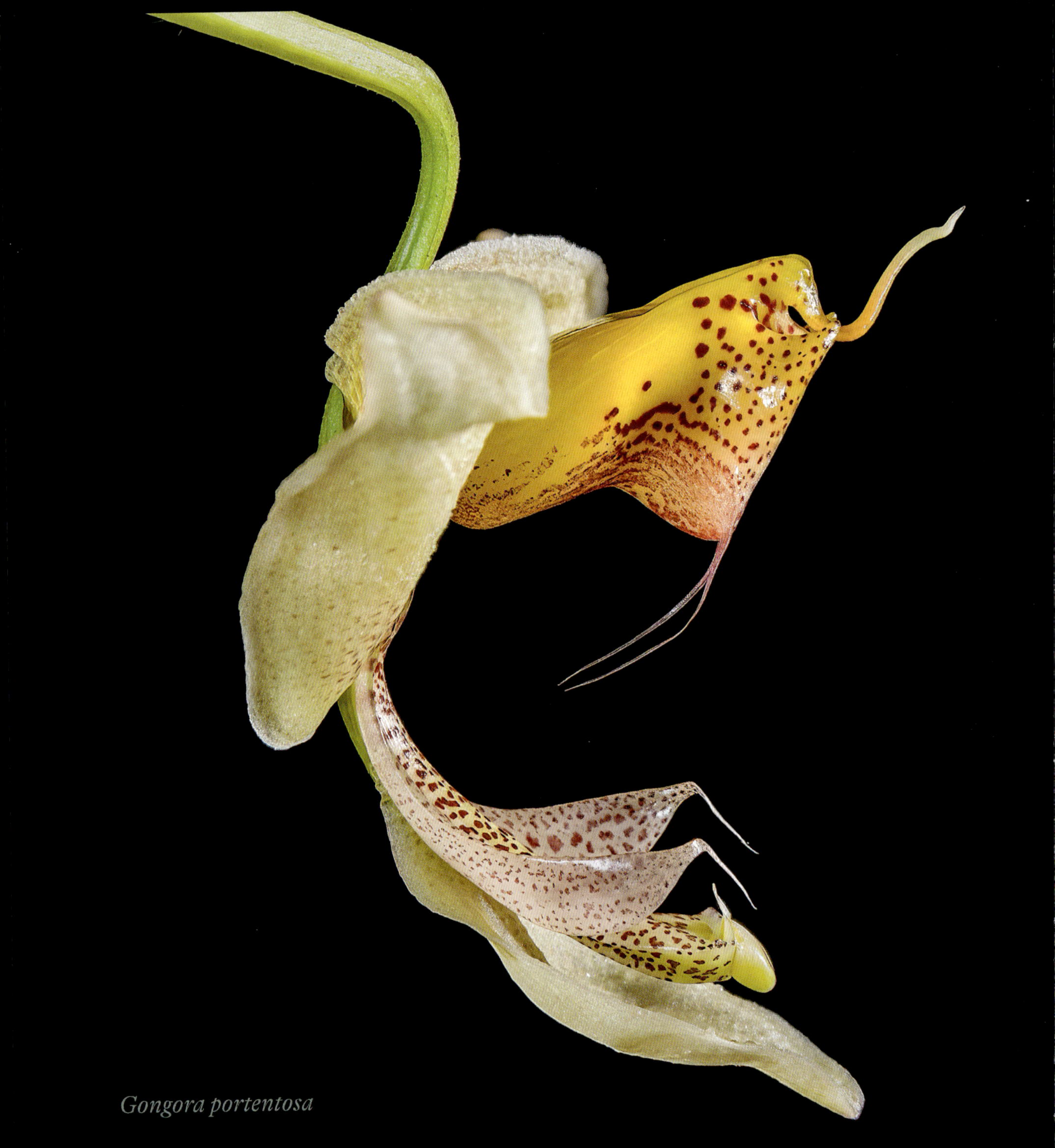

Gongora portentosa

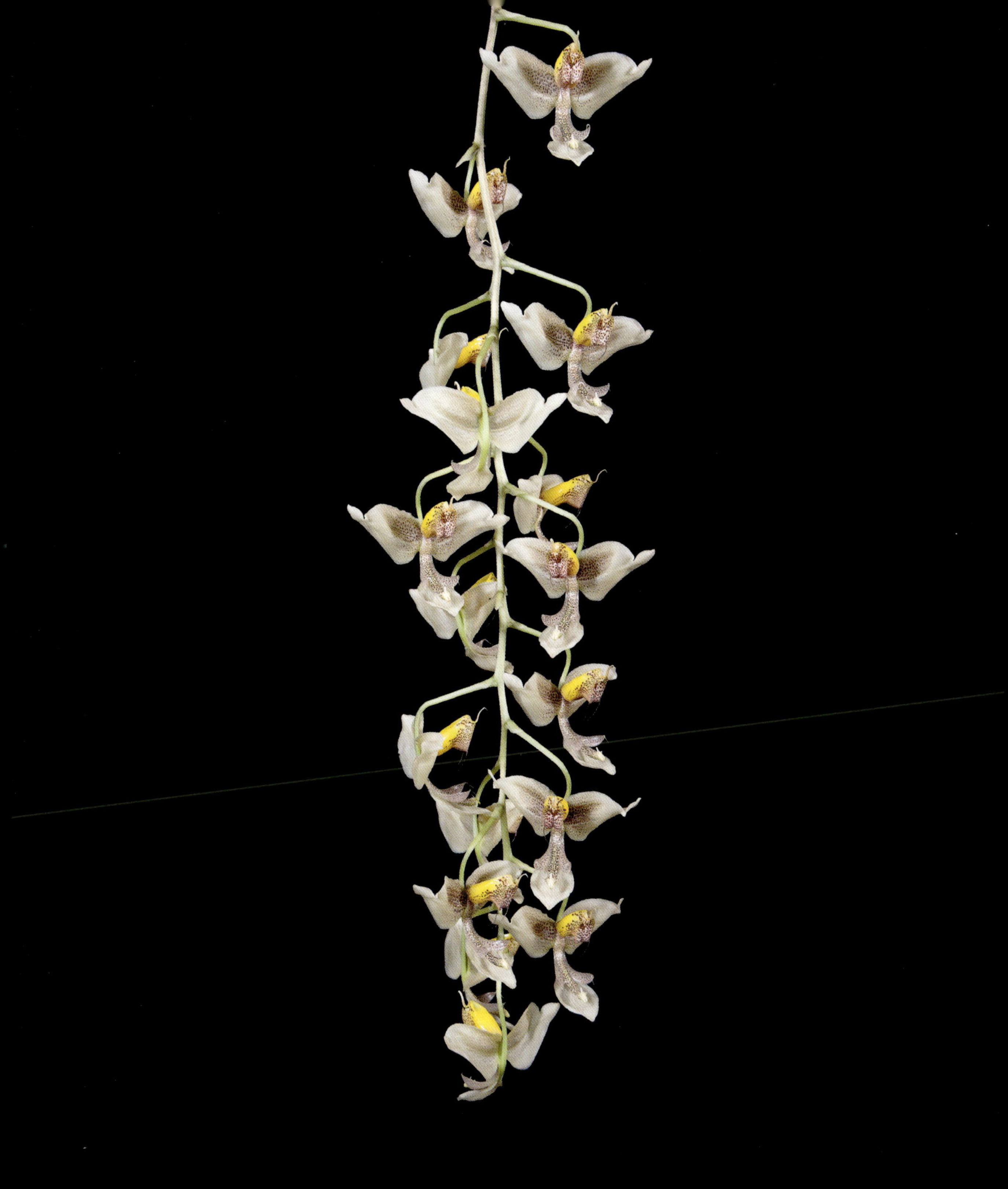

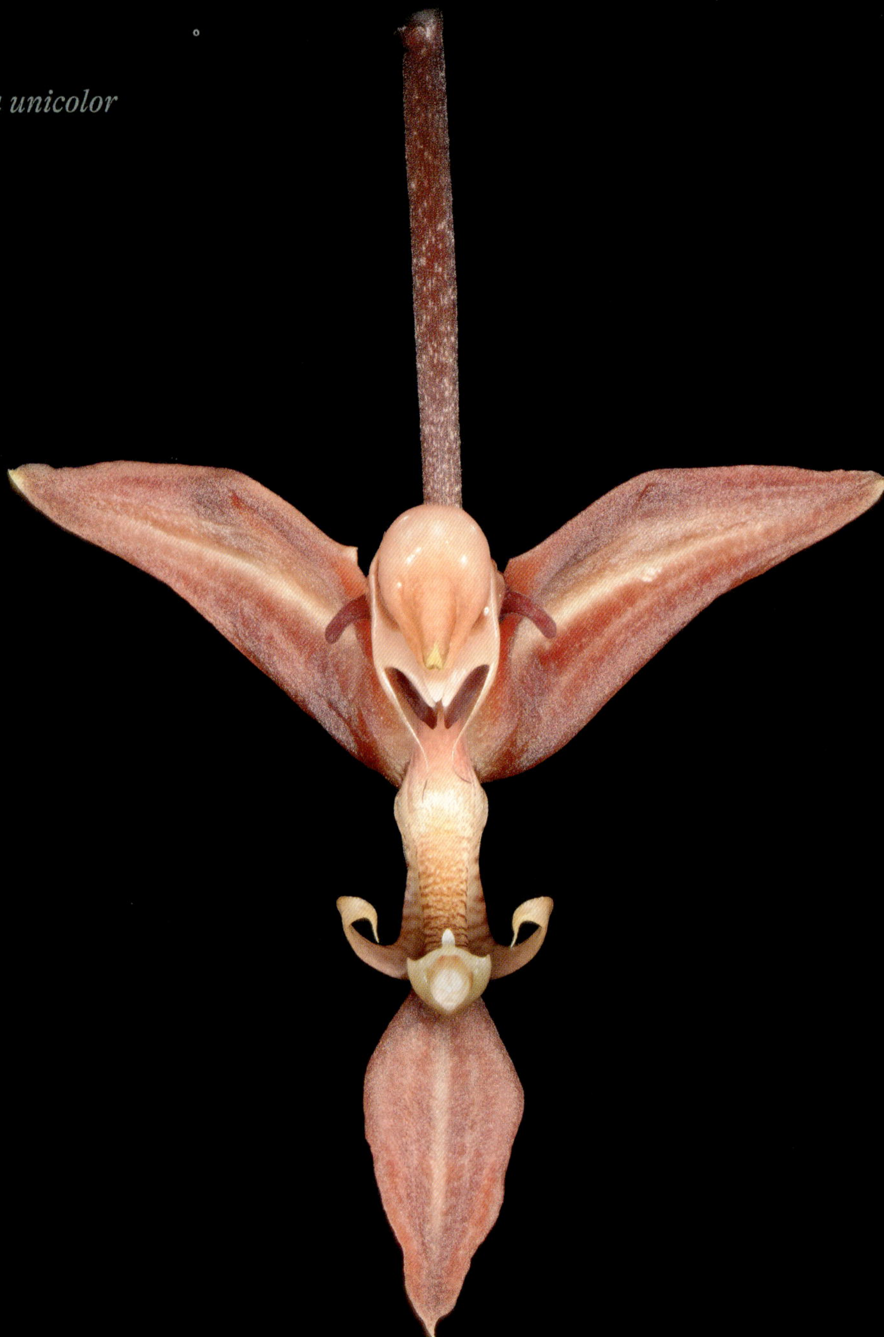

Gongora unicolor

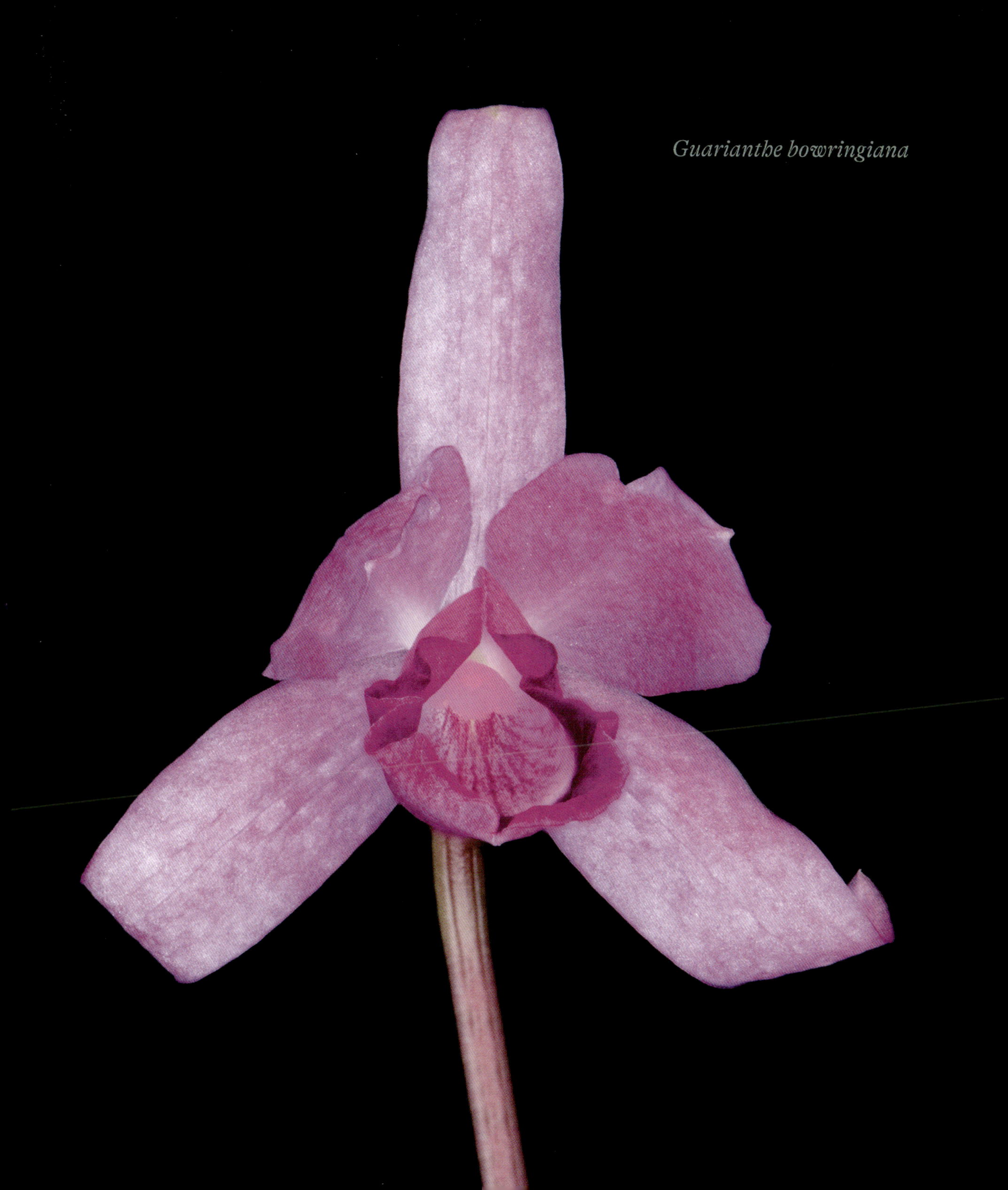

Guarianthe bowringiana

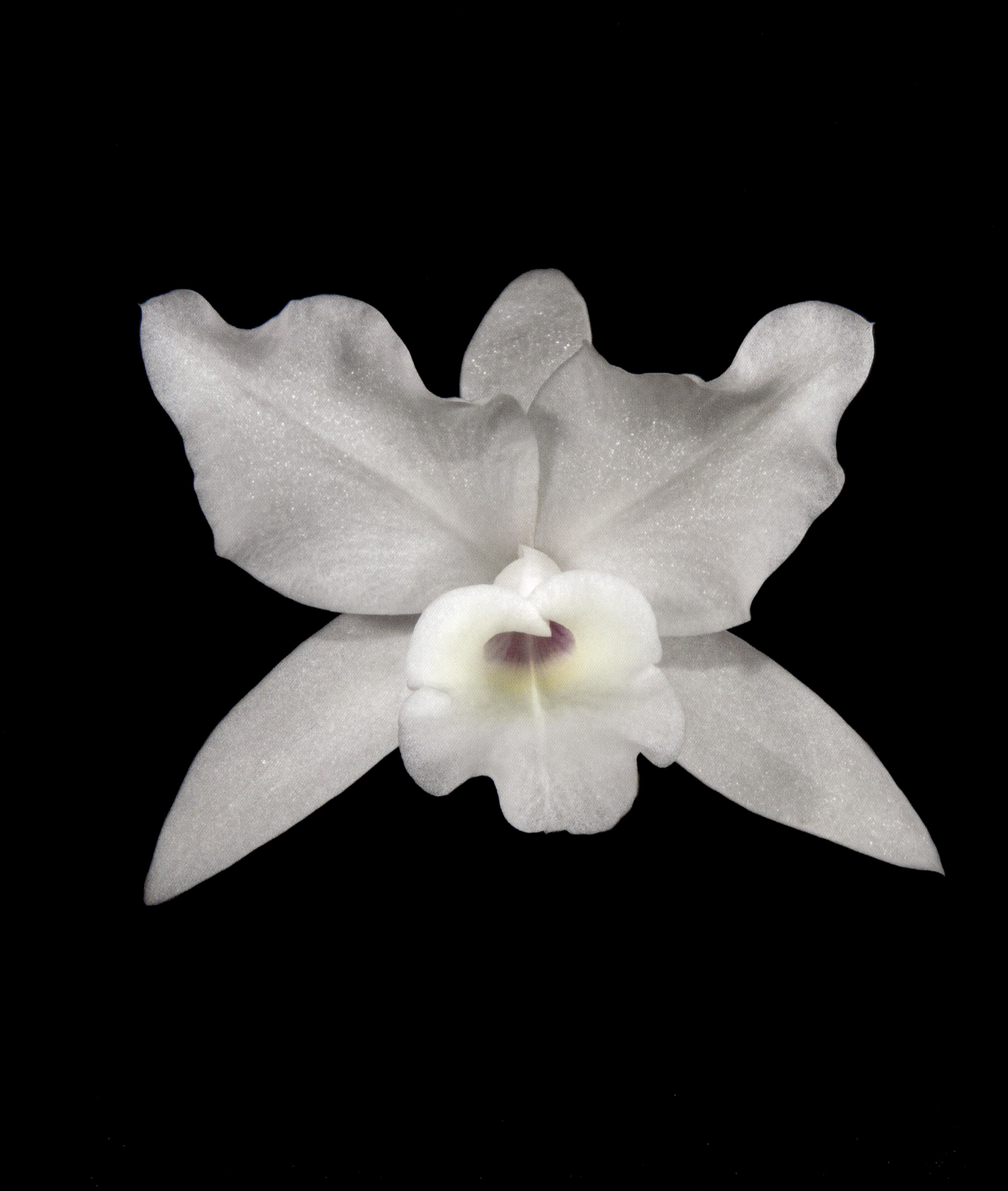

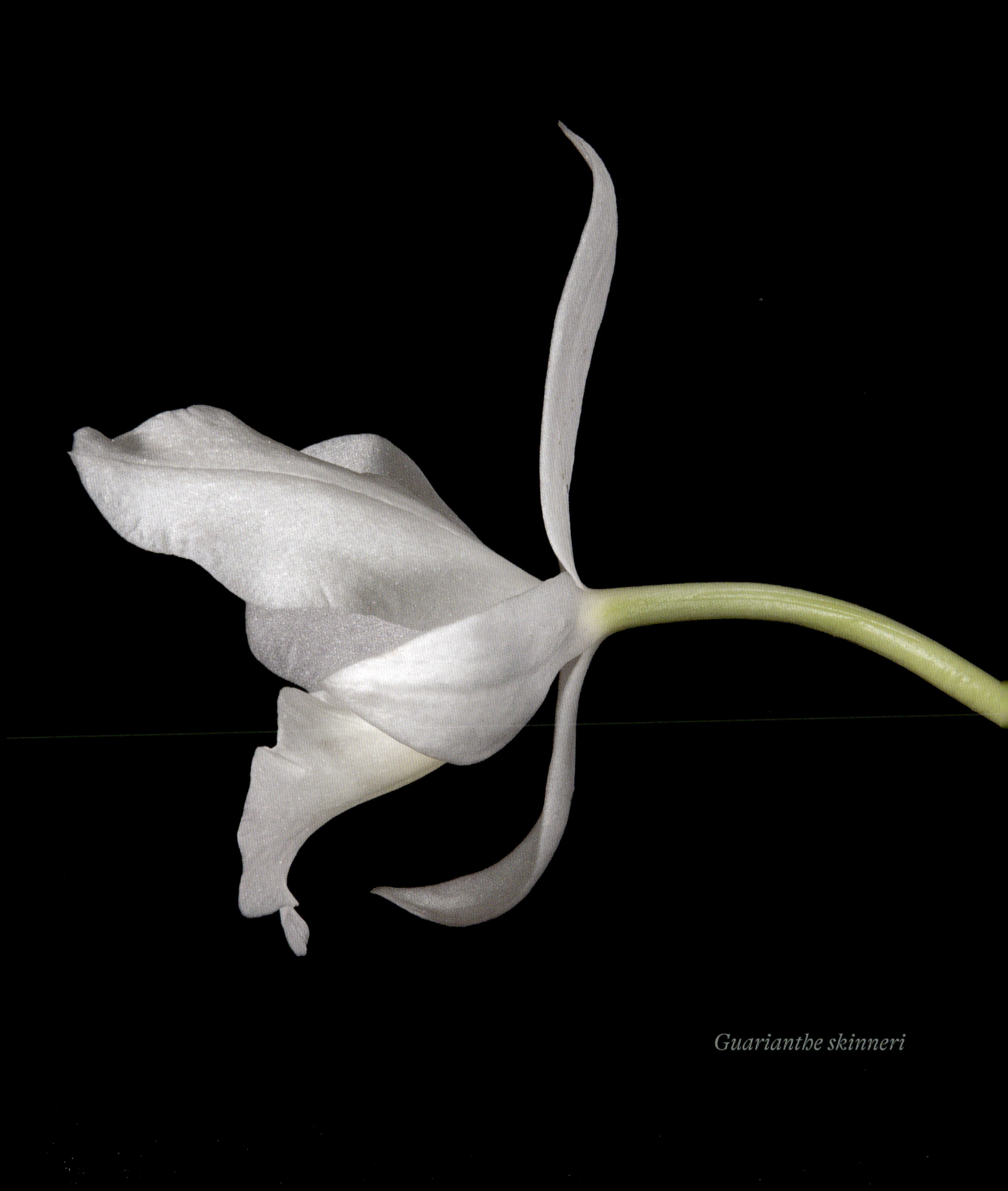

Guarianthe skinneri

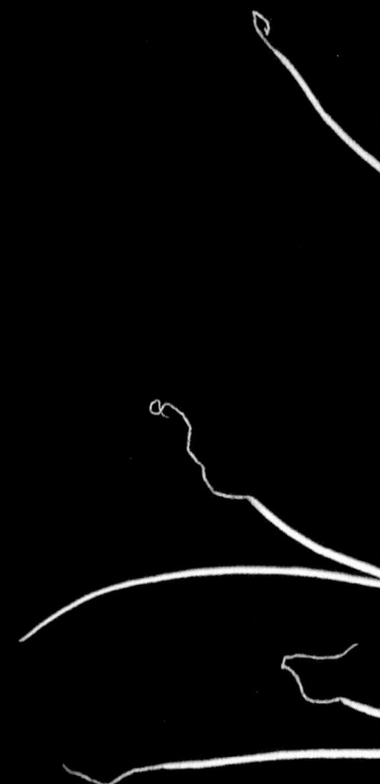

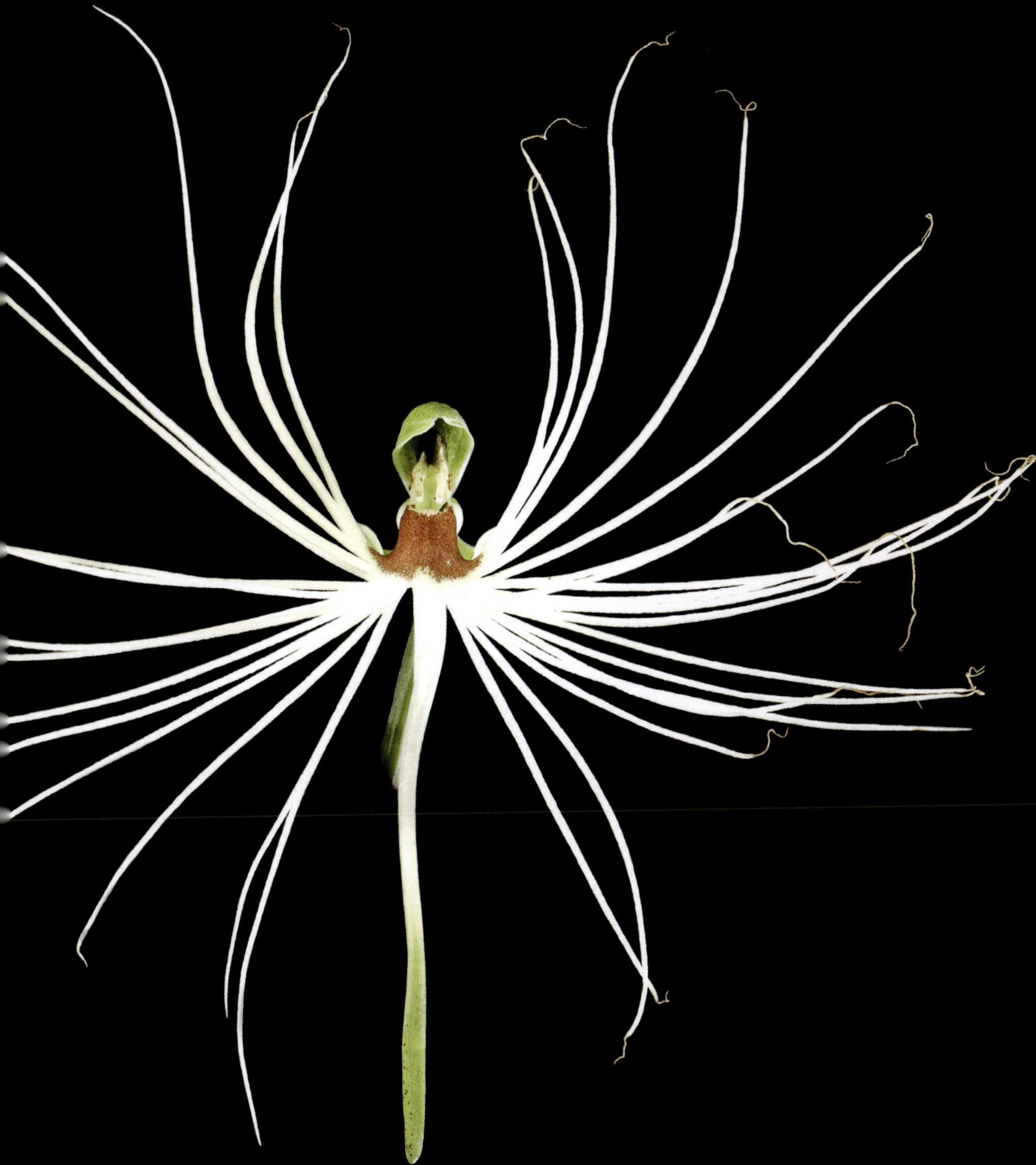

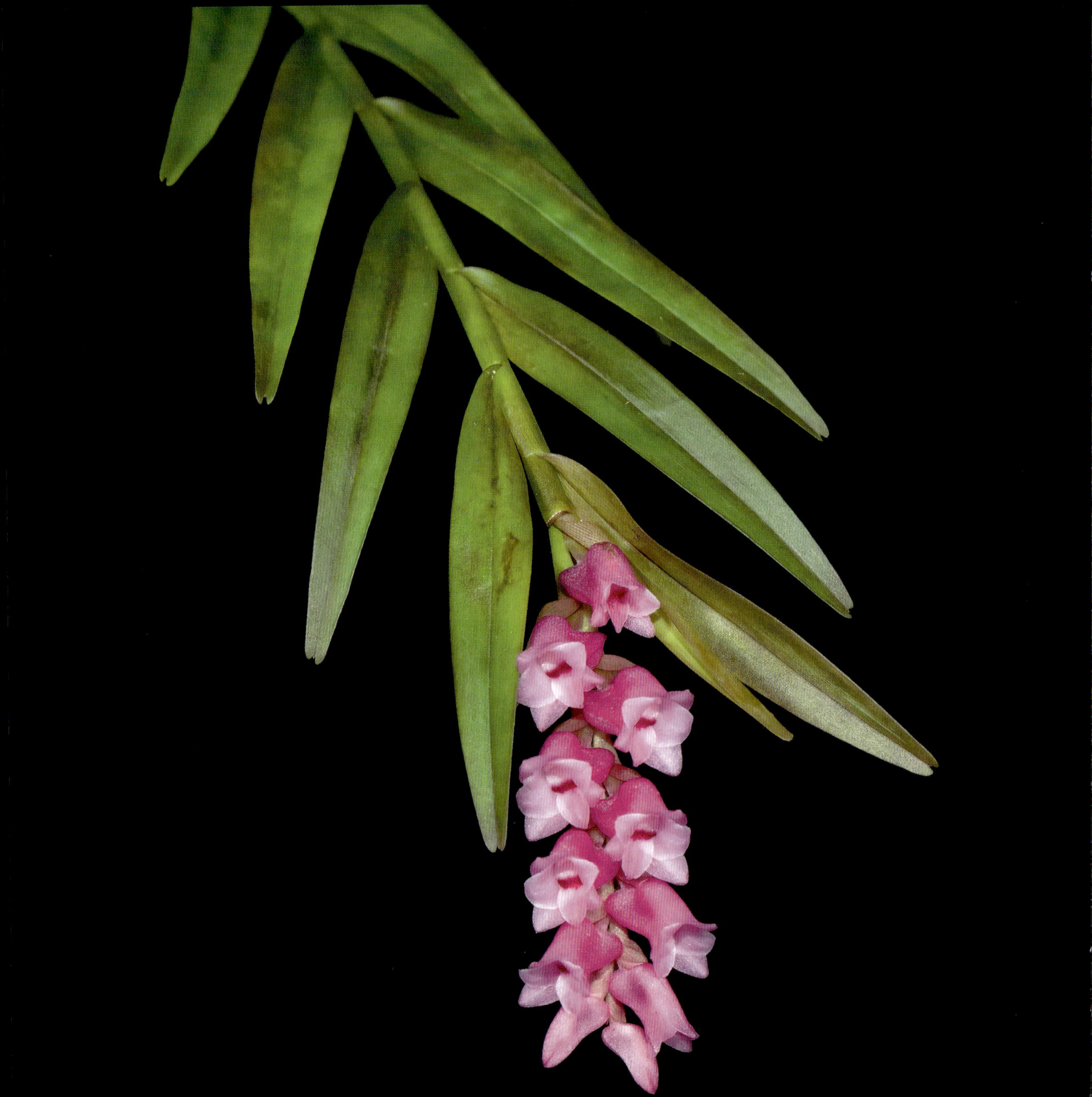

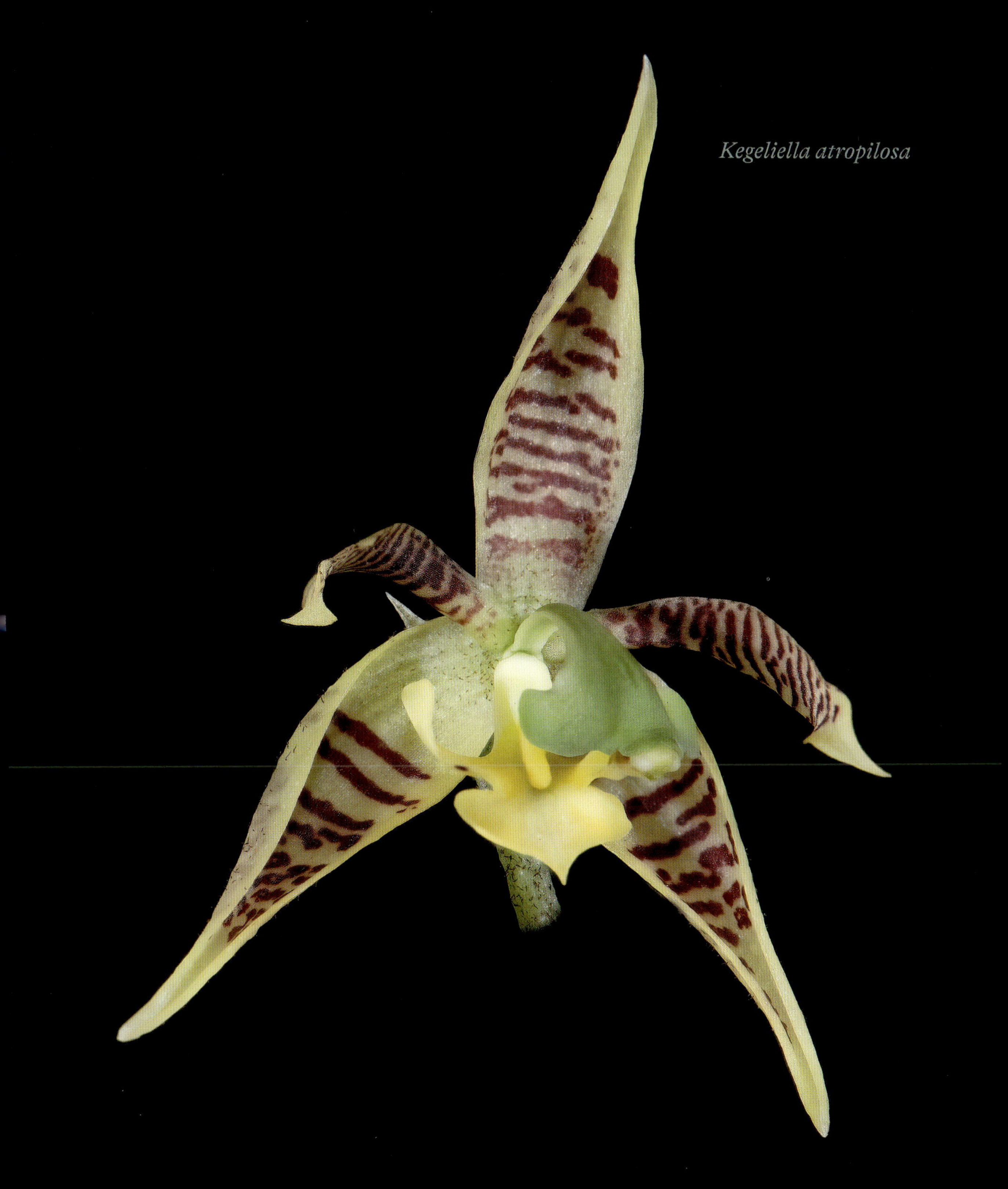

Kegeliella atropilosa

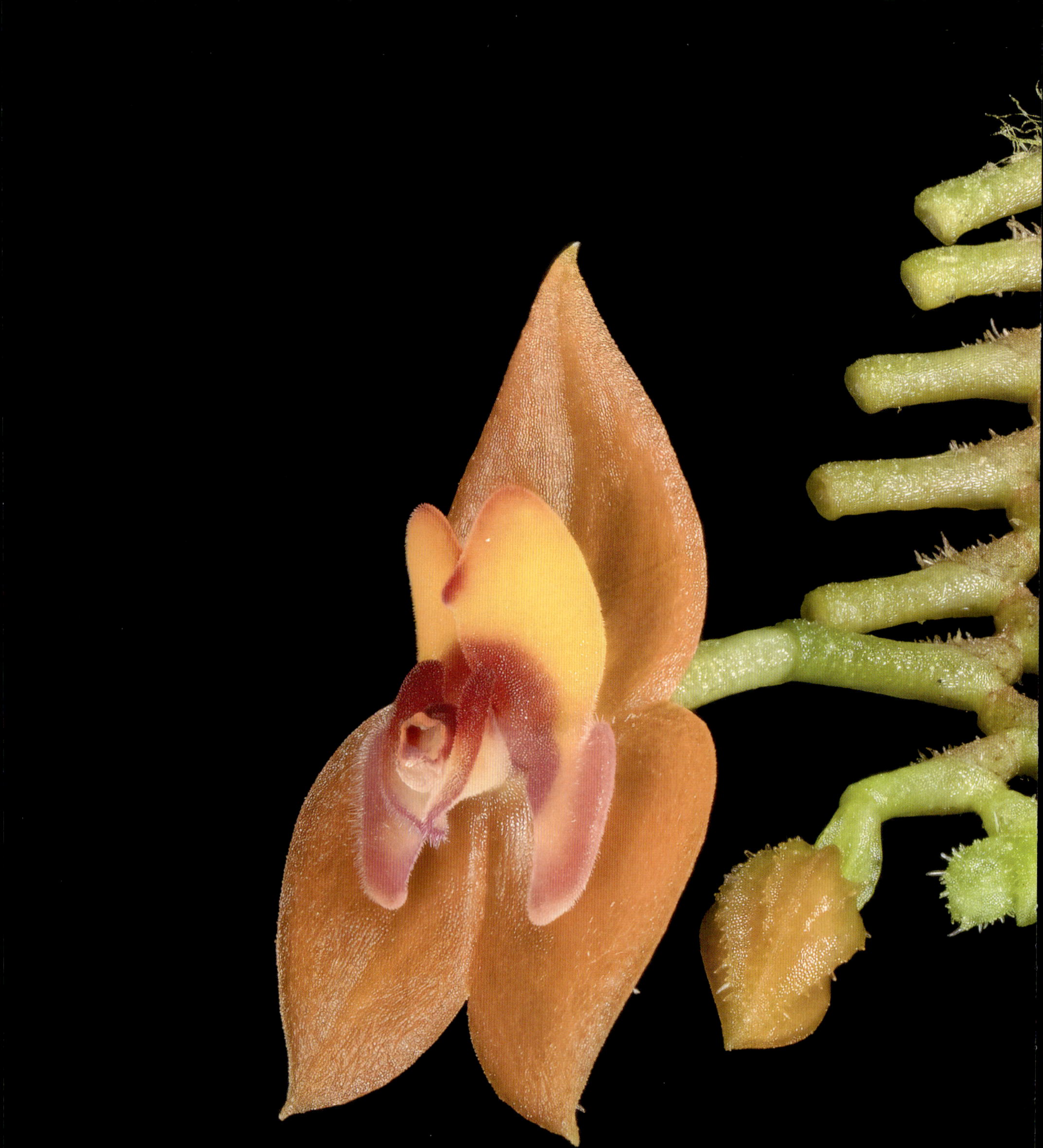

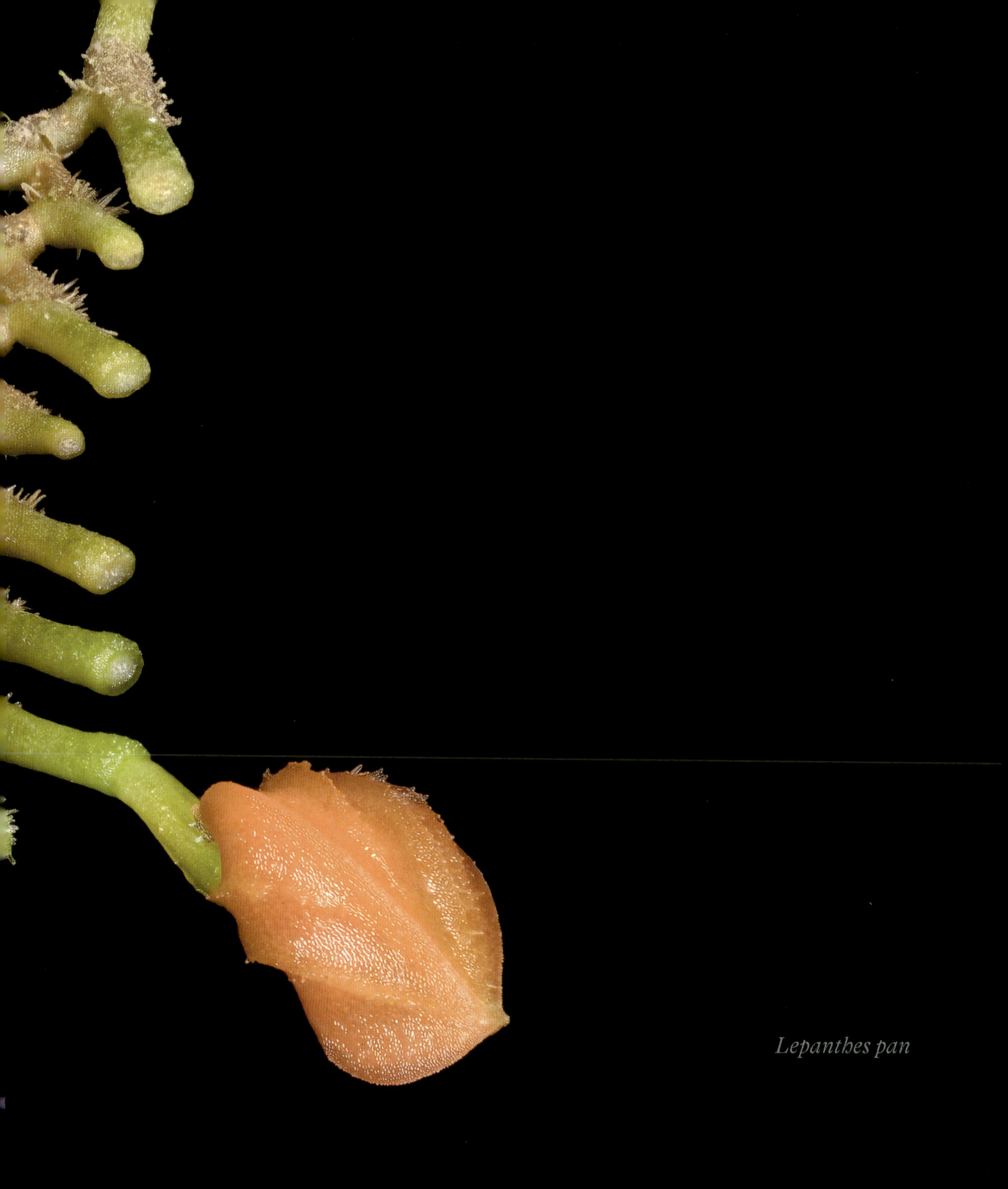

Lepanthes pan

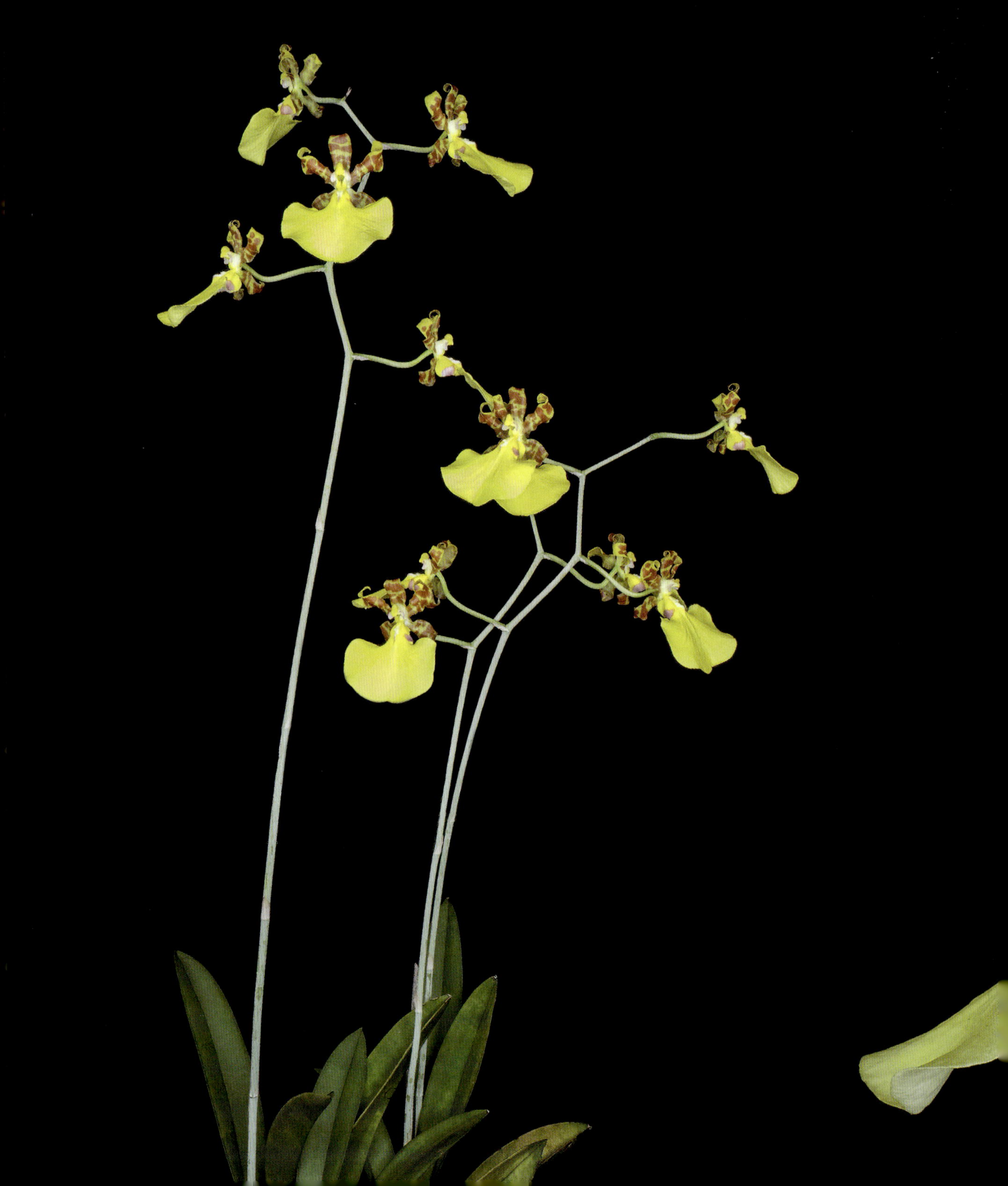

Lophiarella splendida

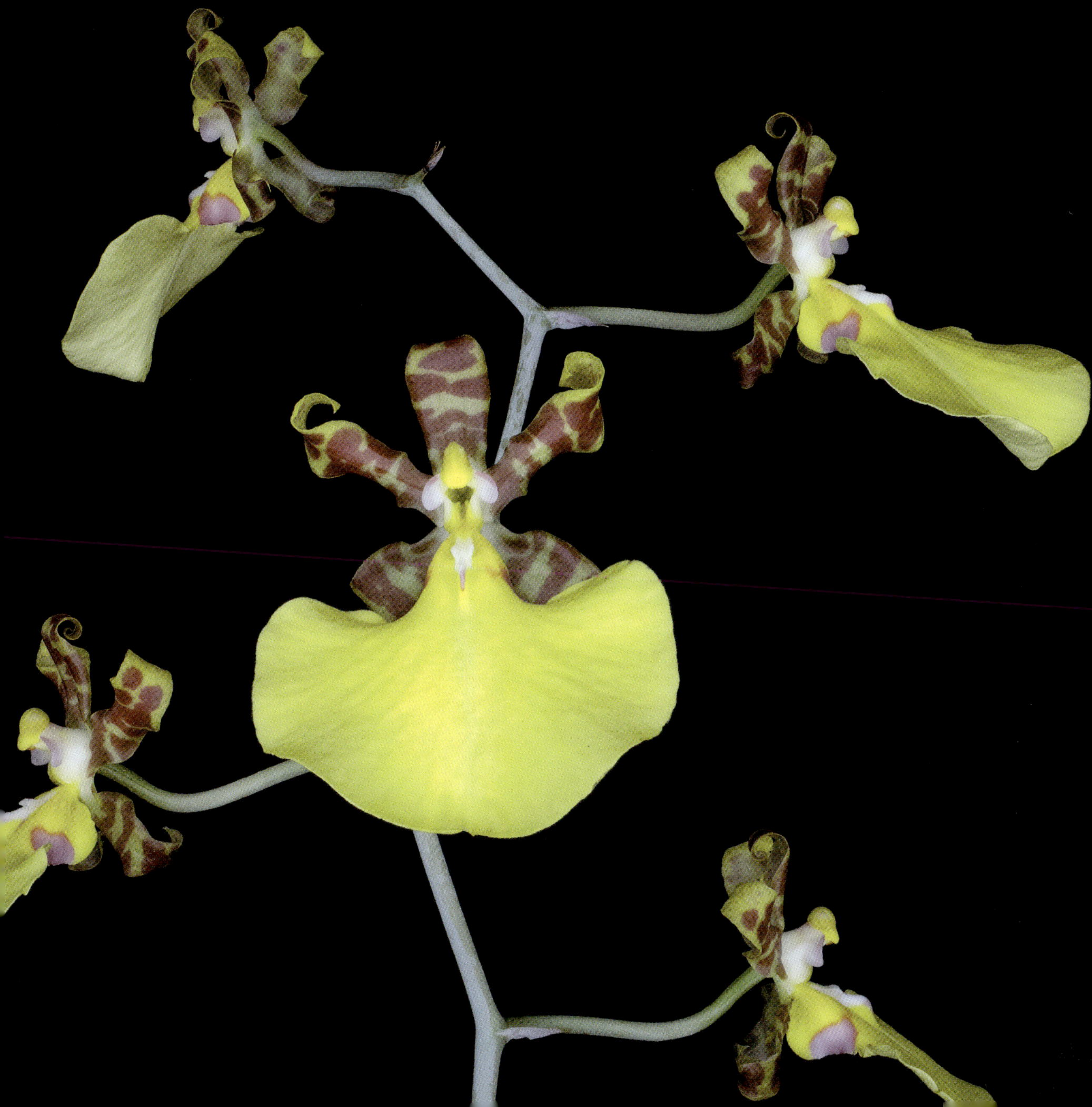

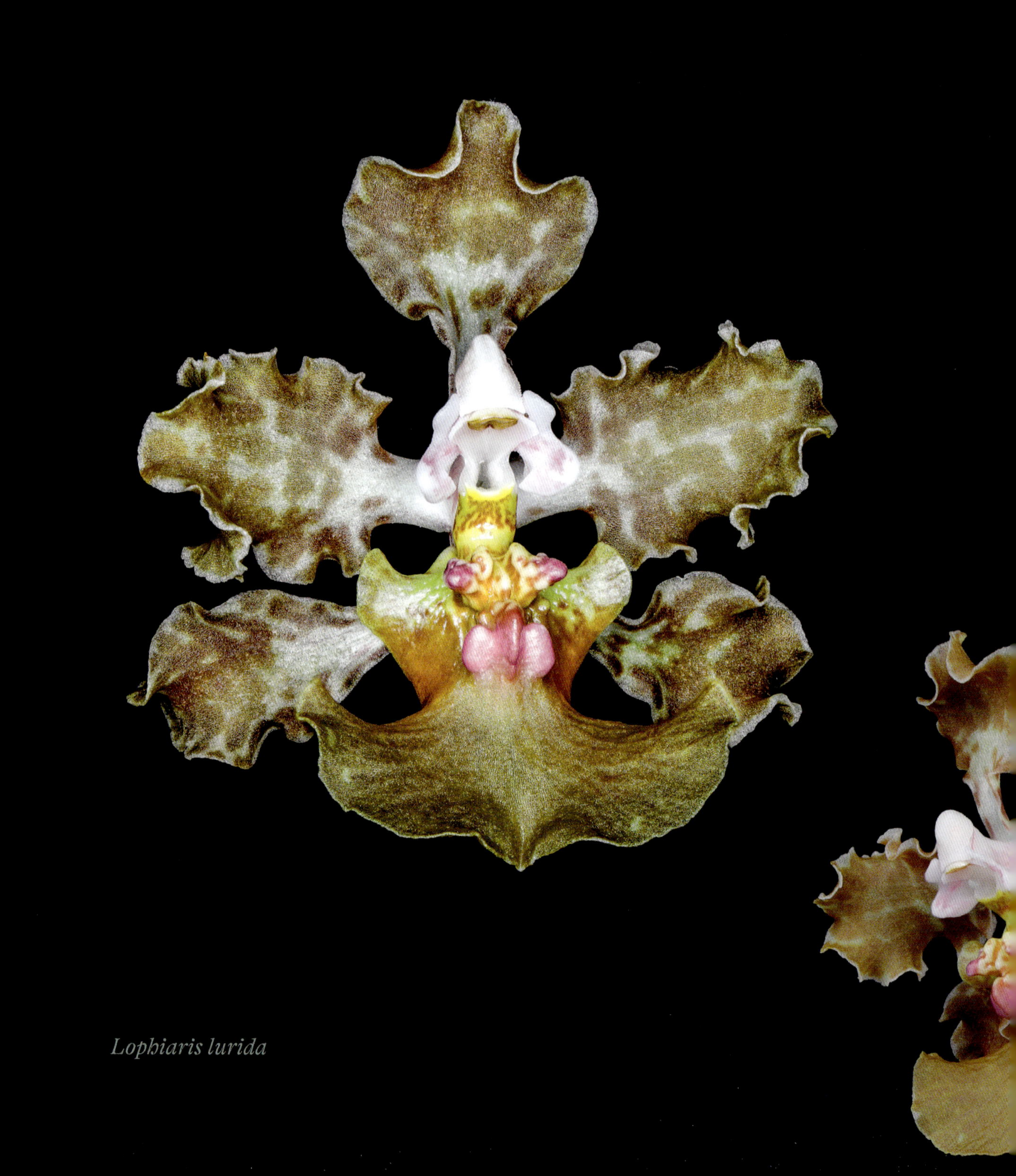

Lophiaris lurida

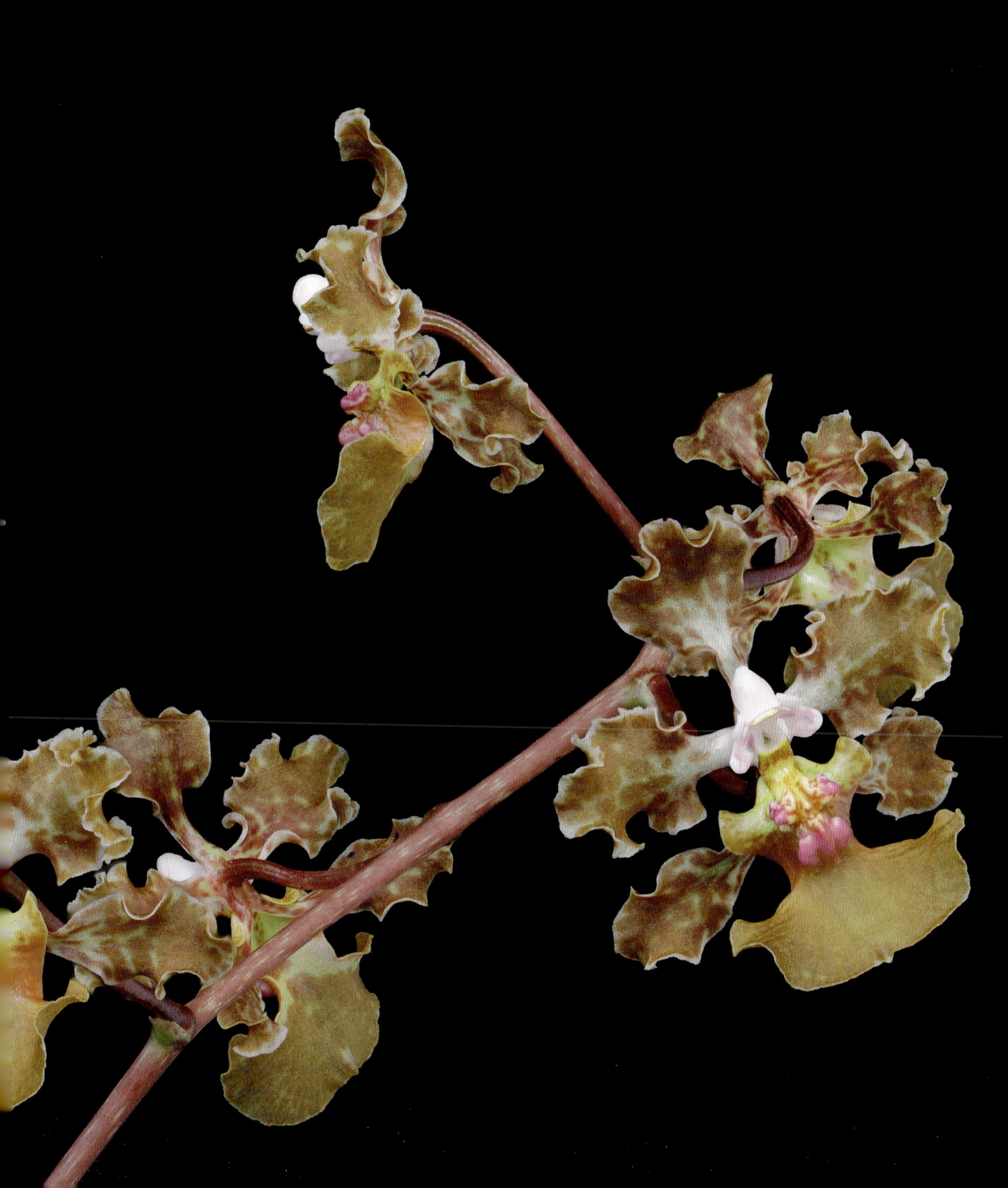

Lophiaris oerstedii

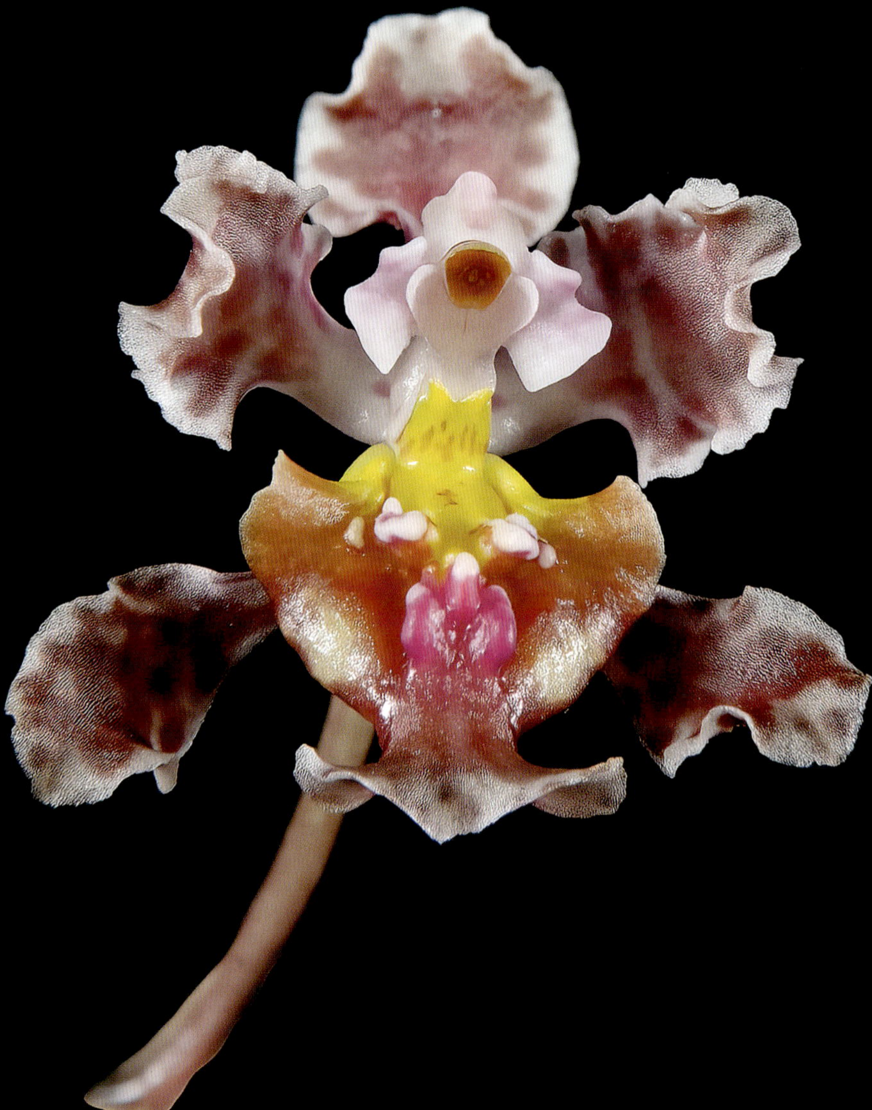

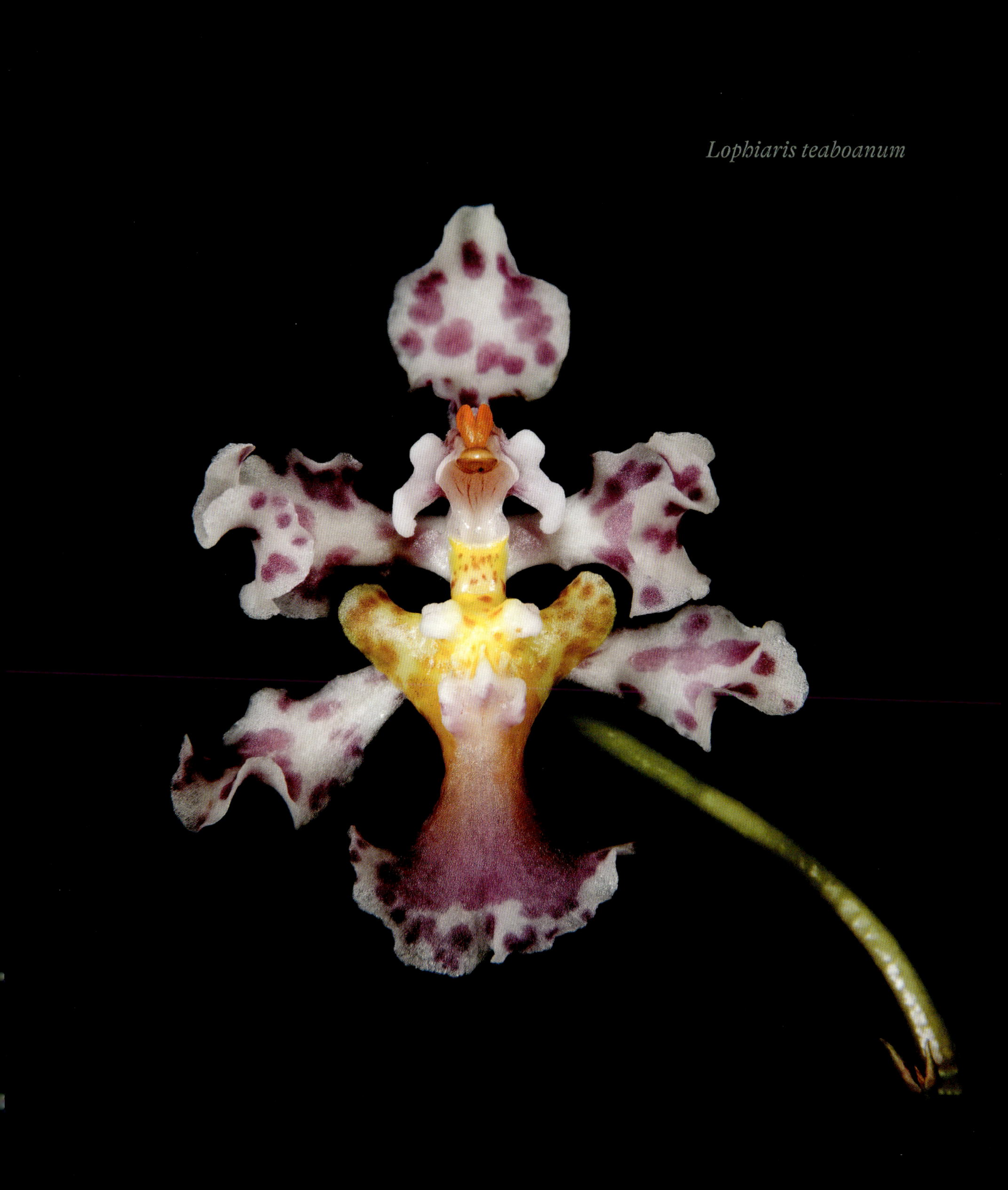

Lophiaris teaboanum

Maxillaria acervata

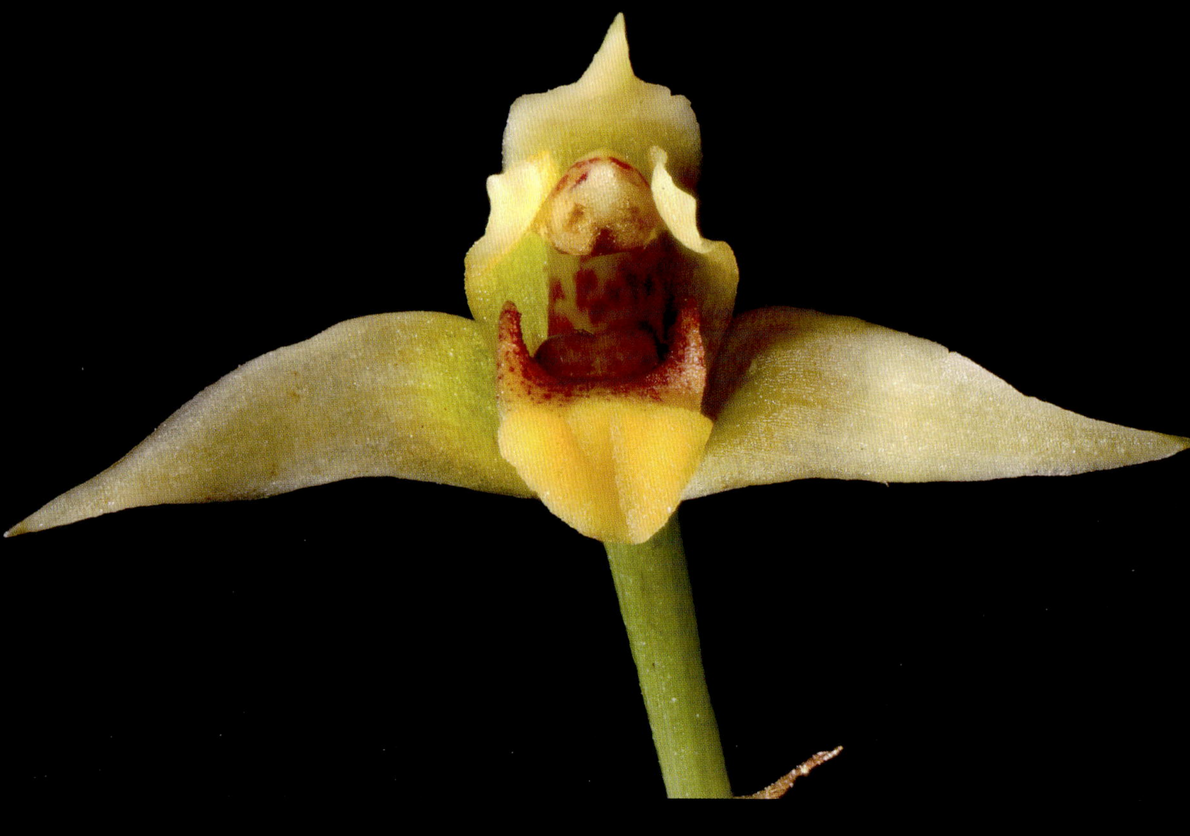

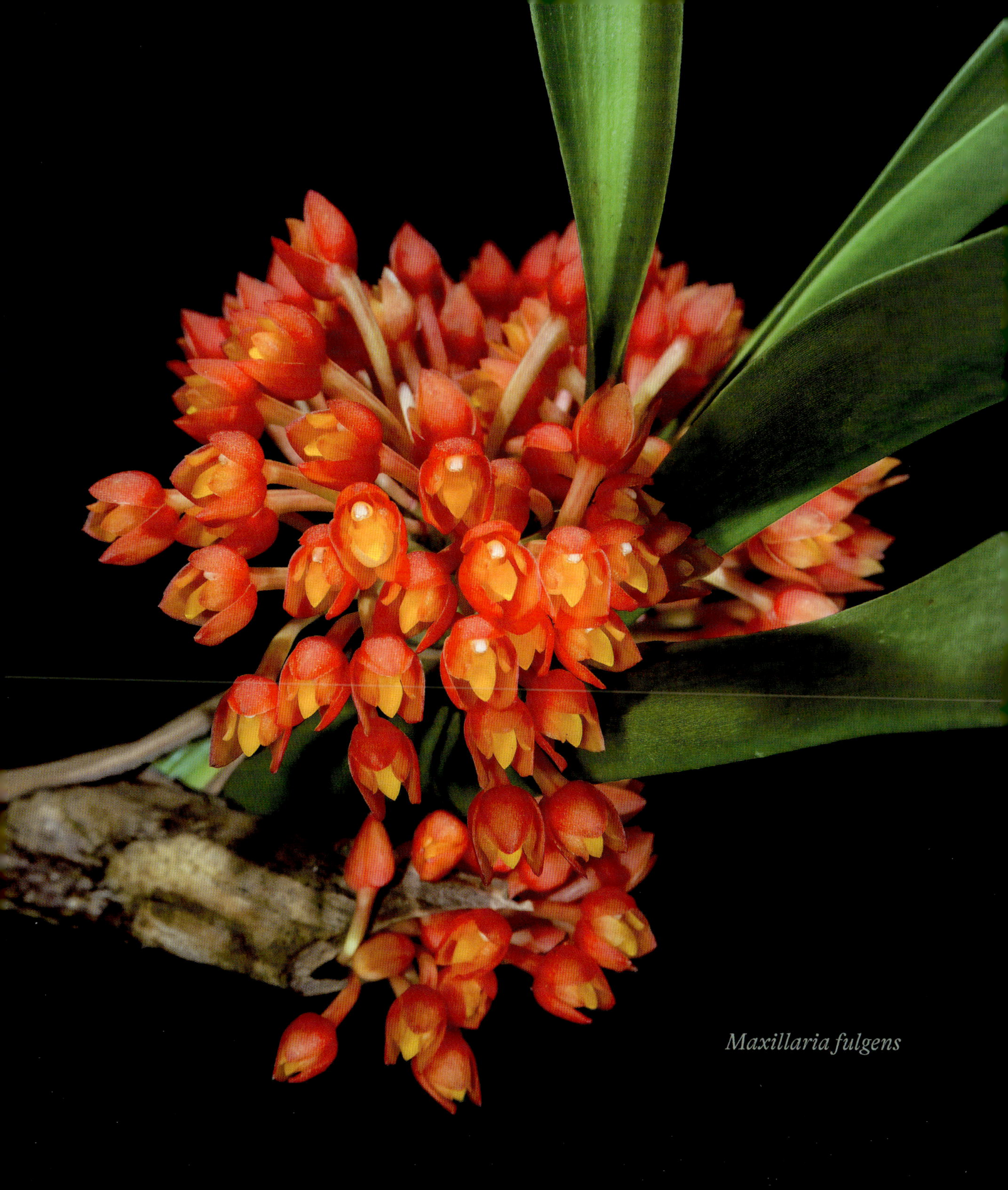

Maxillaria fulgens

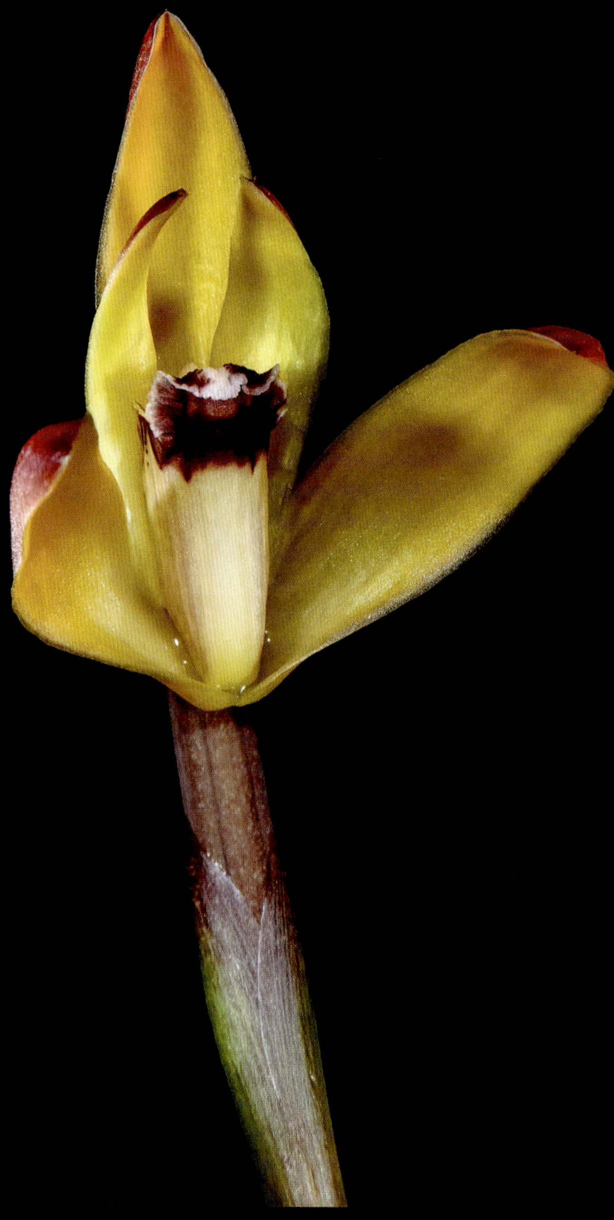

Maxillaria porrecta

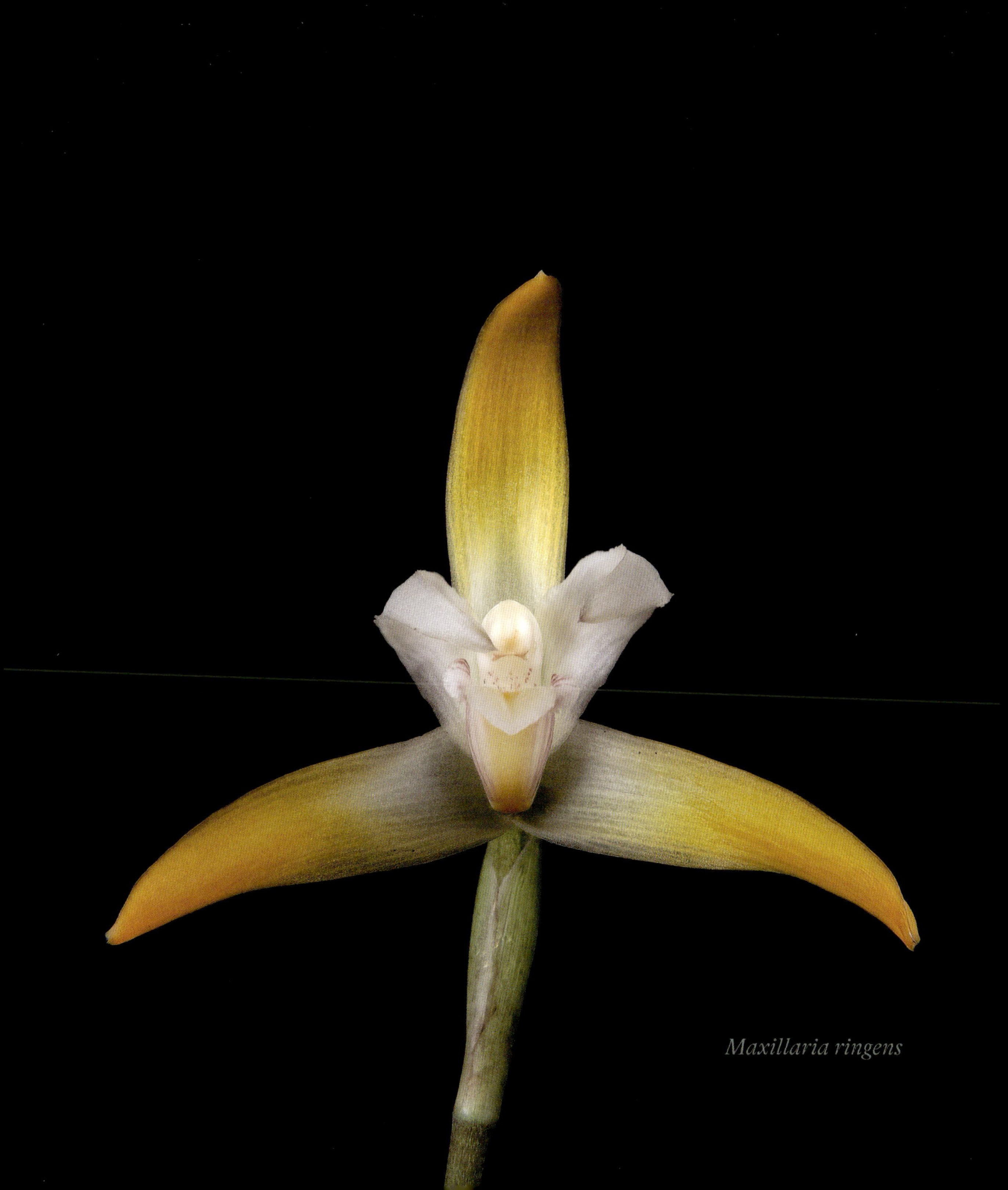

Maxillaria ringens

Mormolyca rufescens

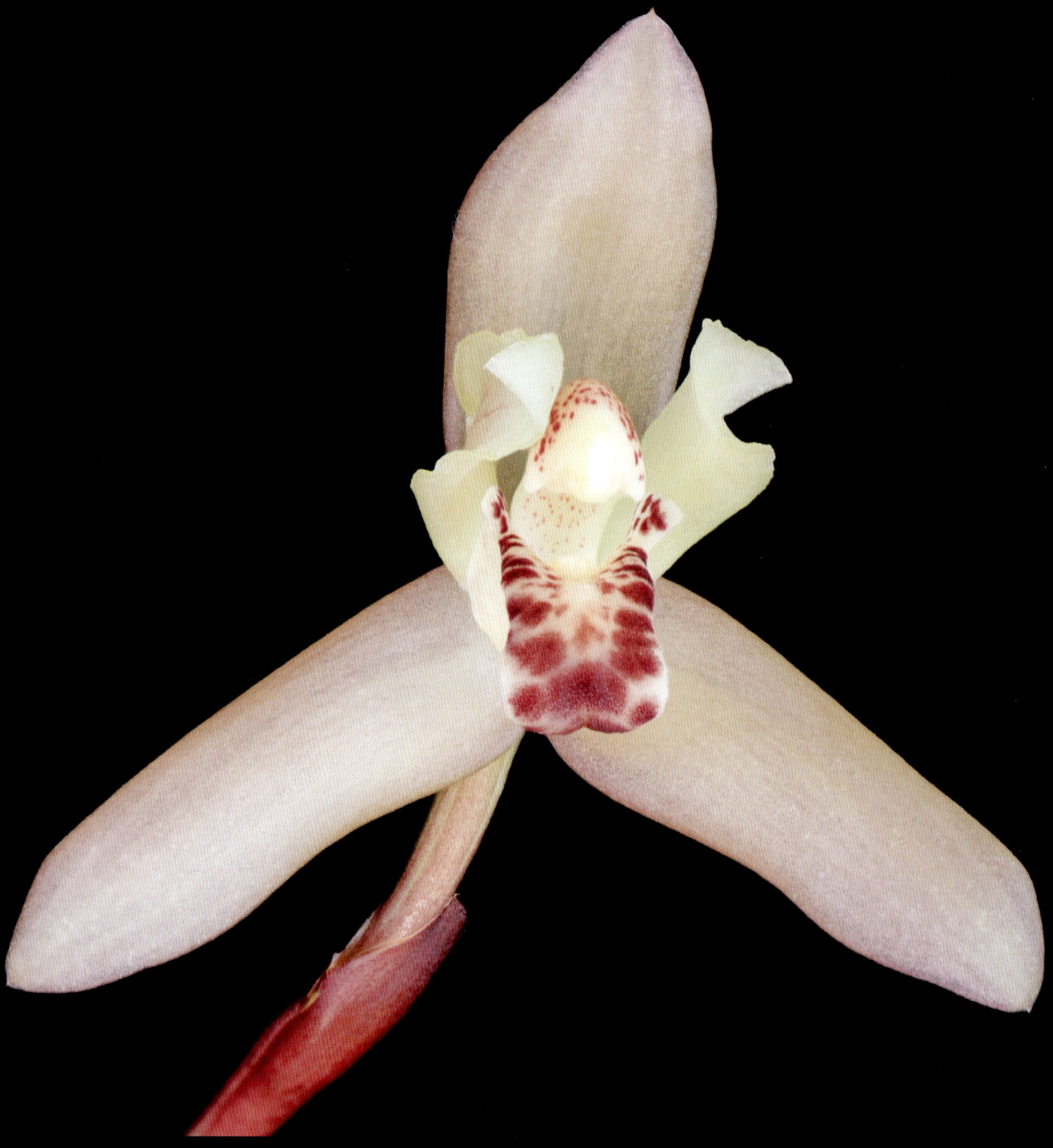

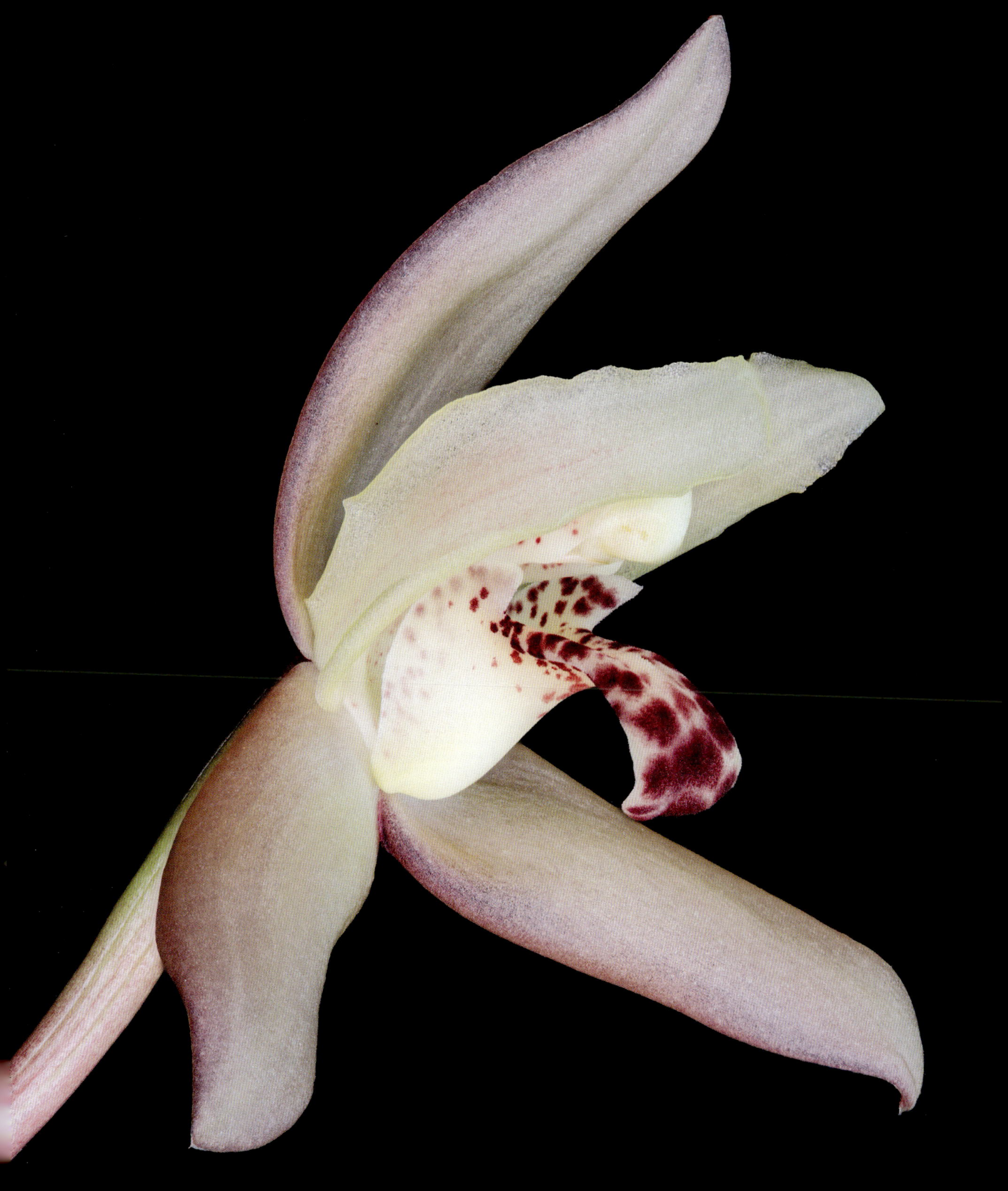

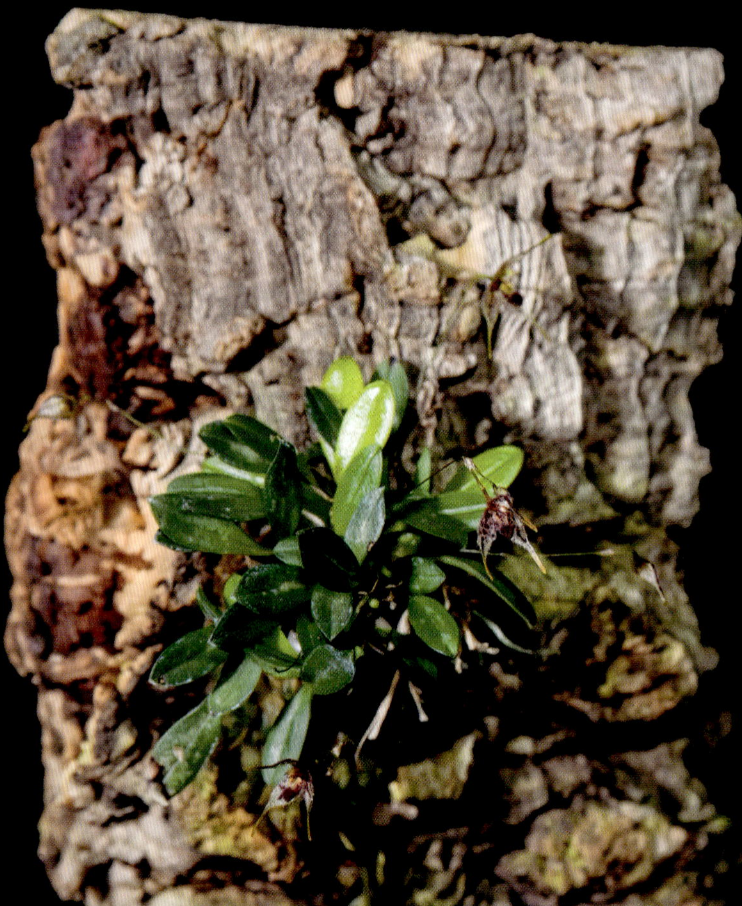

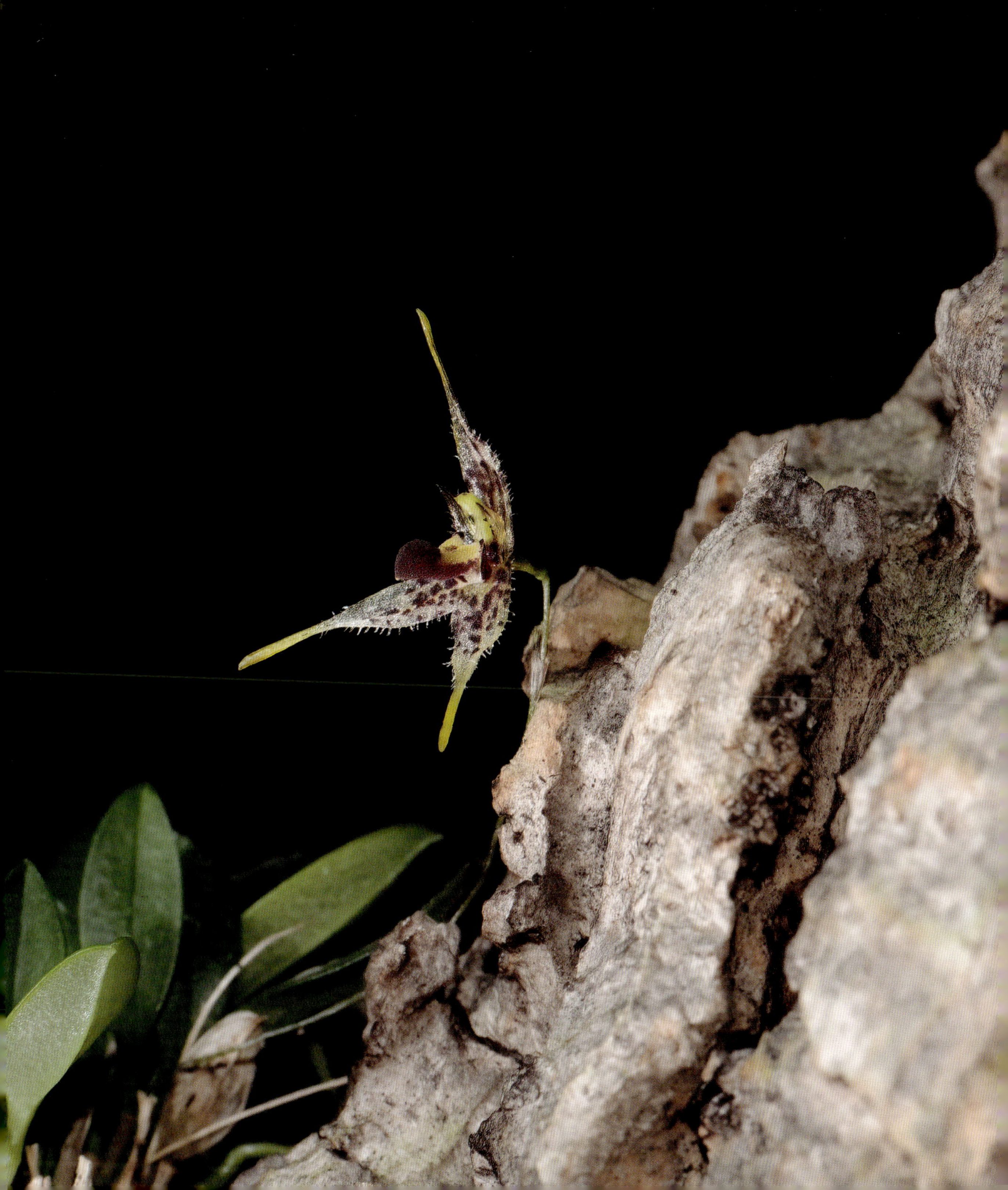

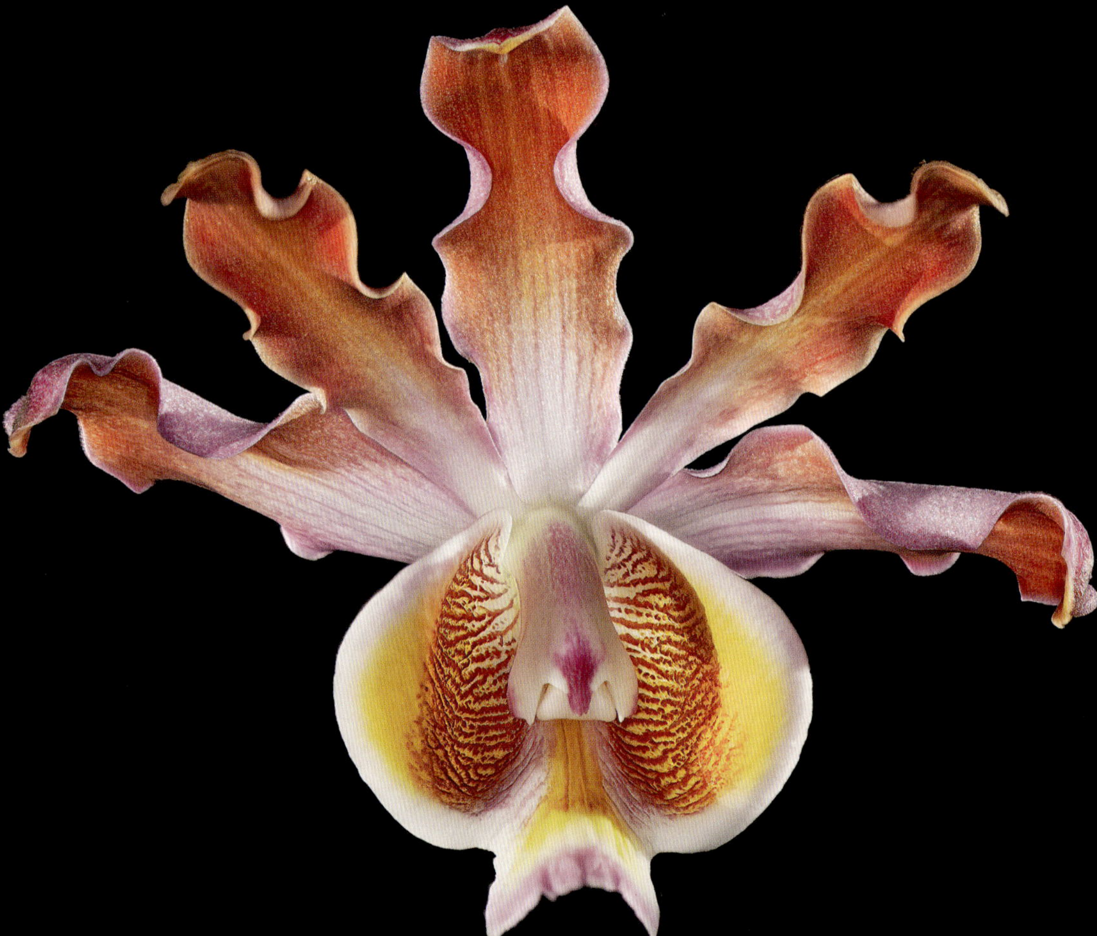

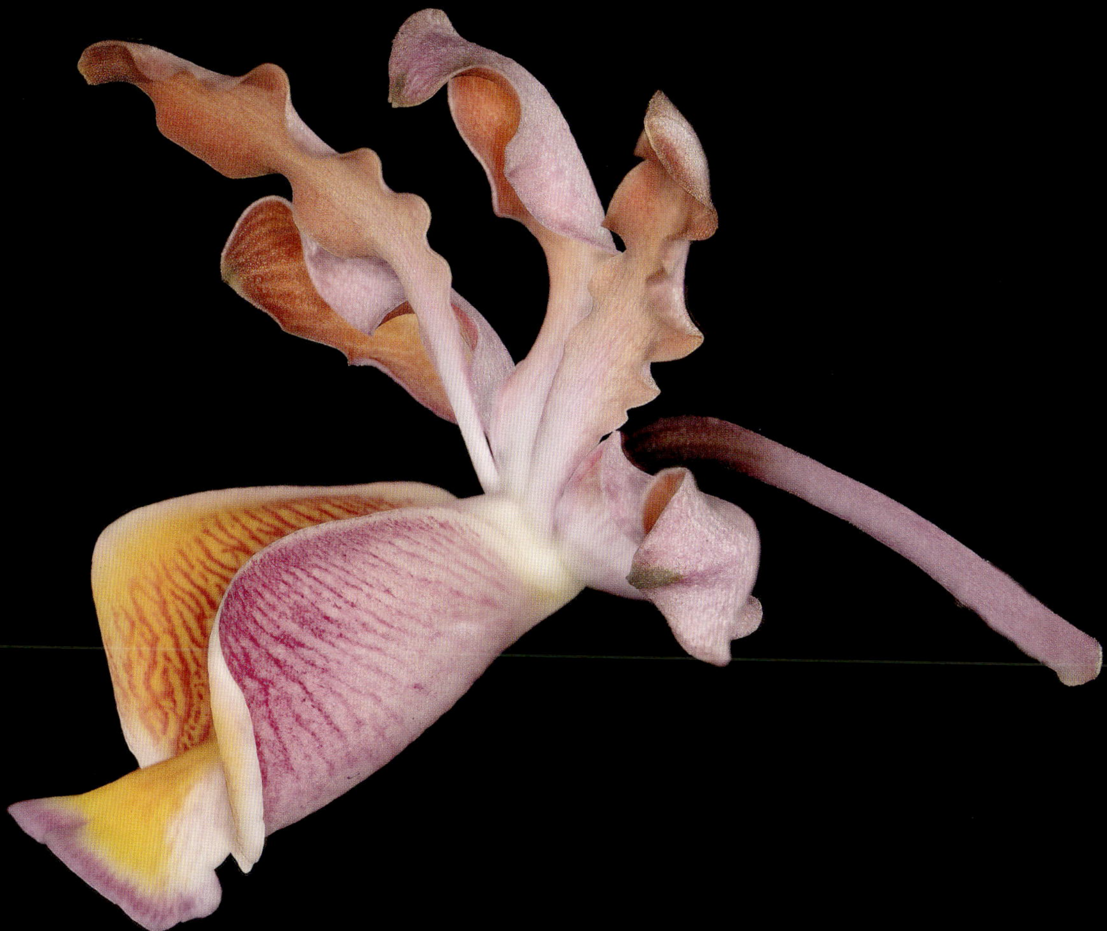

Myrmecophila tibicinis

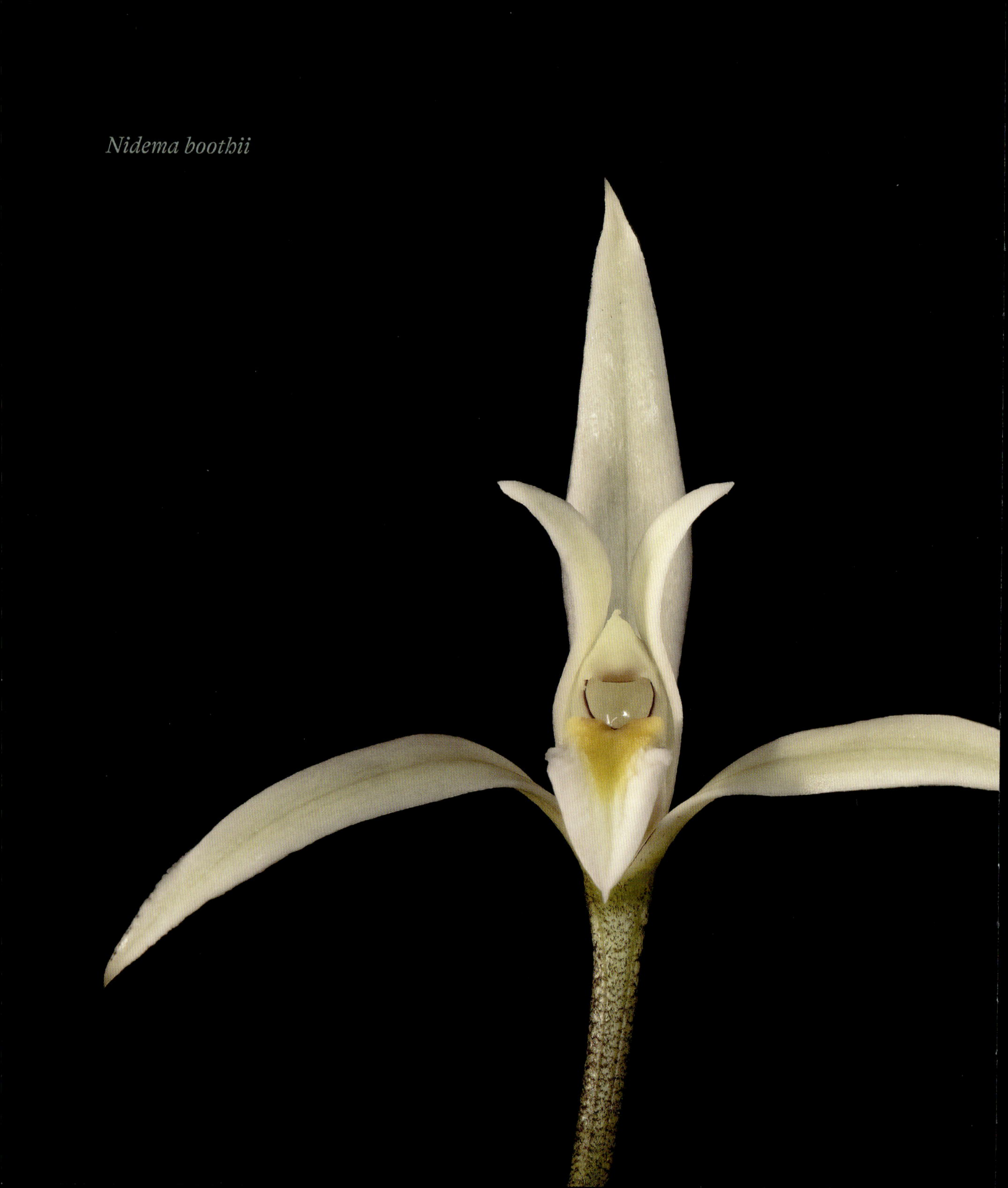

Nidema boothii

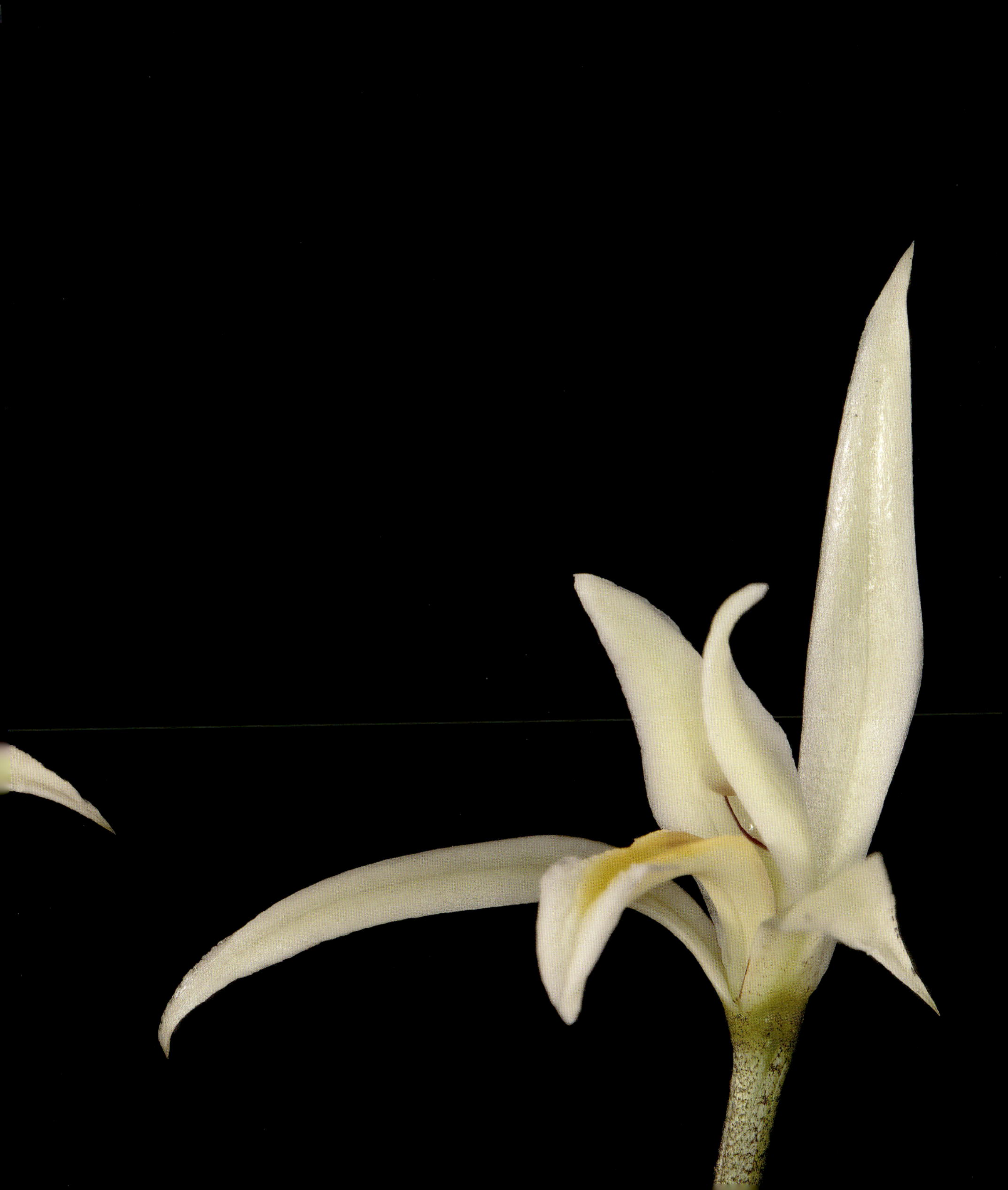

Octomeria juncifolia

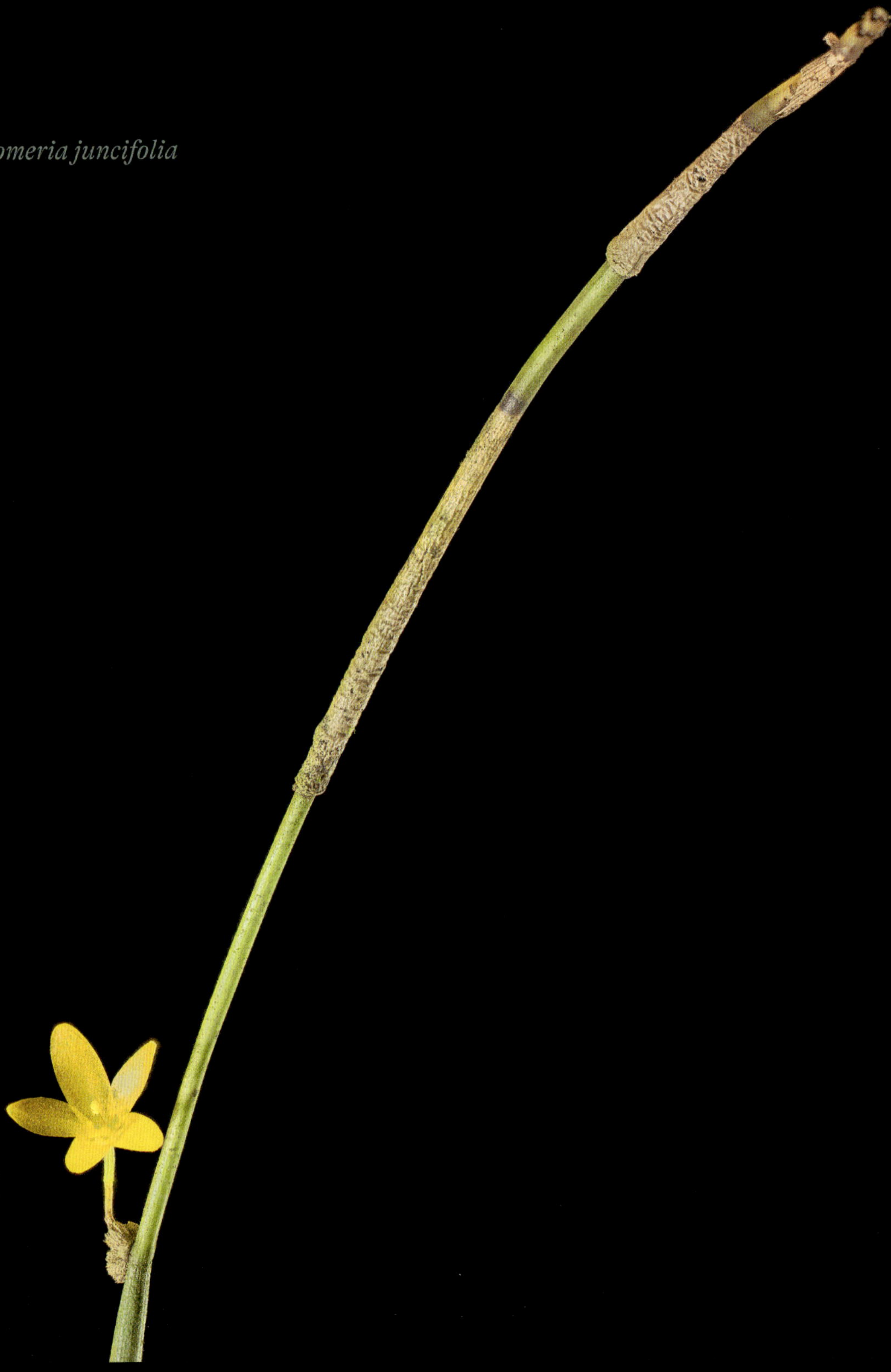

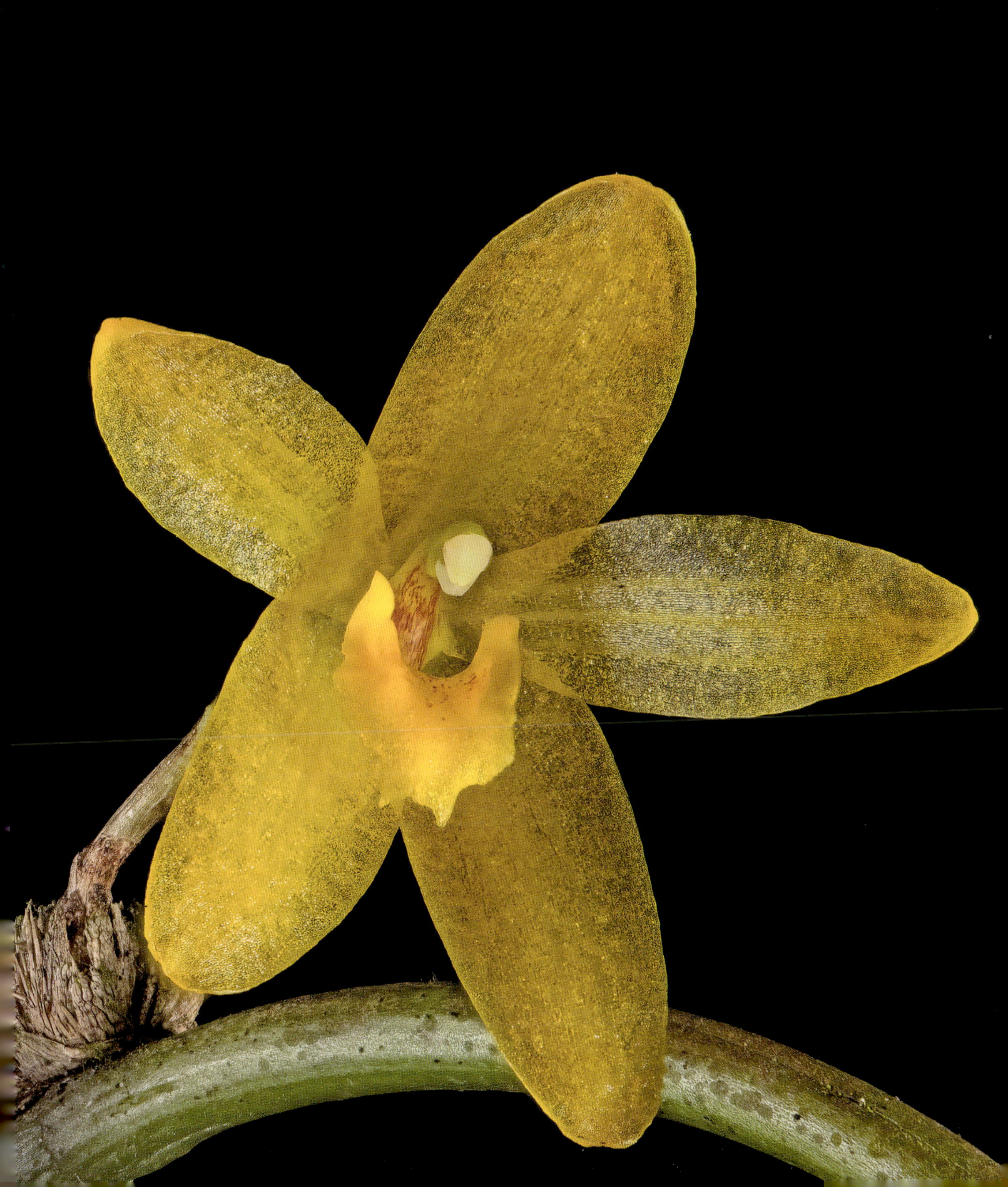

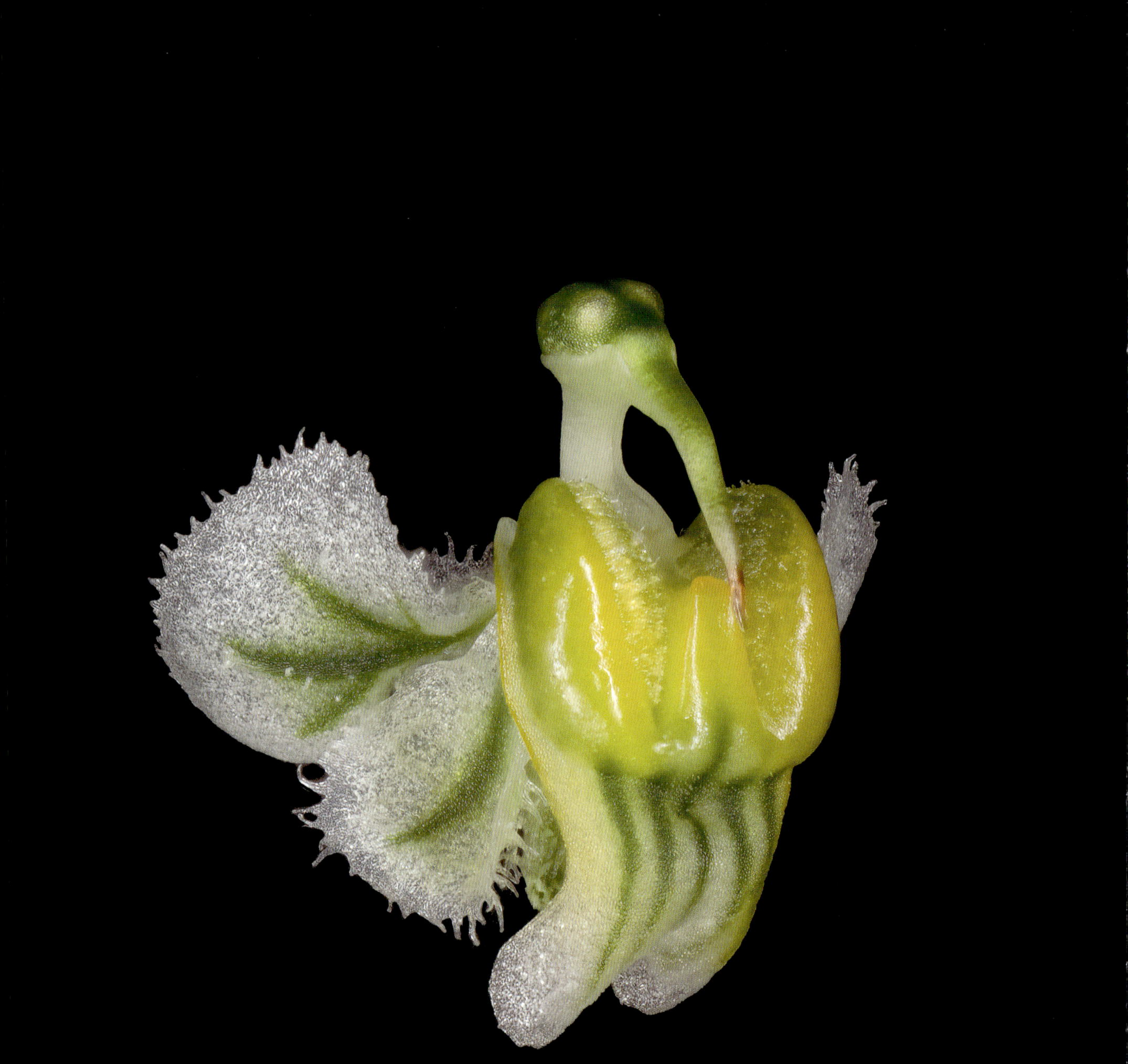

Pabstiella tripterantha

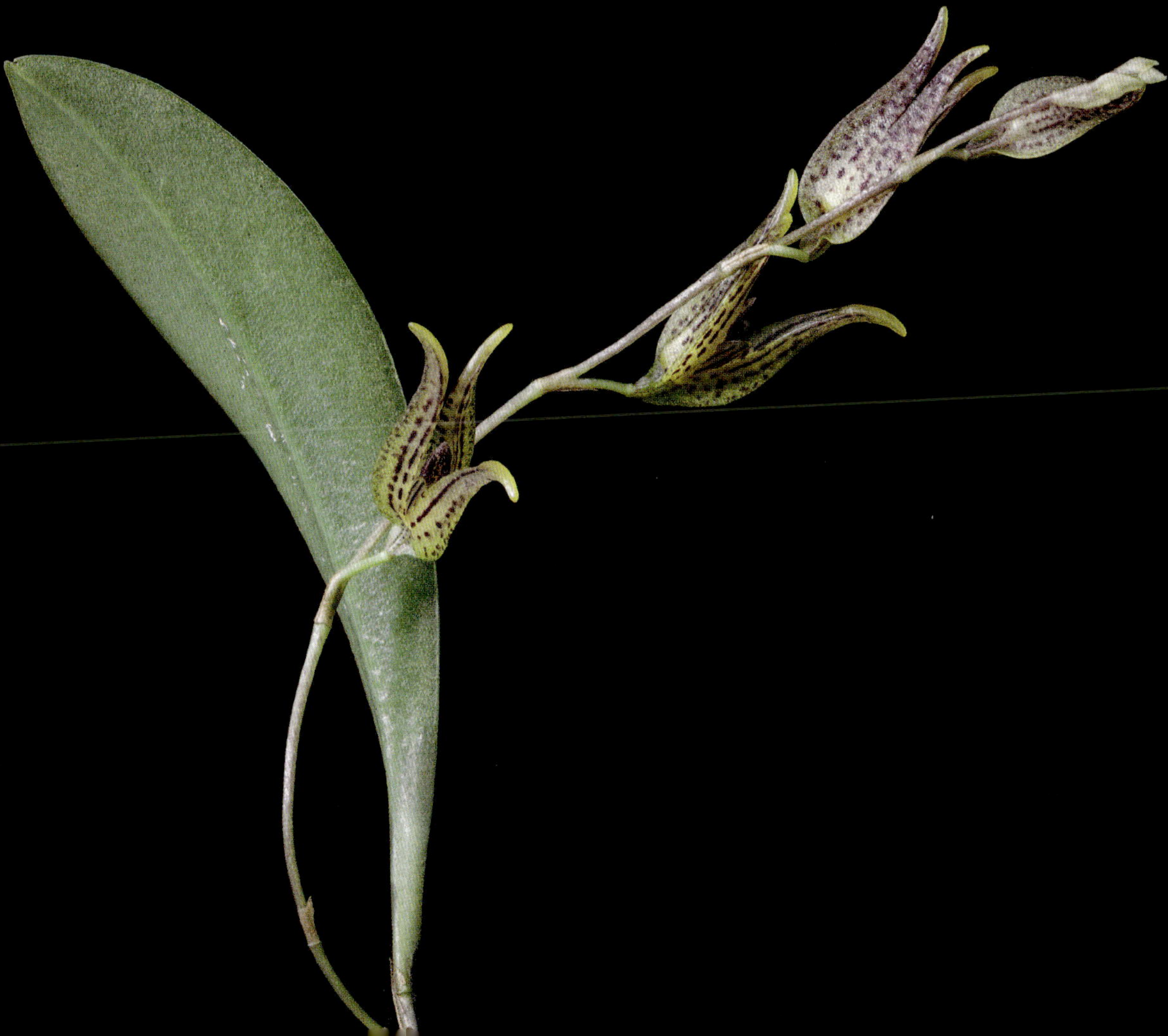

Paphinia herrerae

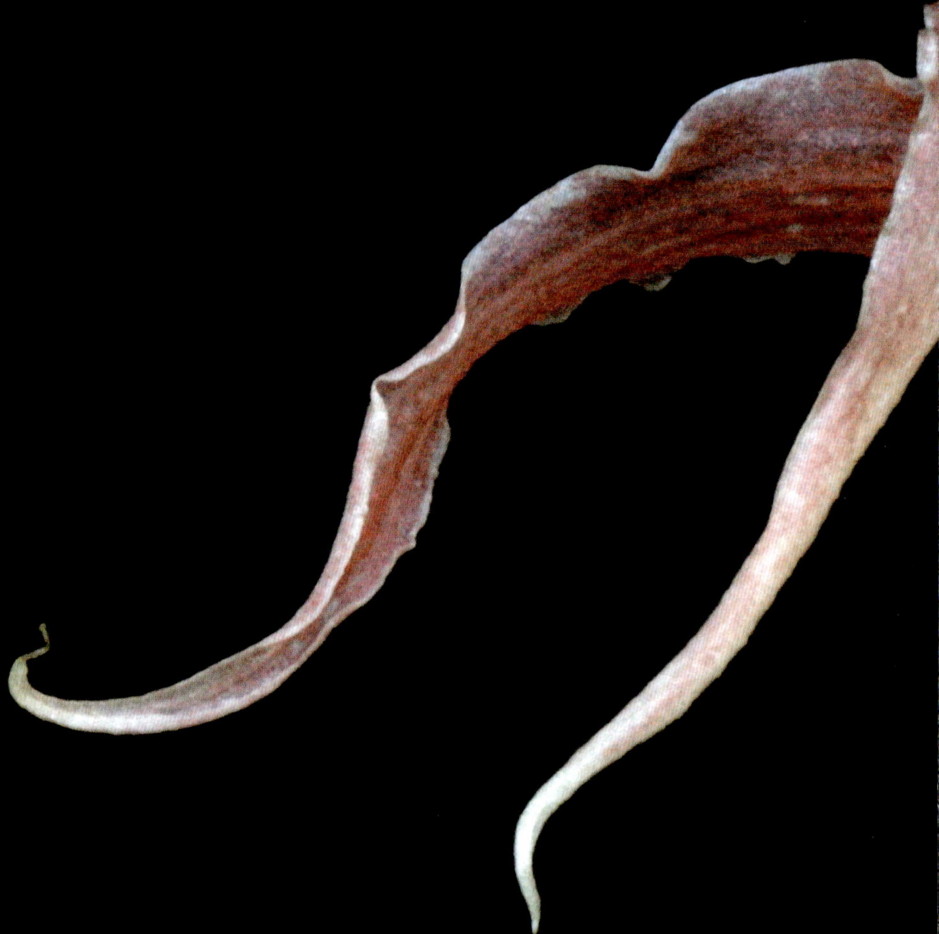

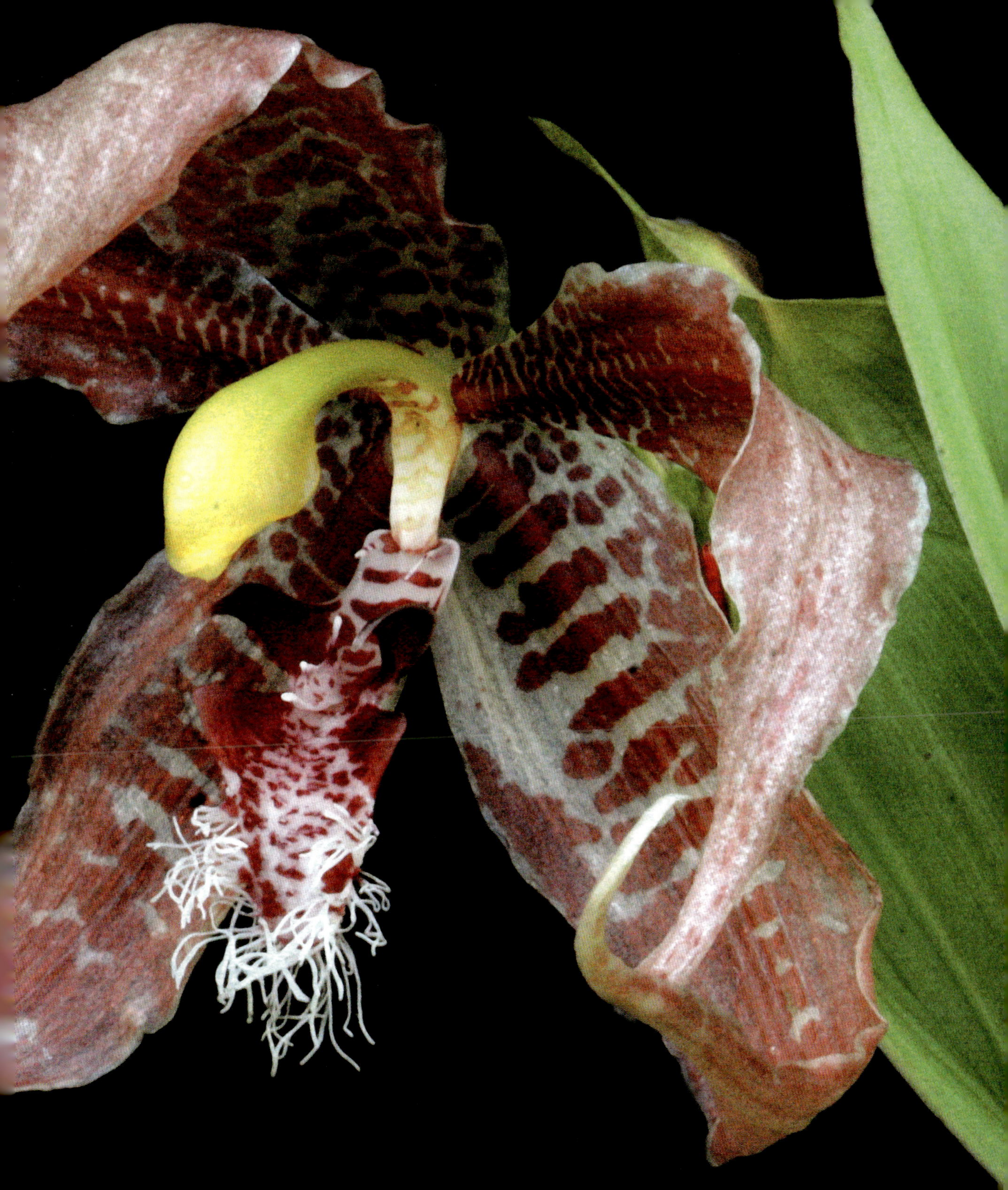

Paphiopedilum callosum

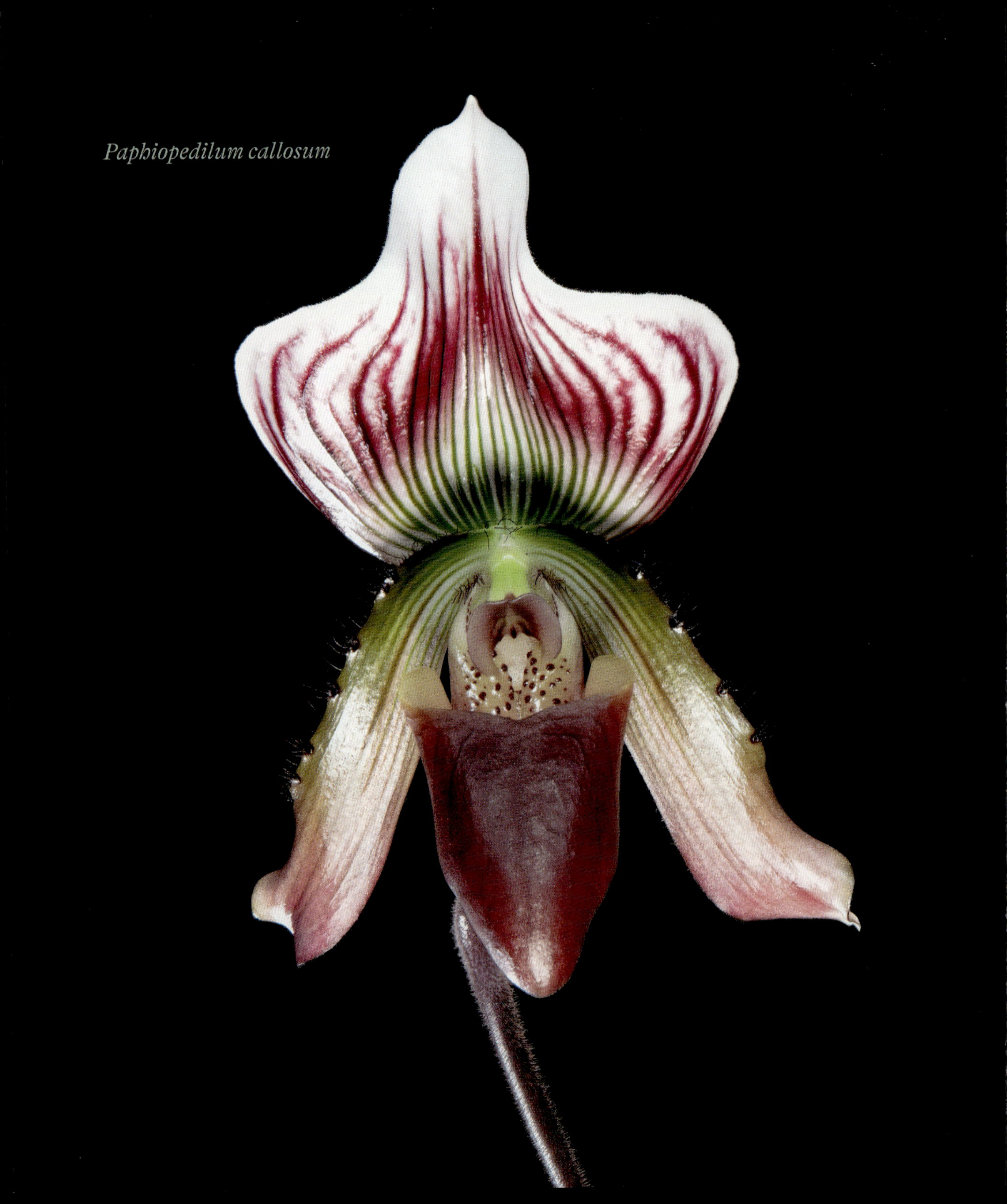

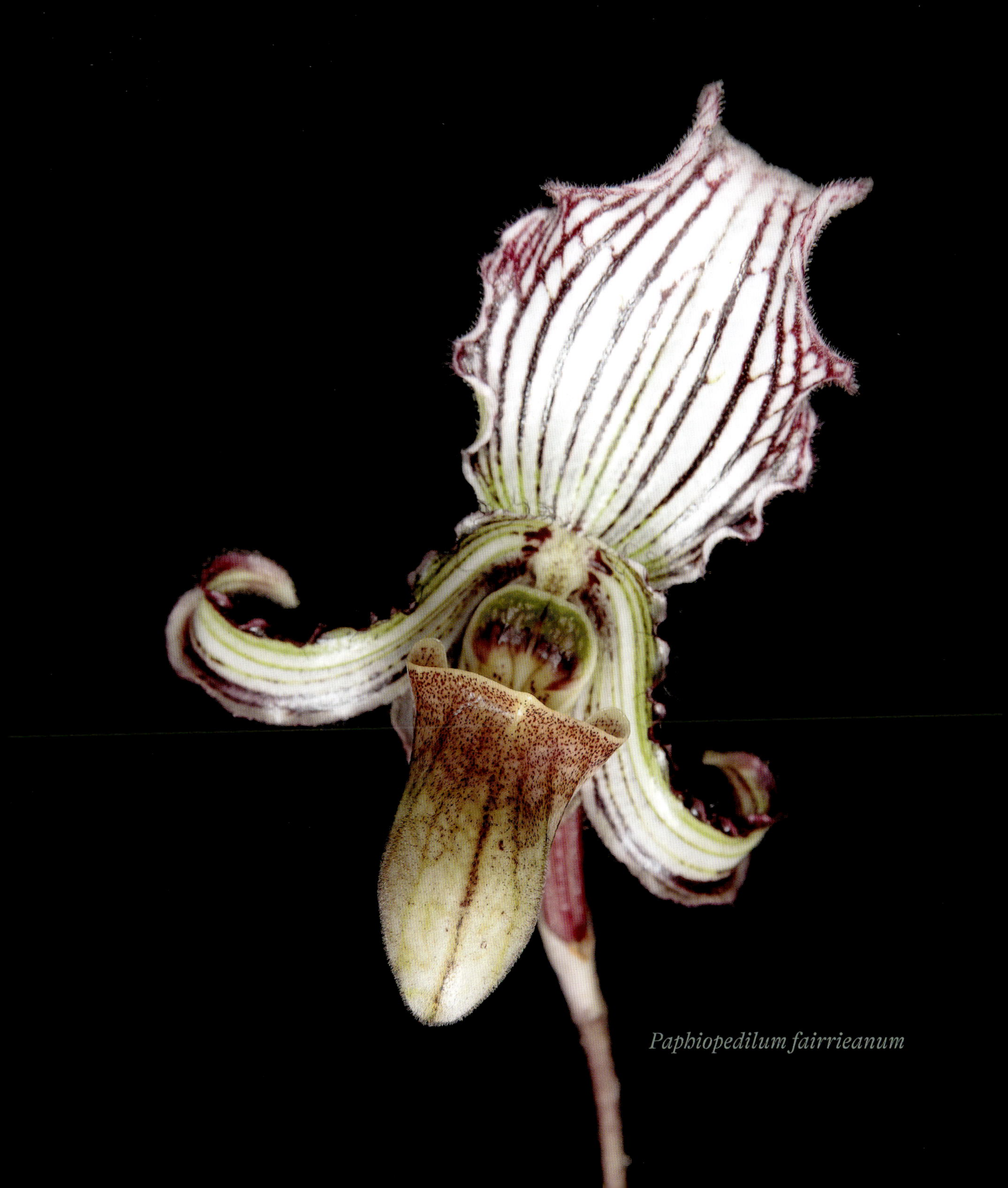

Paphiopedilum fairrieanum

Phalaenopsis amabilis

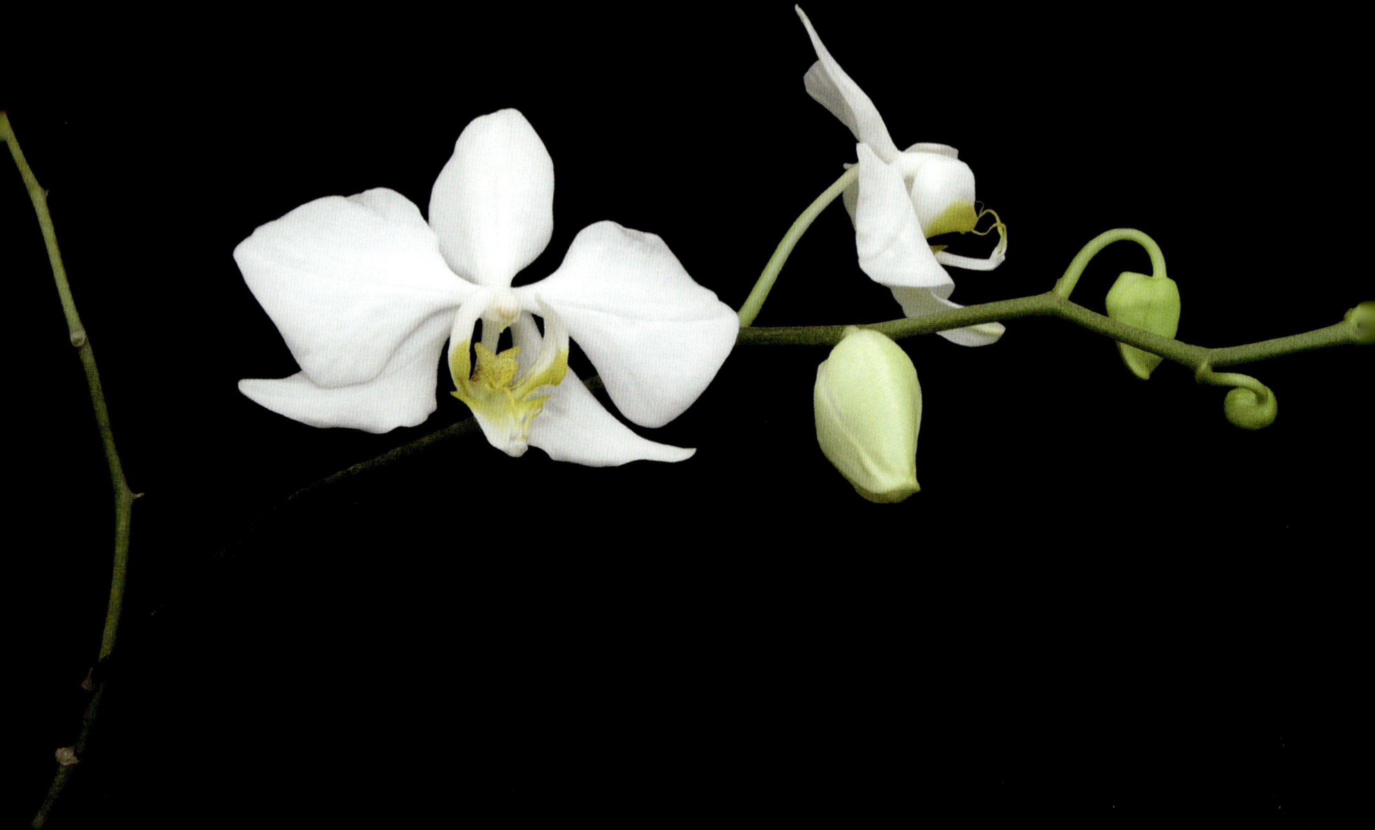

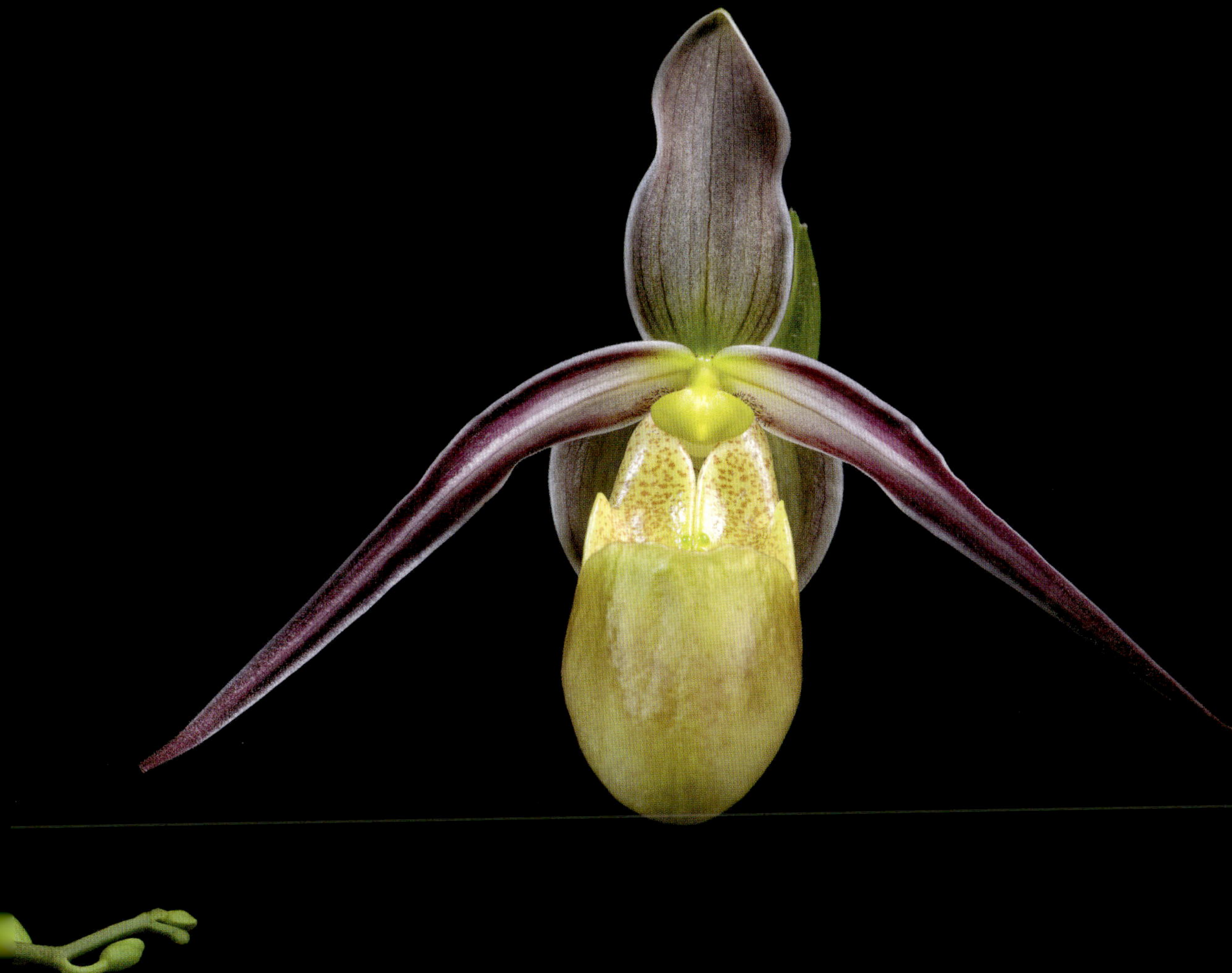

Phragmipedium longifolium

Pleurothallis aspergillum

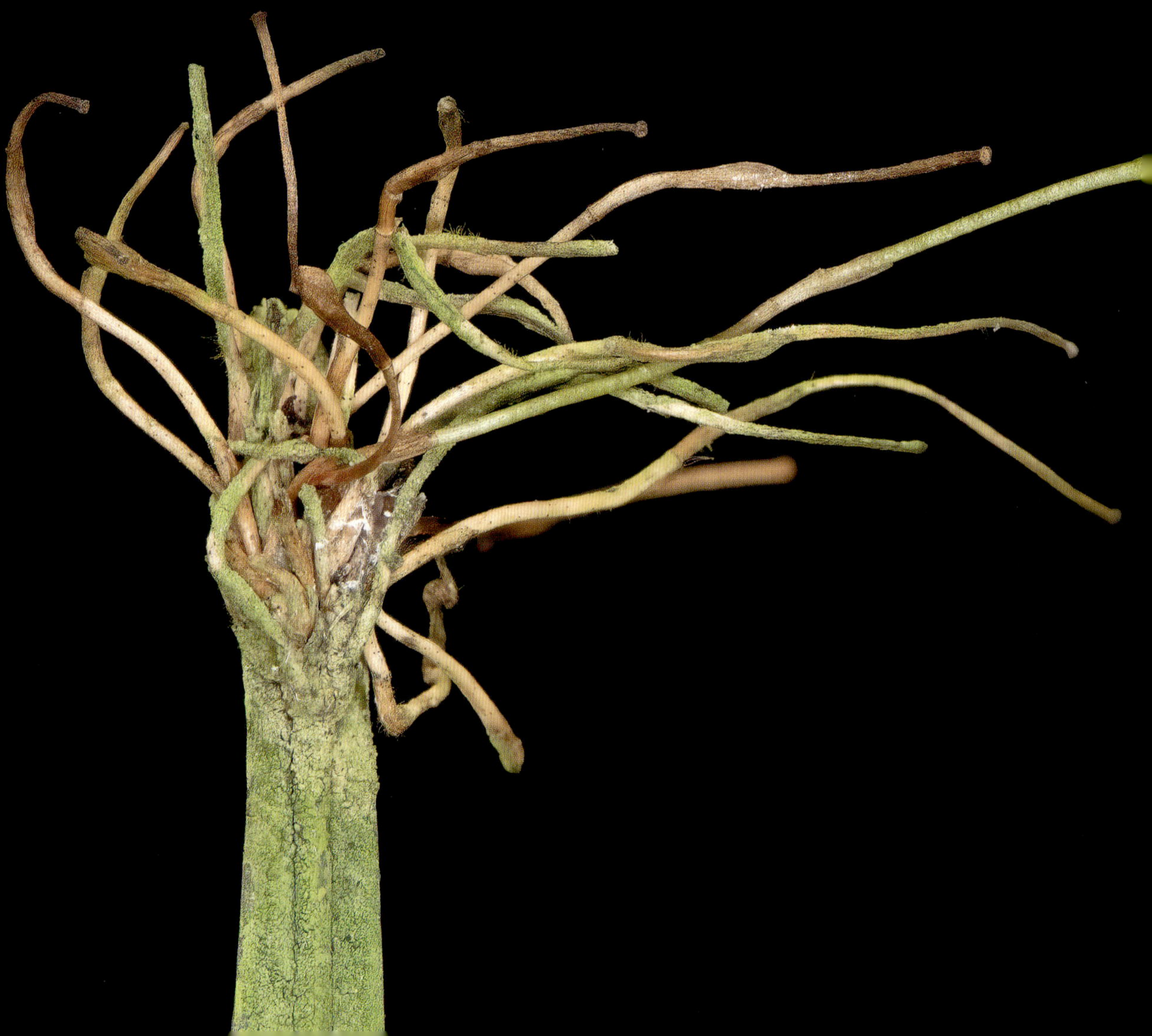

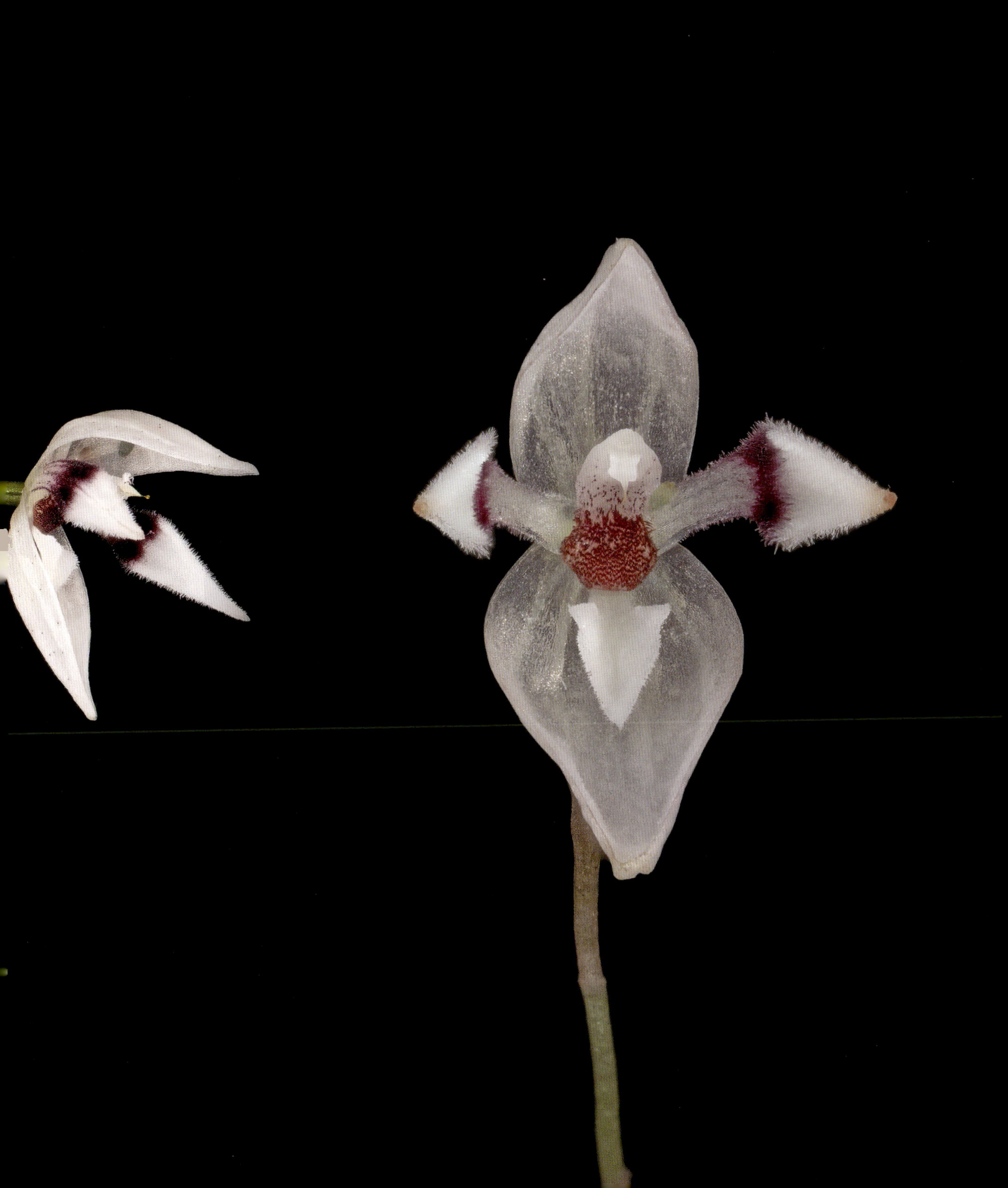

Pleurothallis cardiothallis

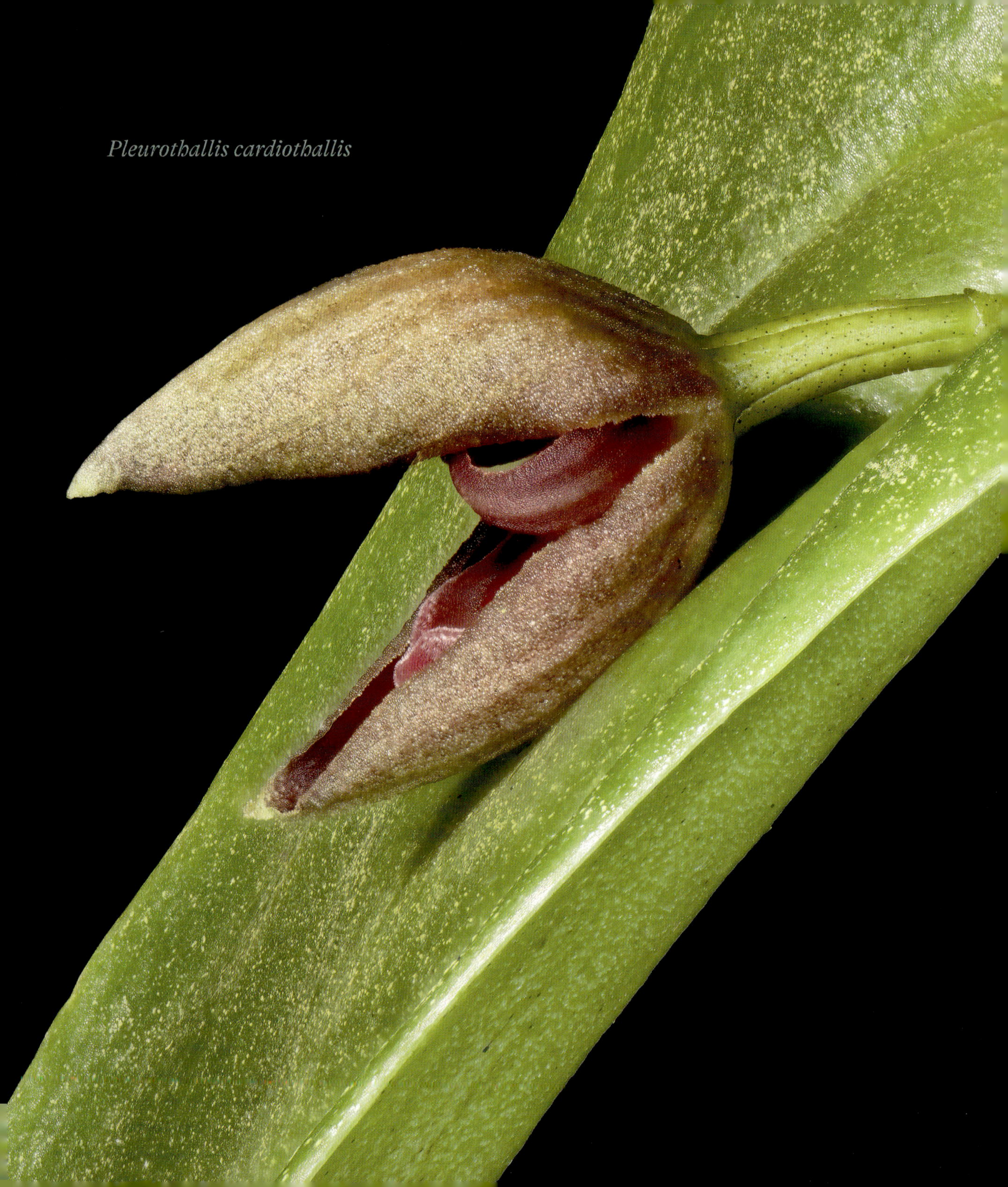

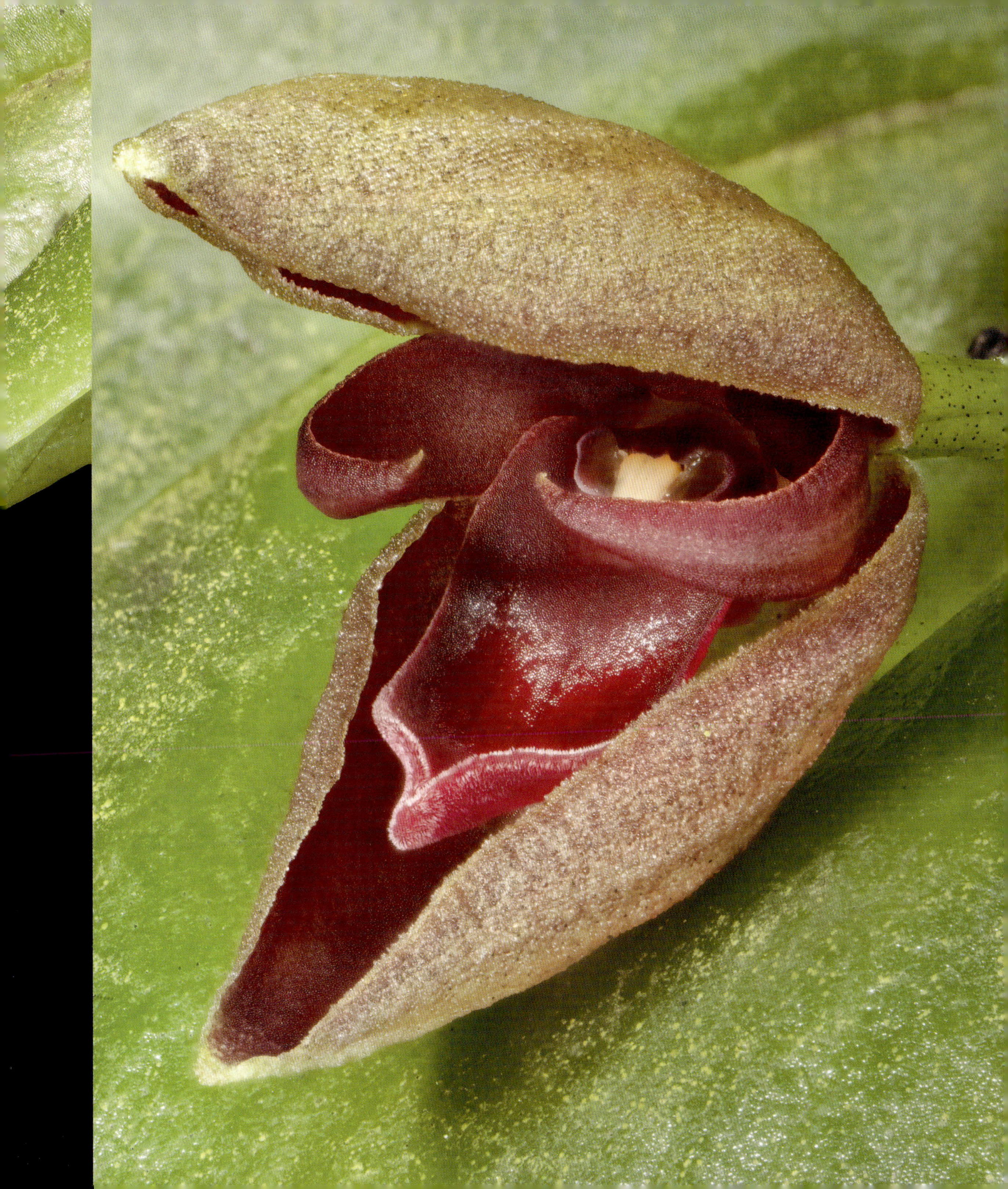

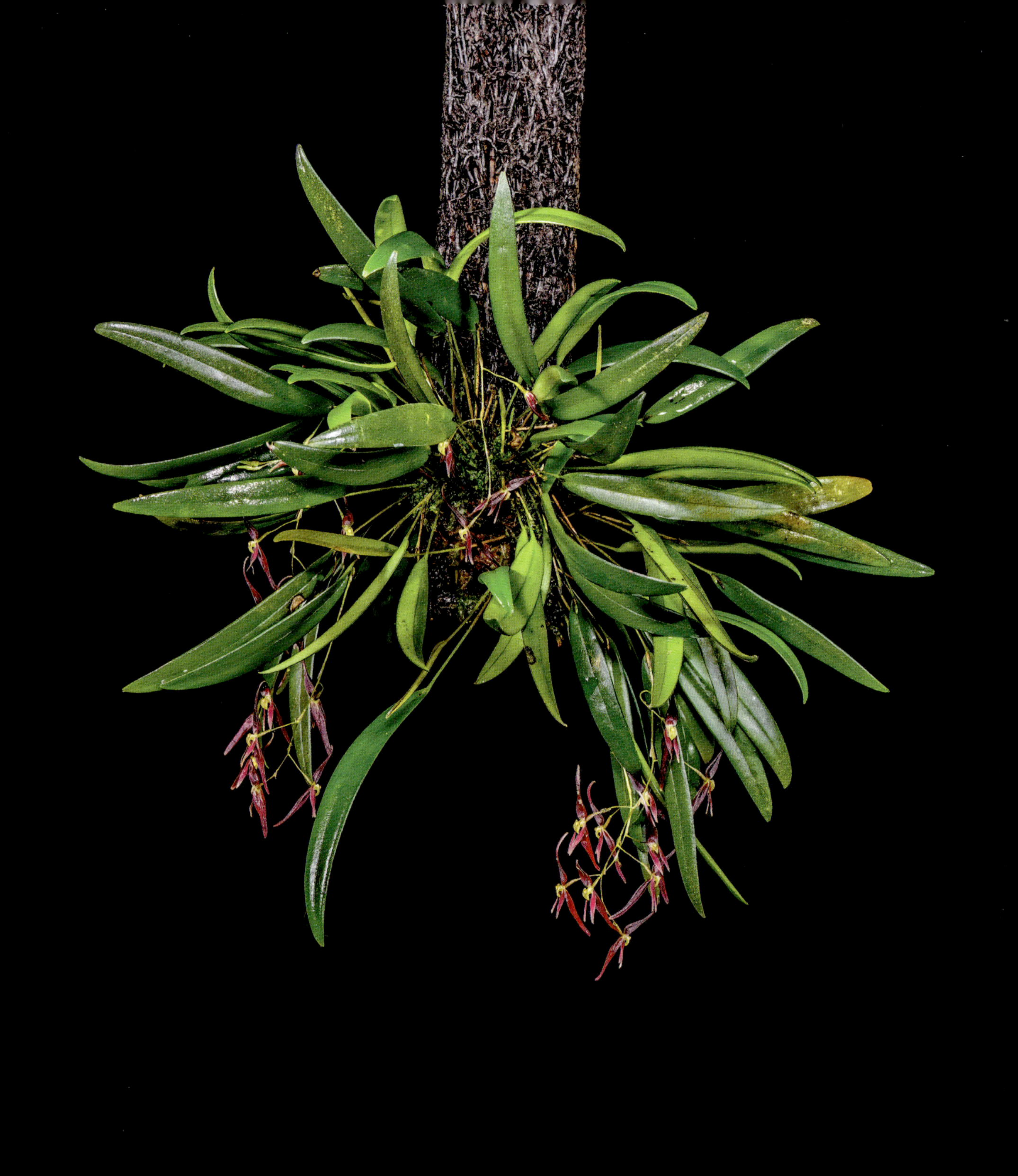

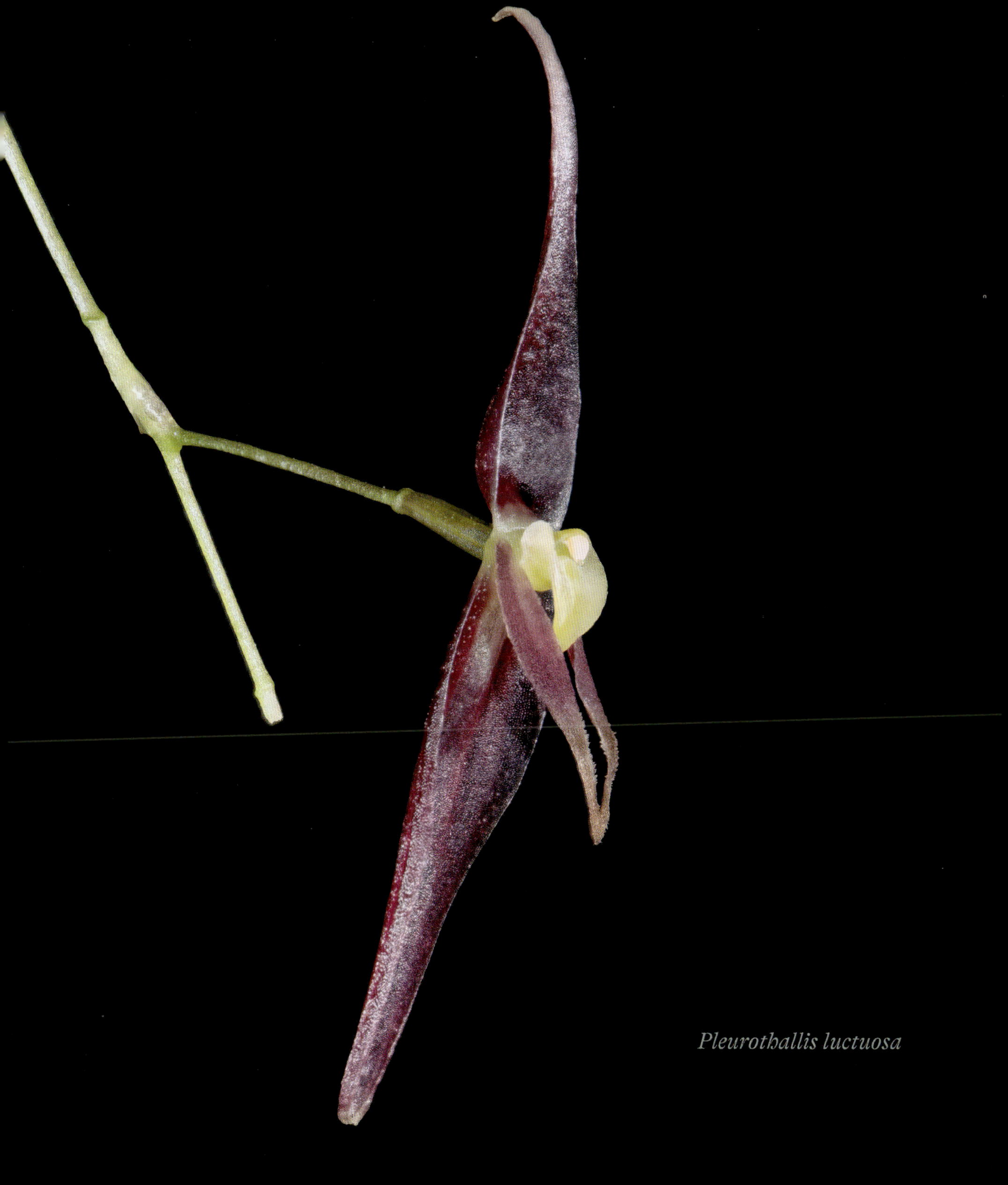

Pleurothallis luctuosa

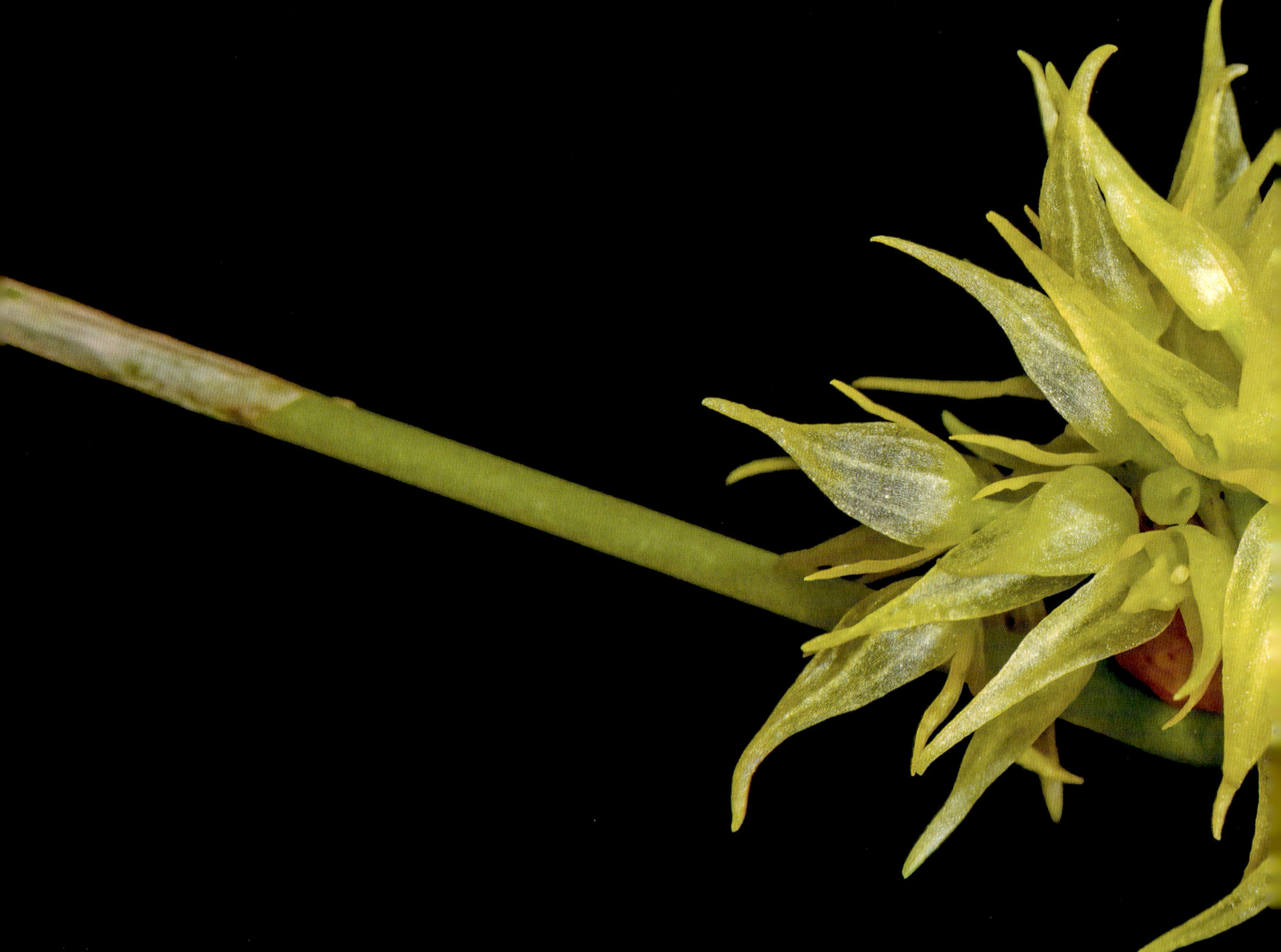

Pleurothallis ruscifolia

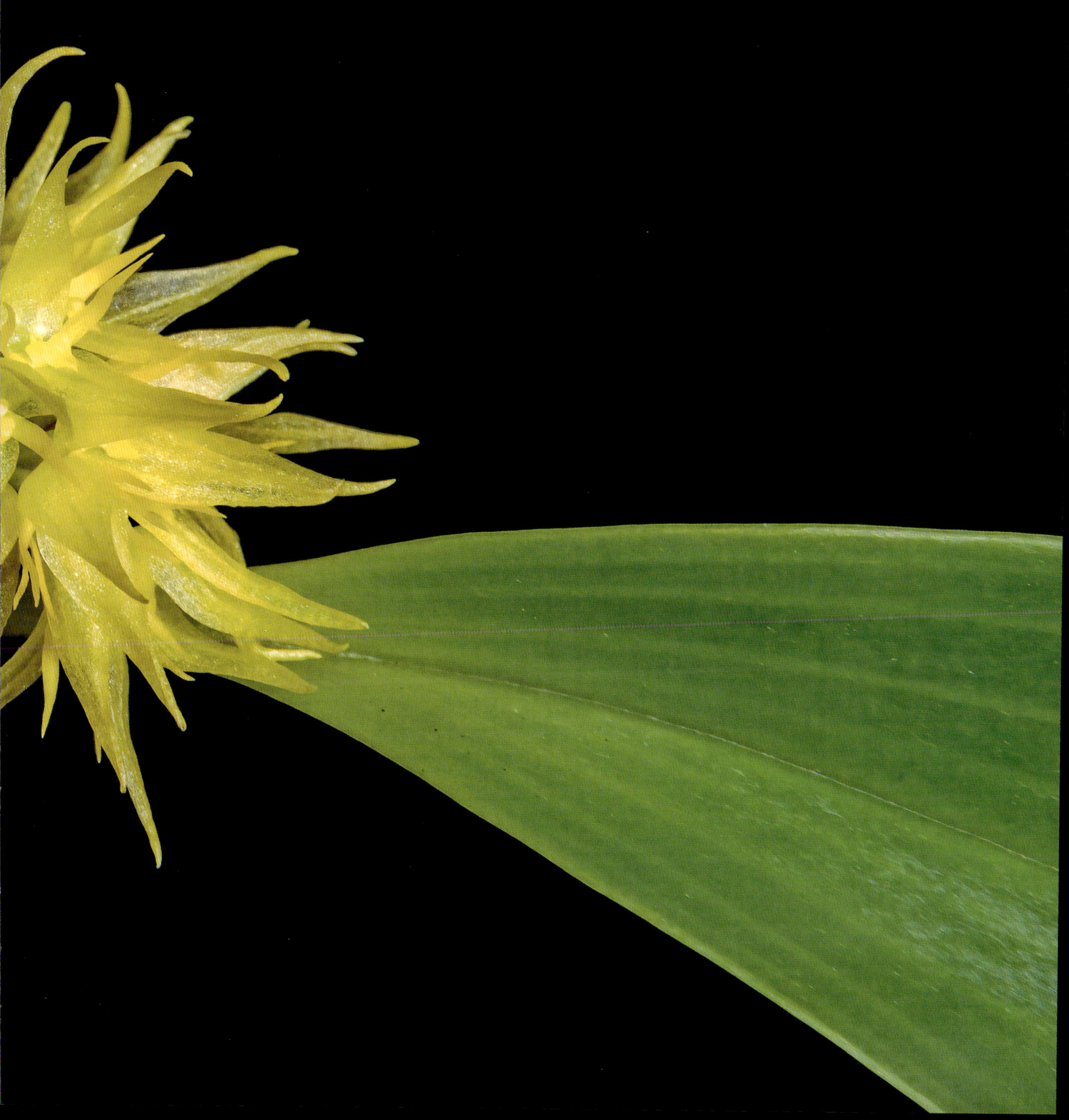

Polystachya paniculata

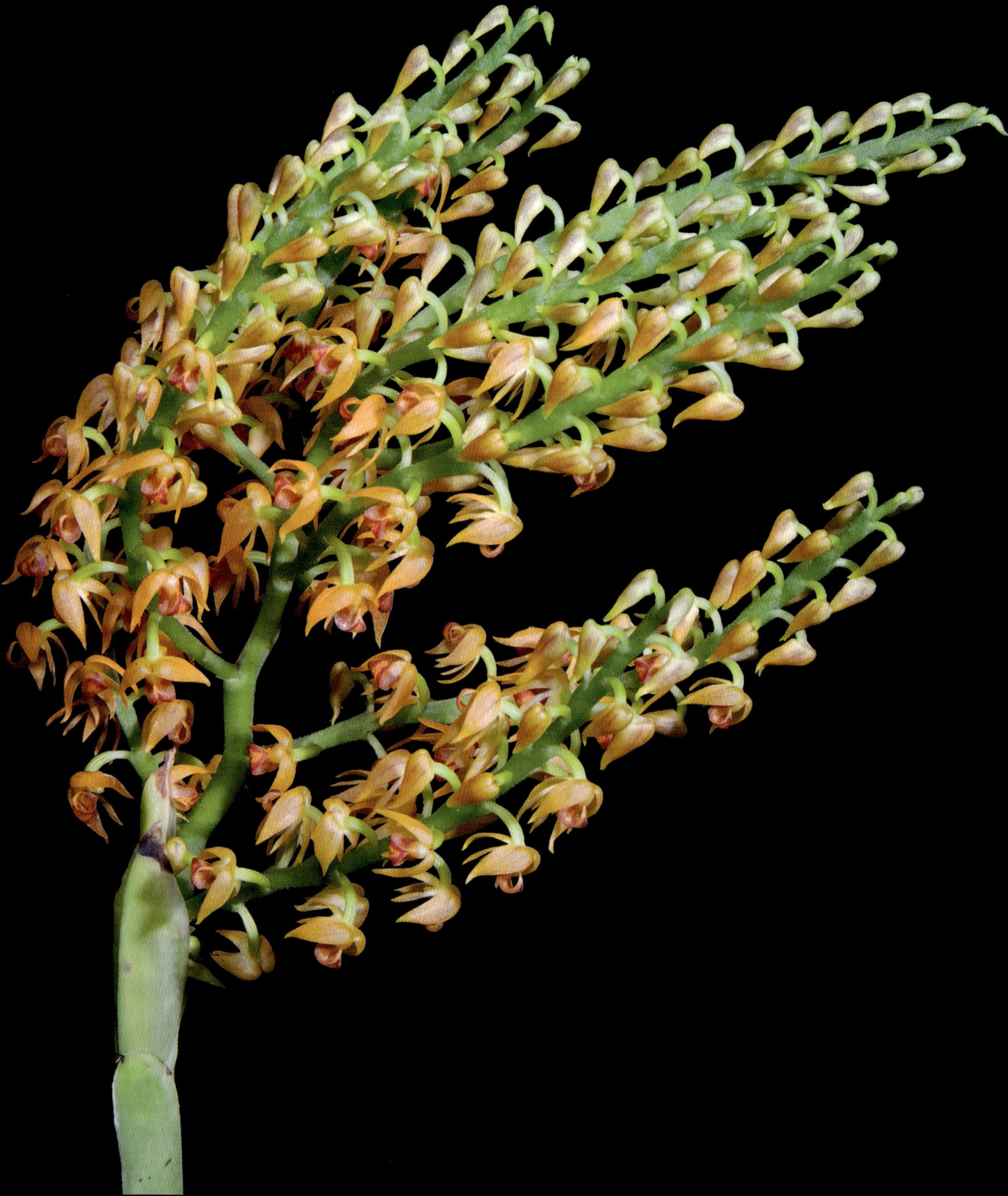

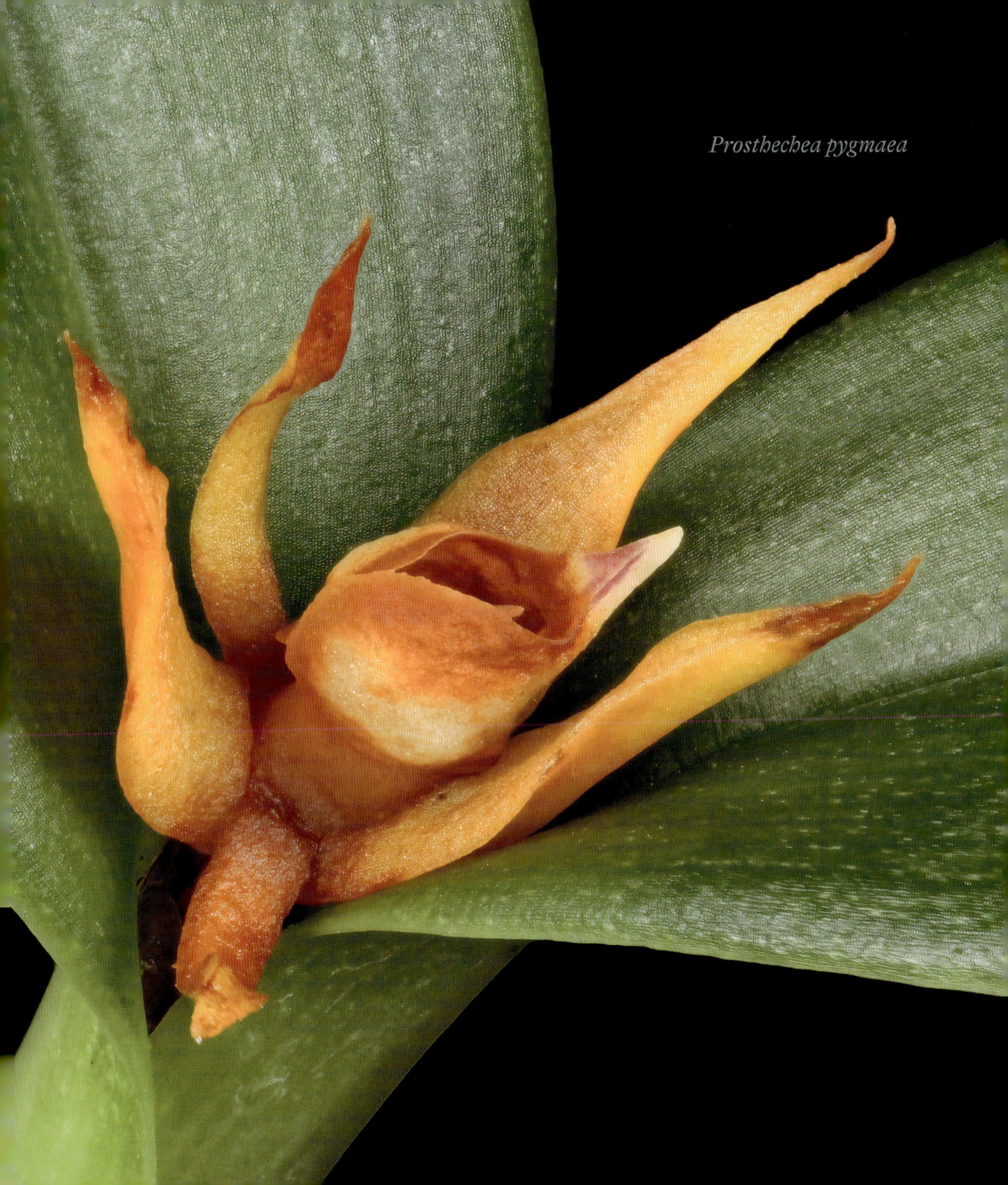

Prosthechea pygmaea

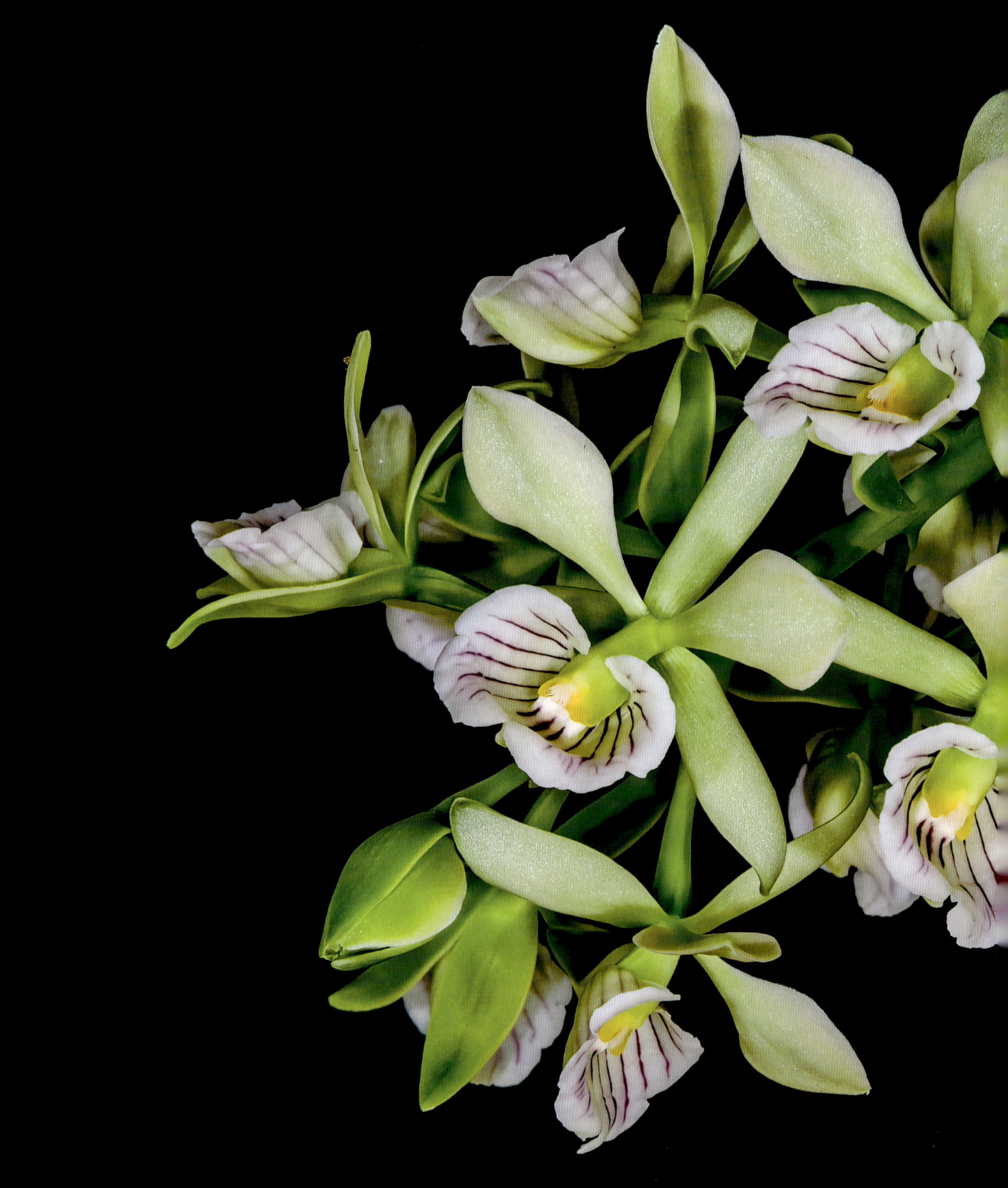

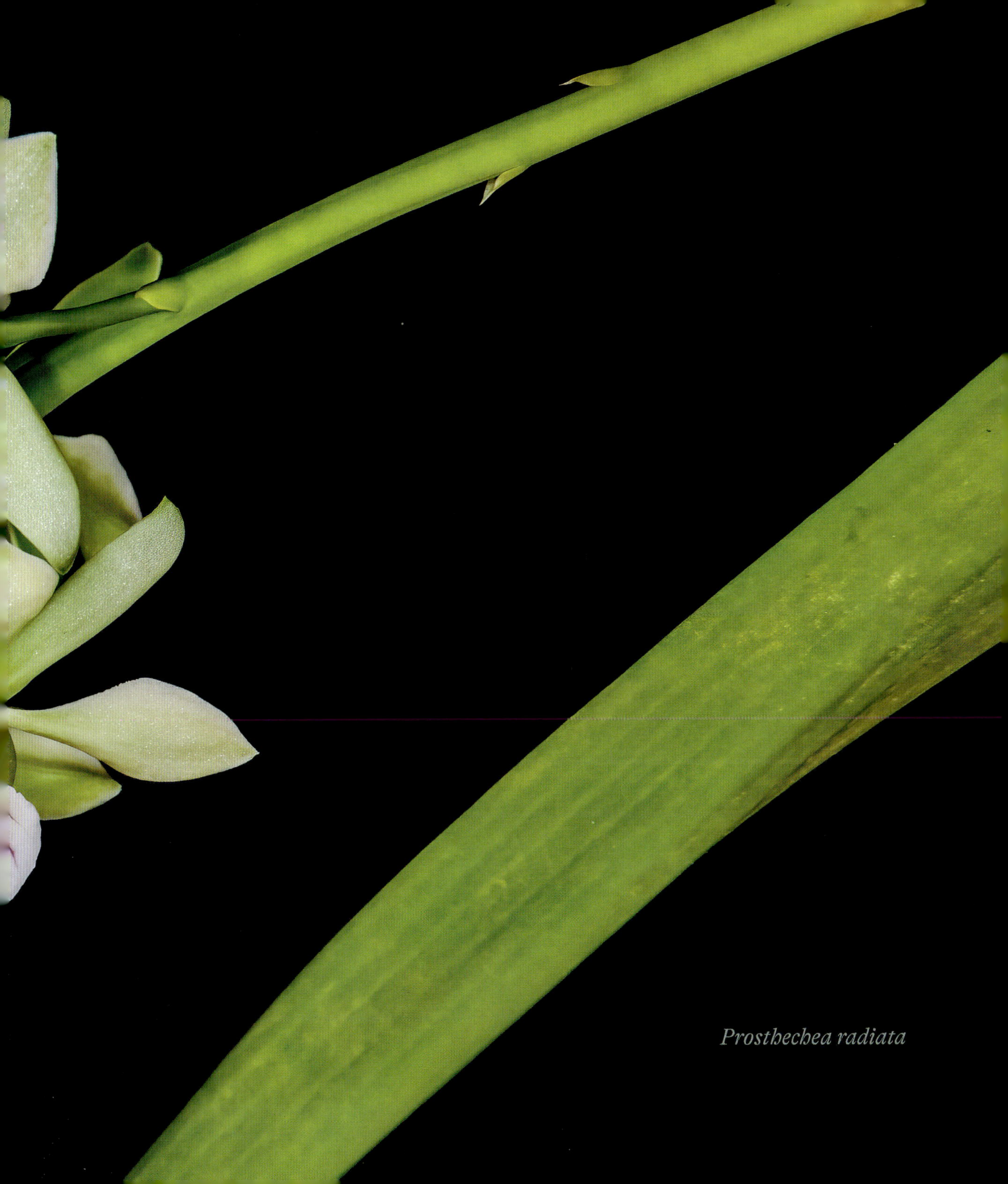

Prosthechea radiata

Rhyncholaelia digbyana

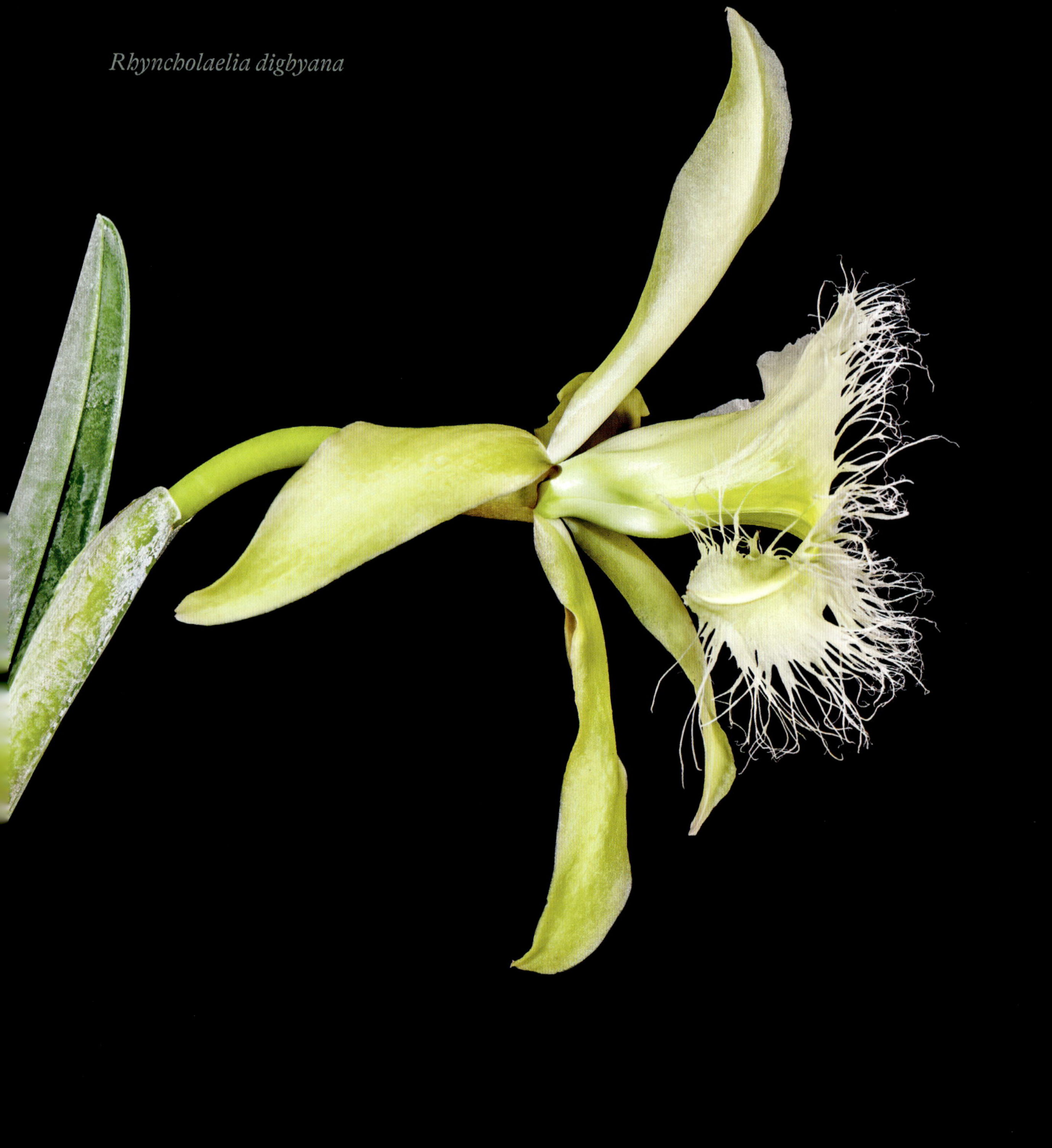

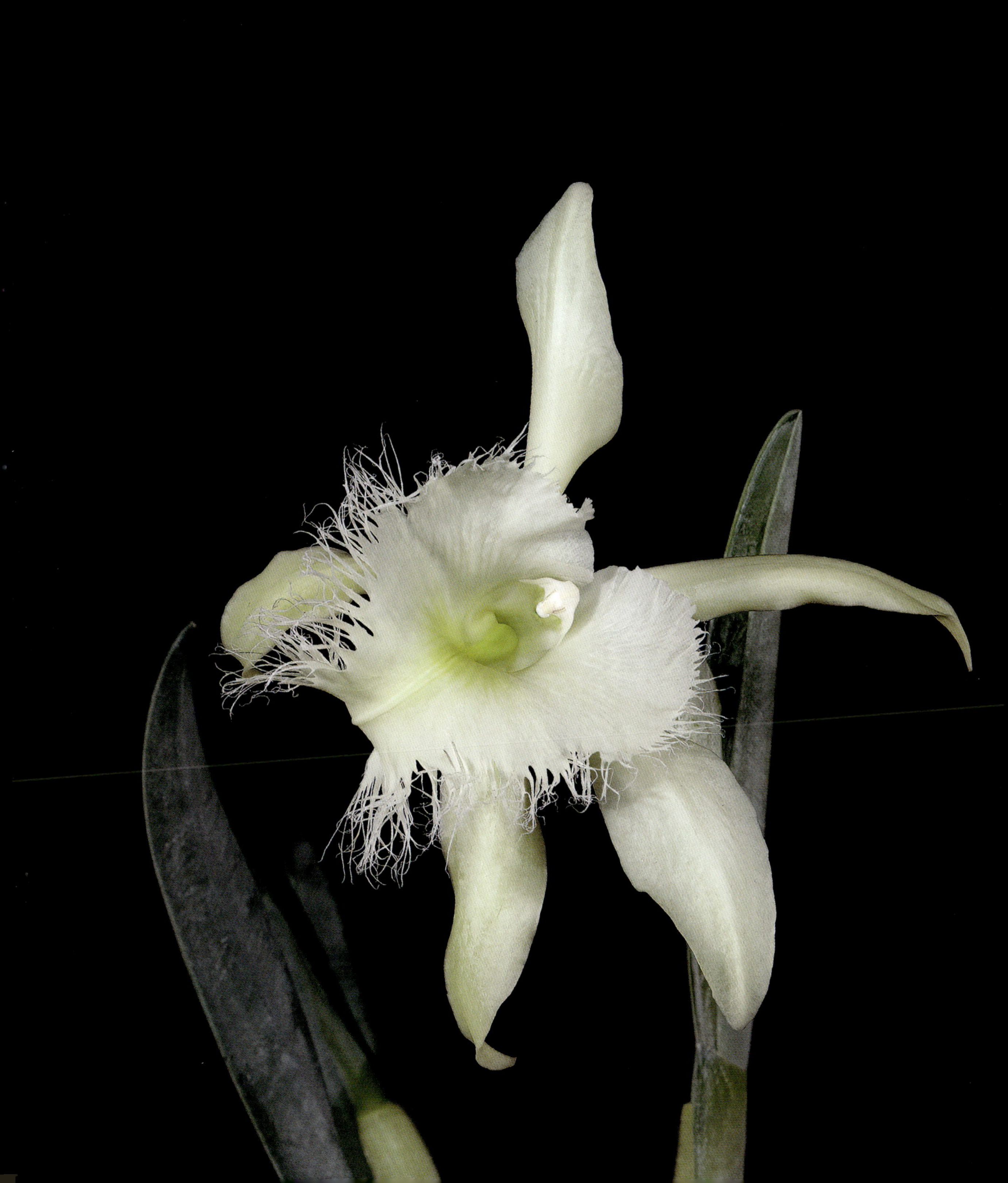

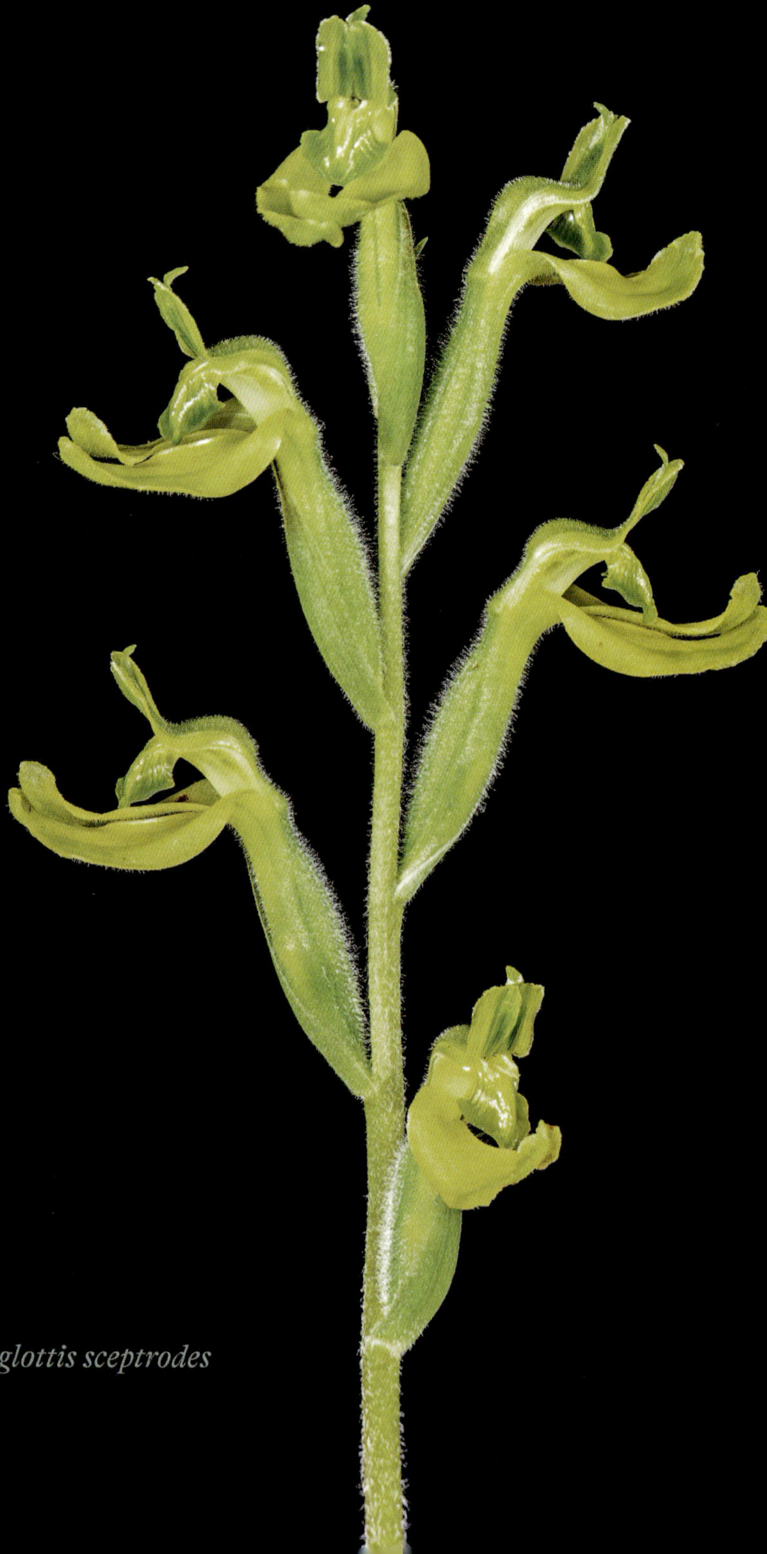

Sarcoglottis sceptrodes

Specklinia brighamii

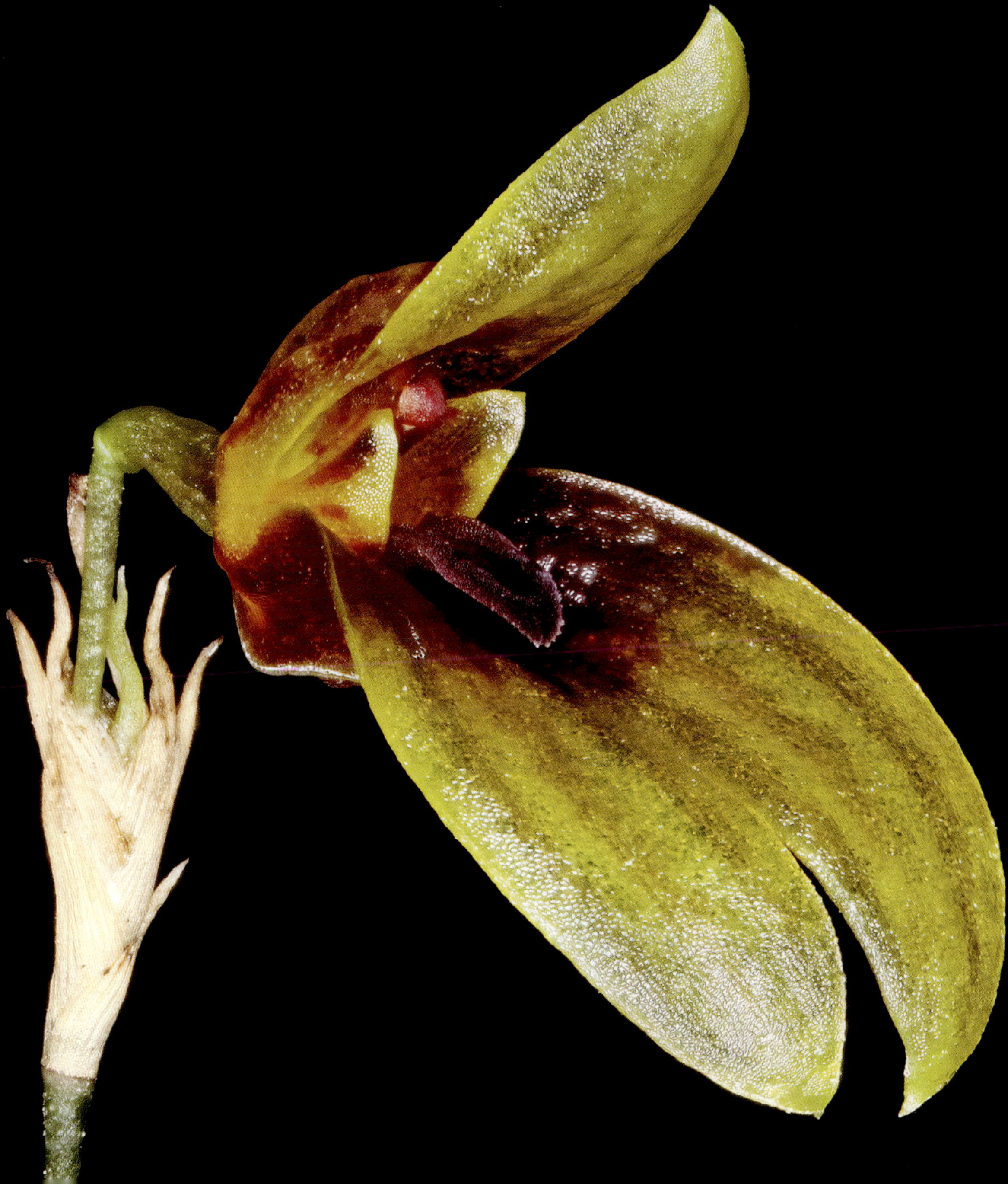

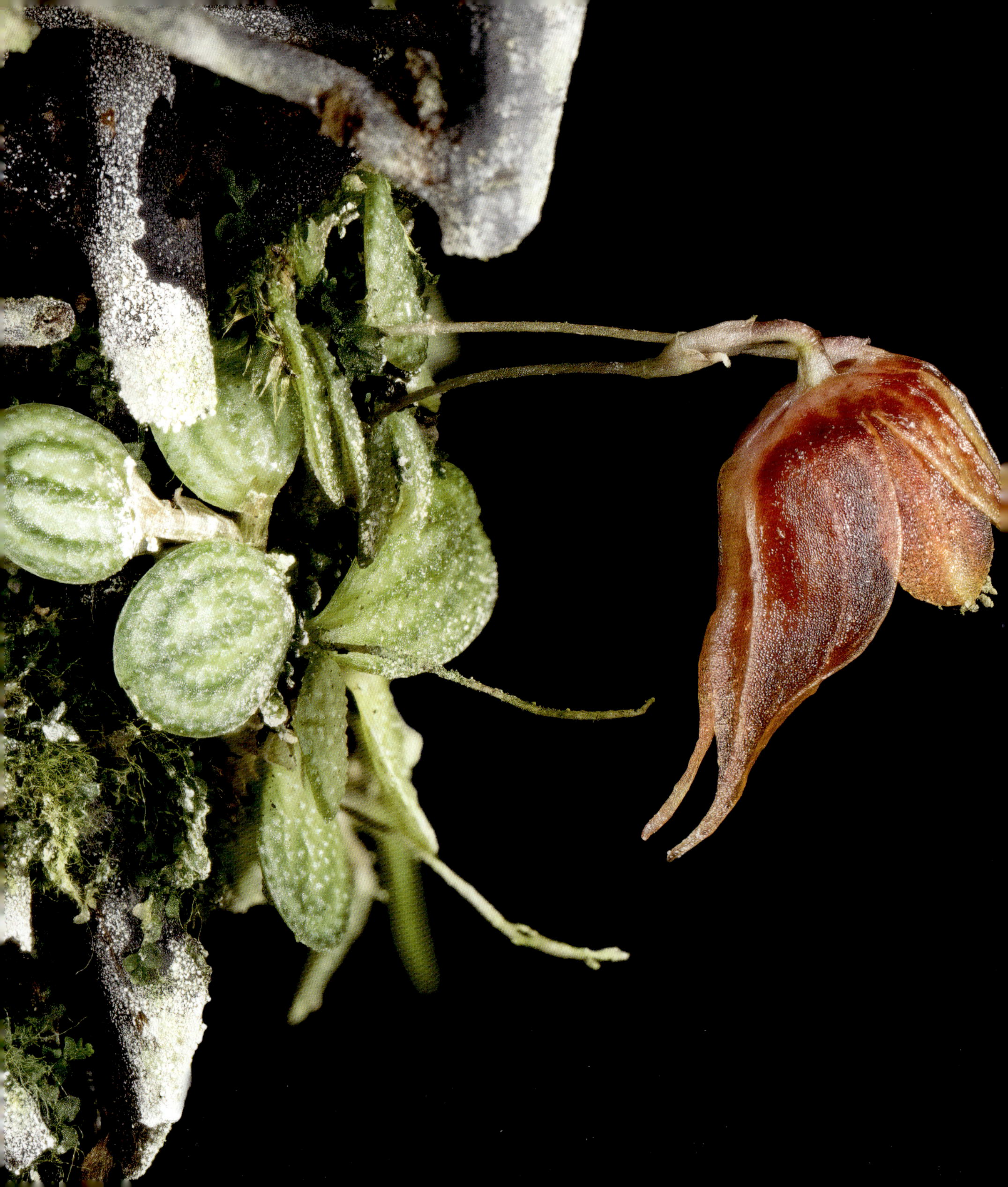

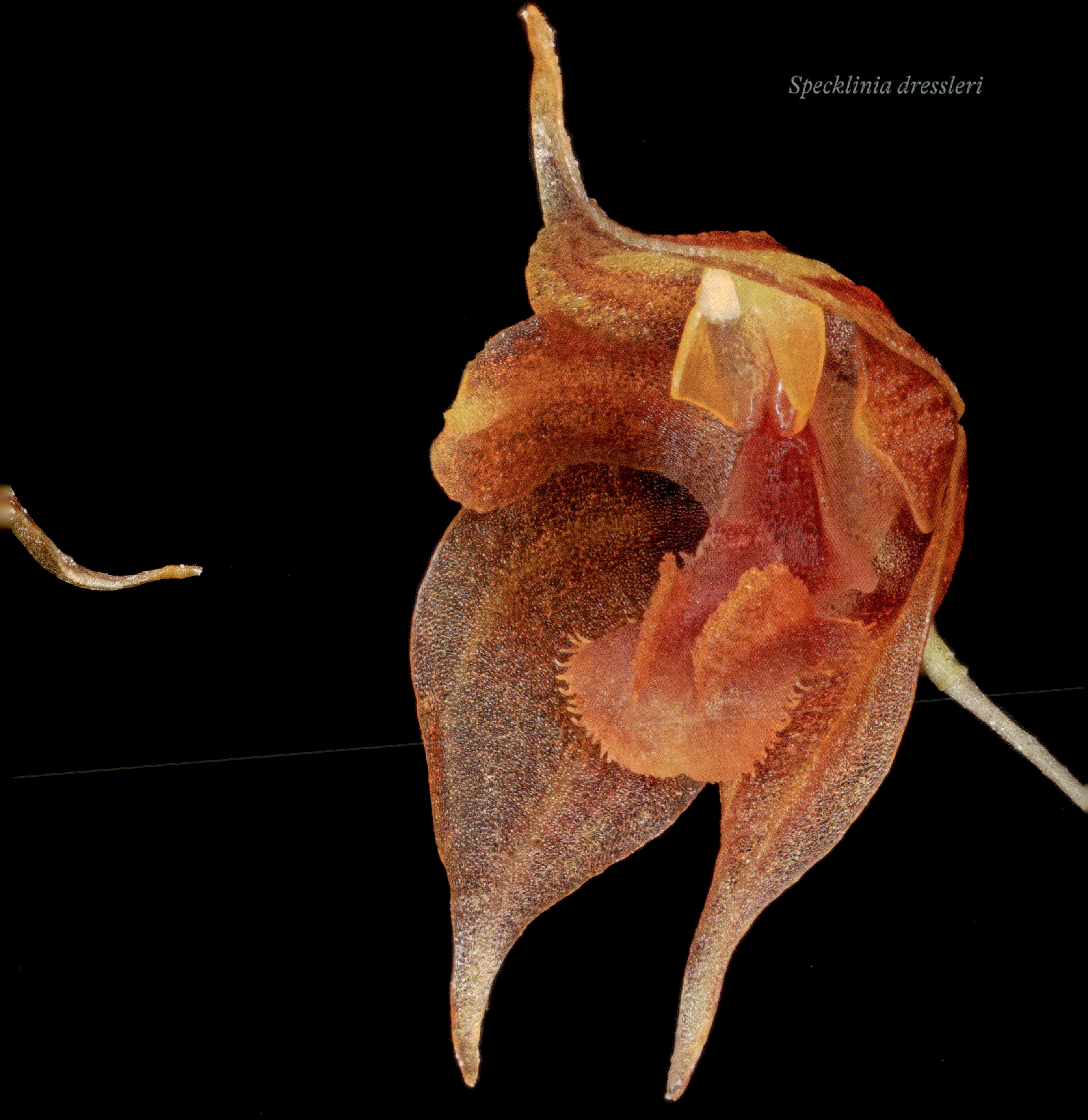

Specklinia dressleri

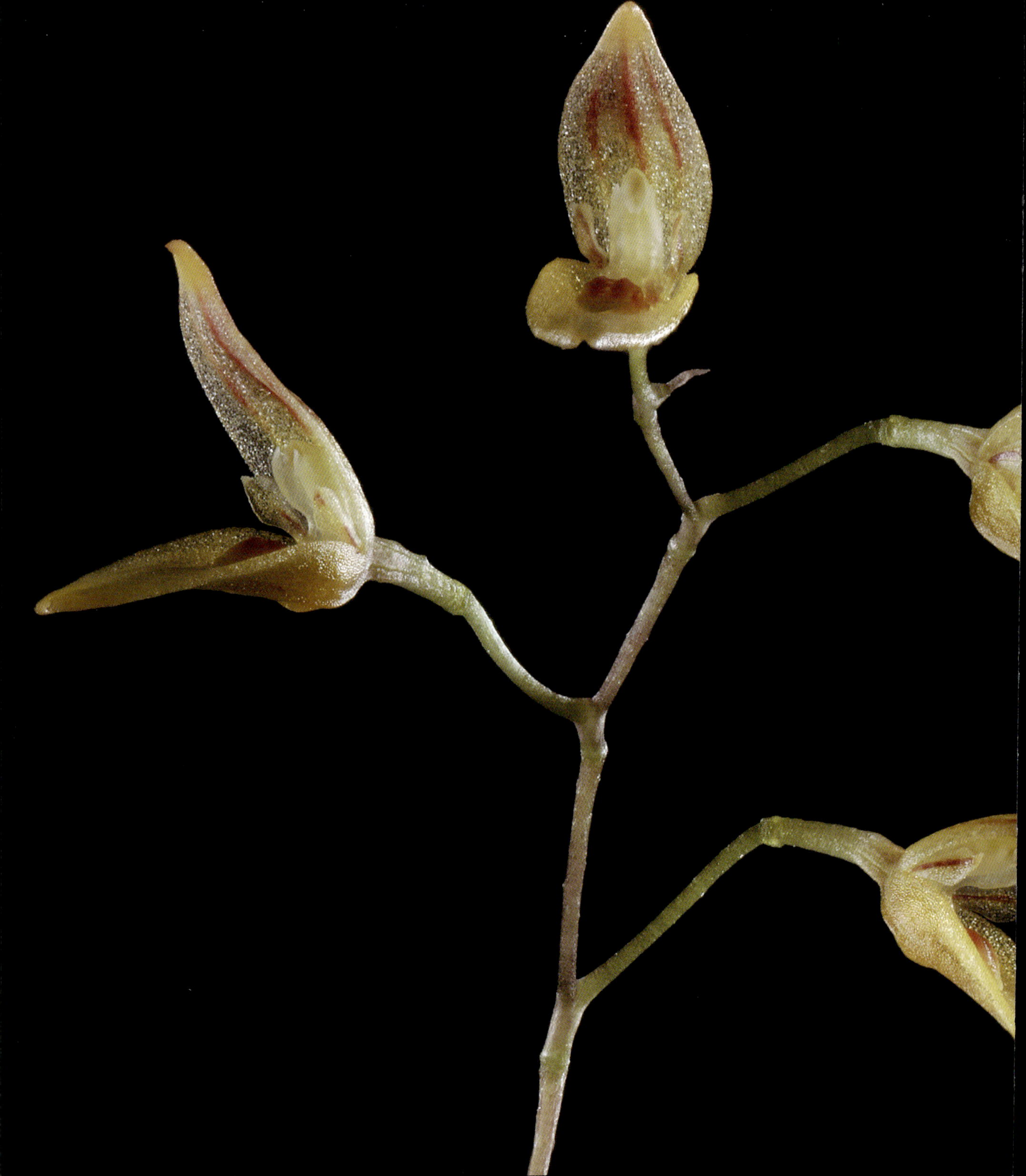

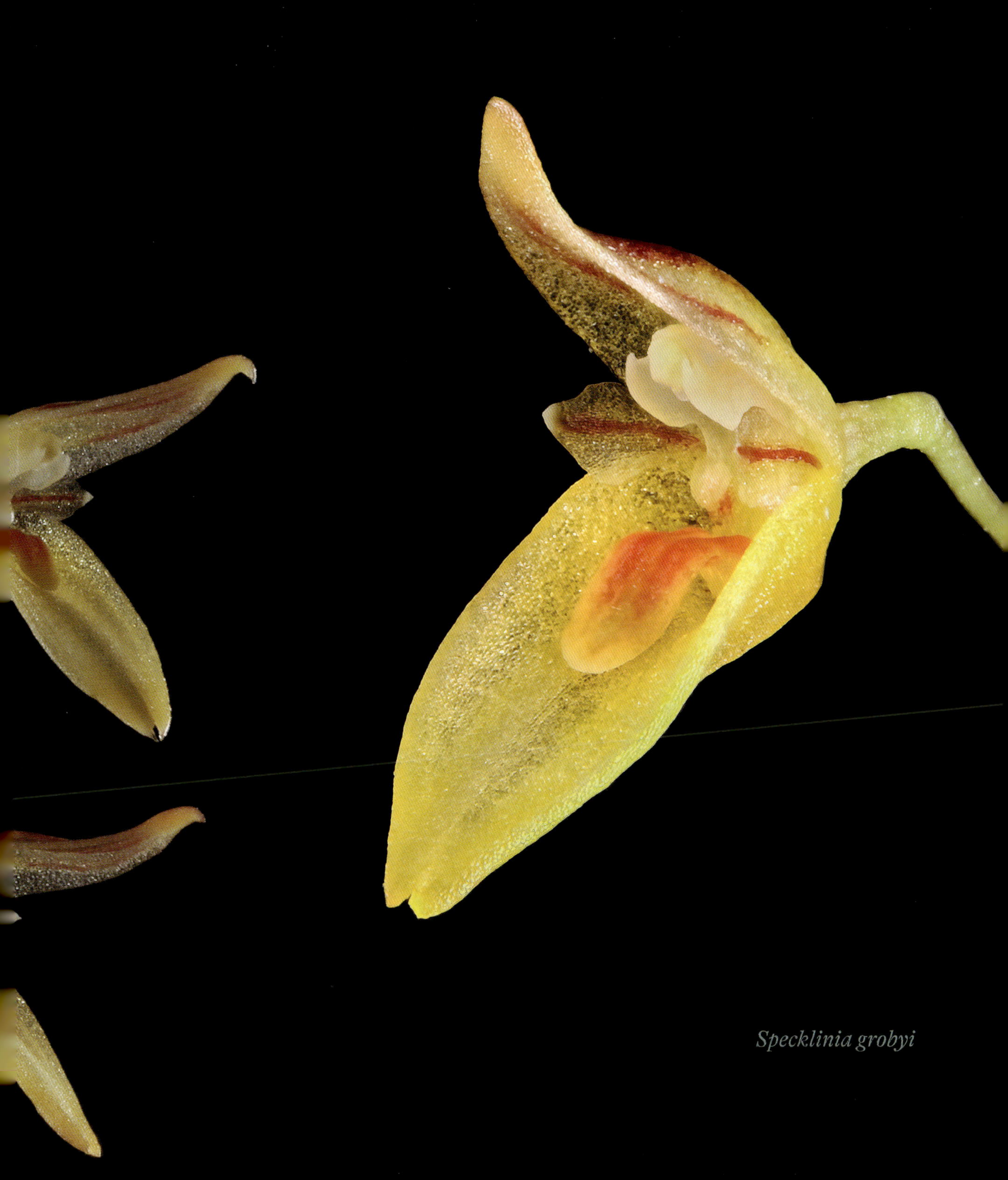

Specklinia grobyi

Specklinia pisinna

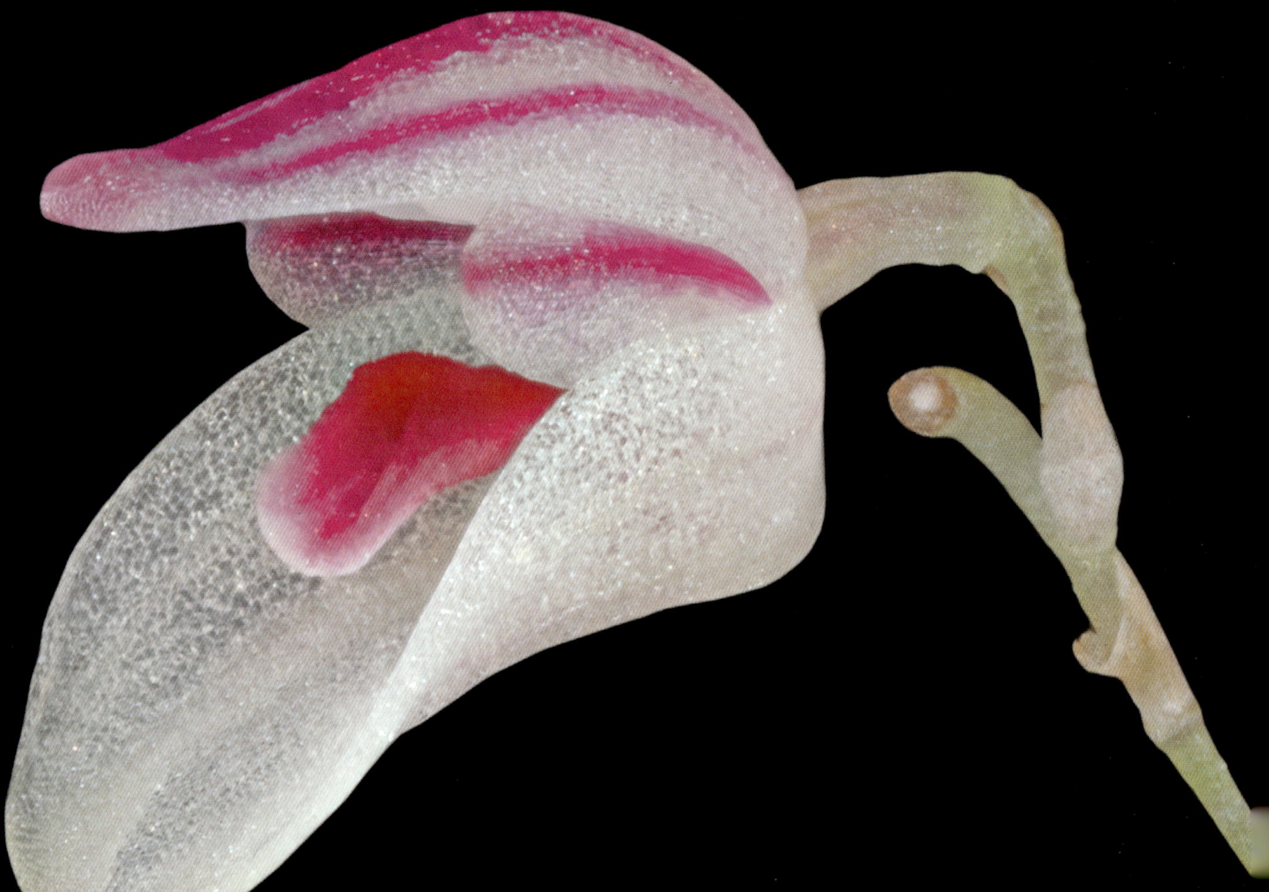

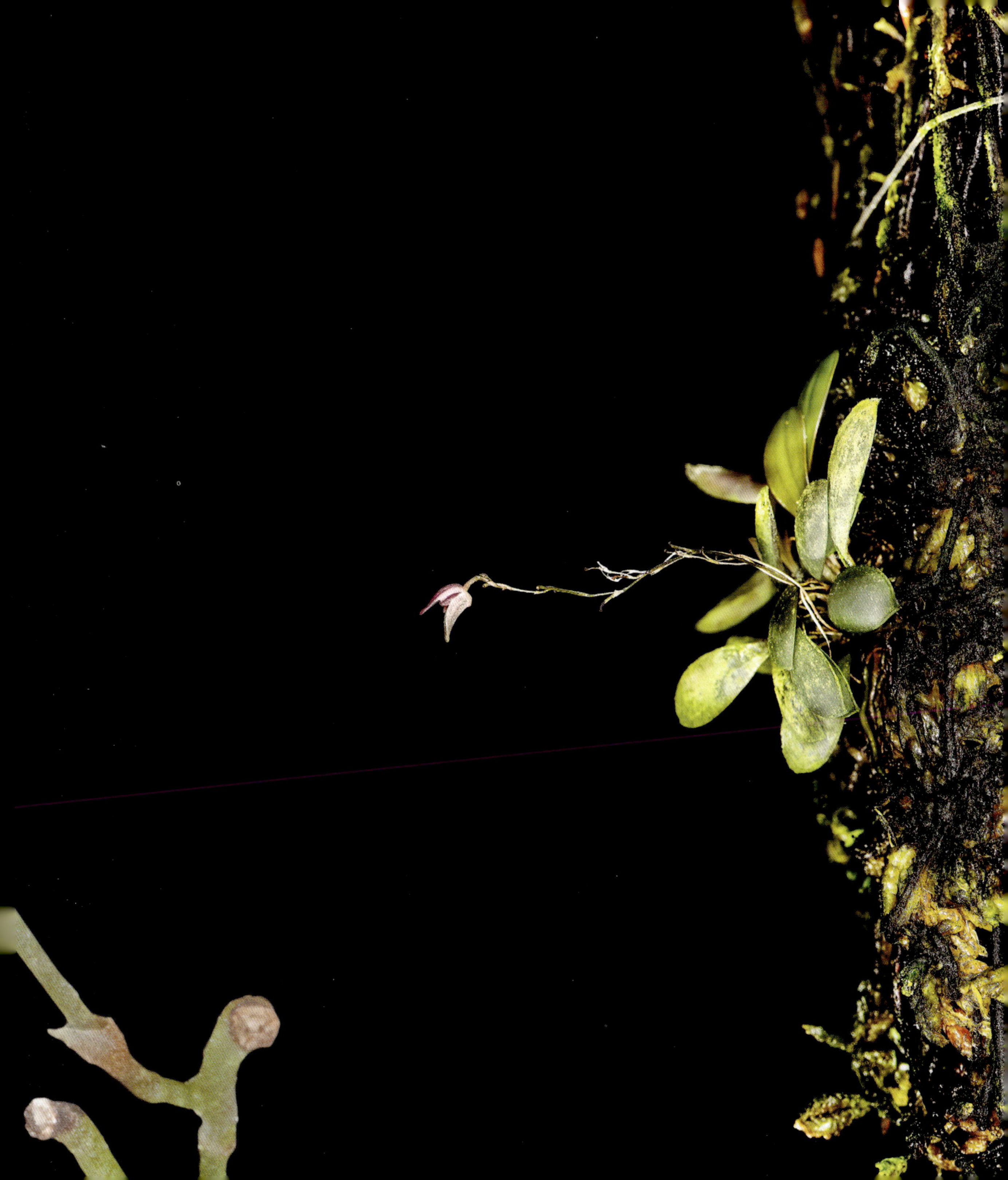

Stanhopea candida

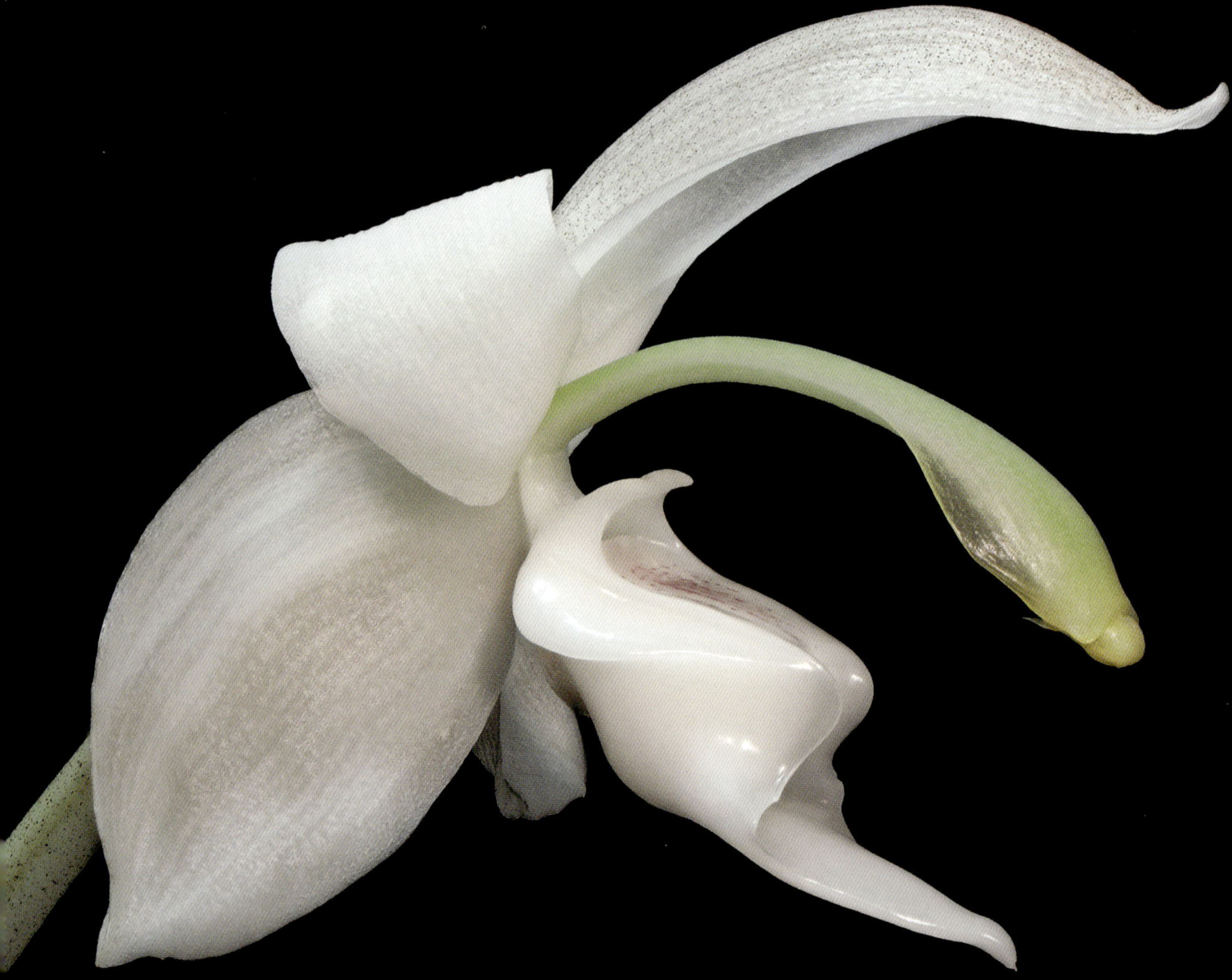

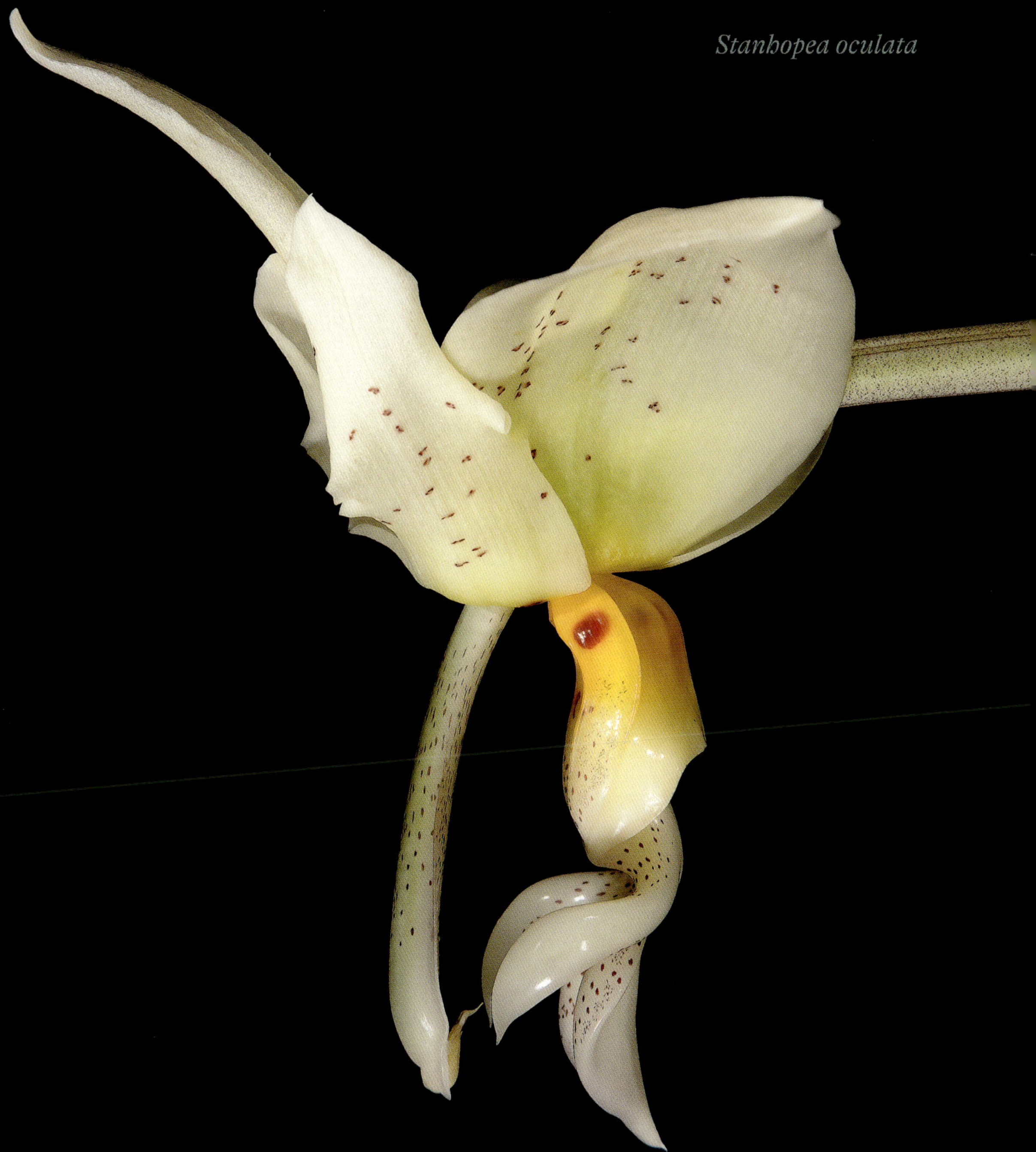

Stanhopea oculata

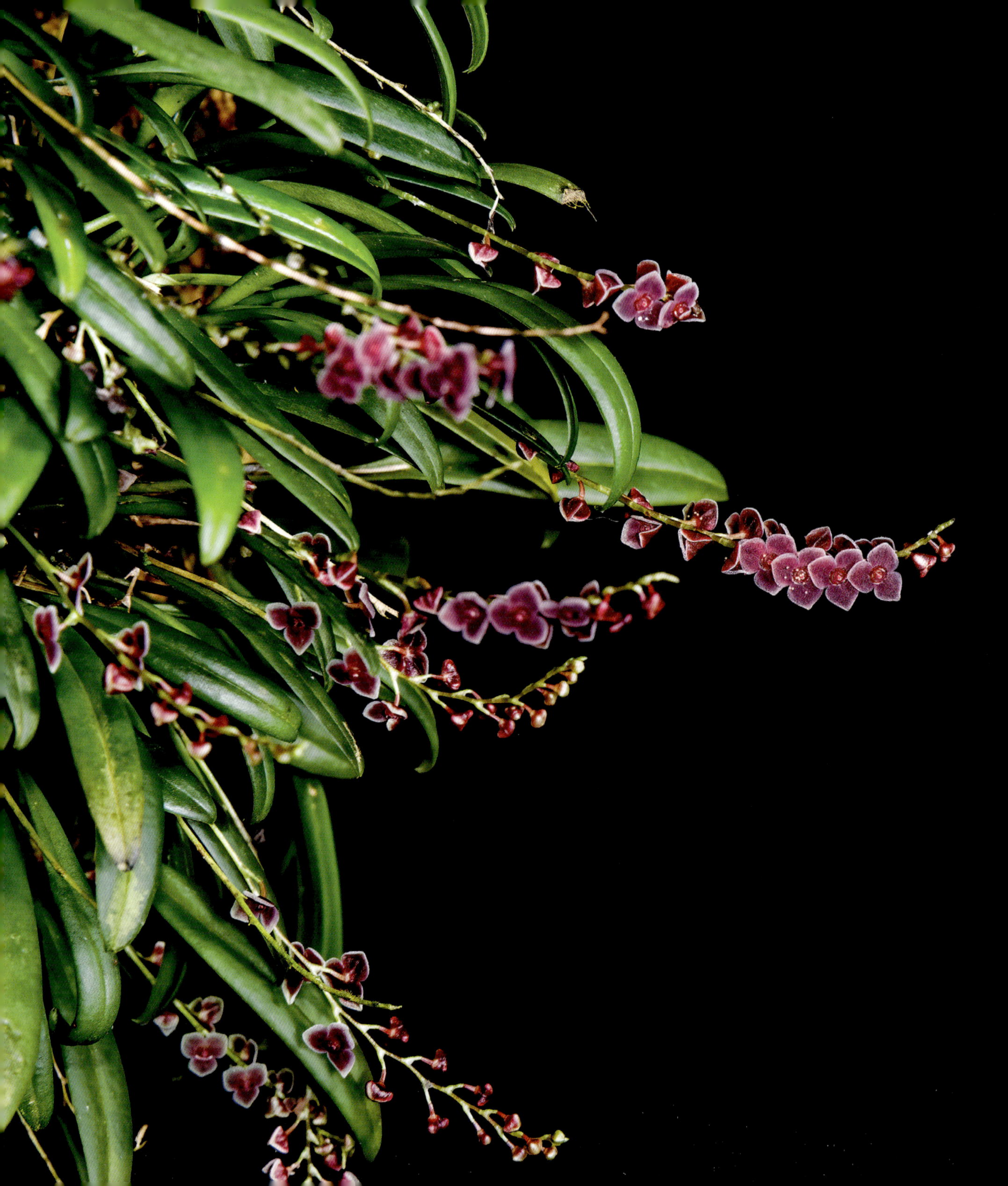

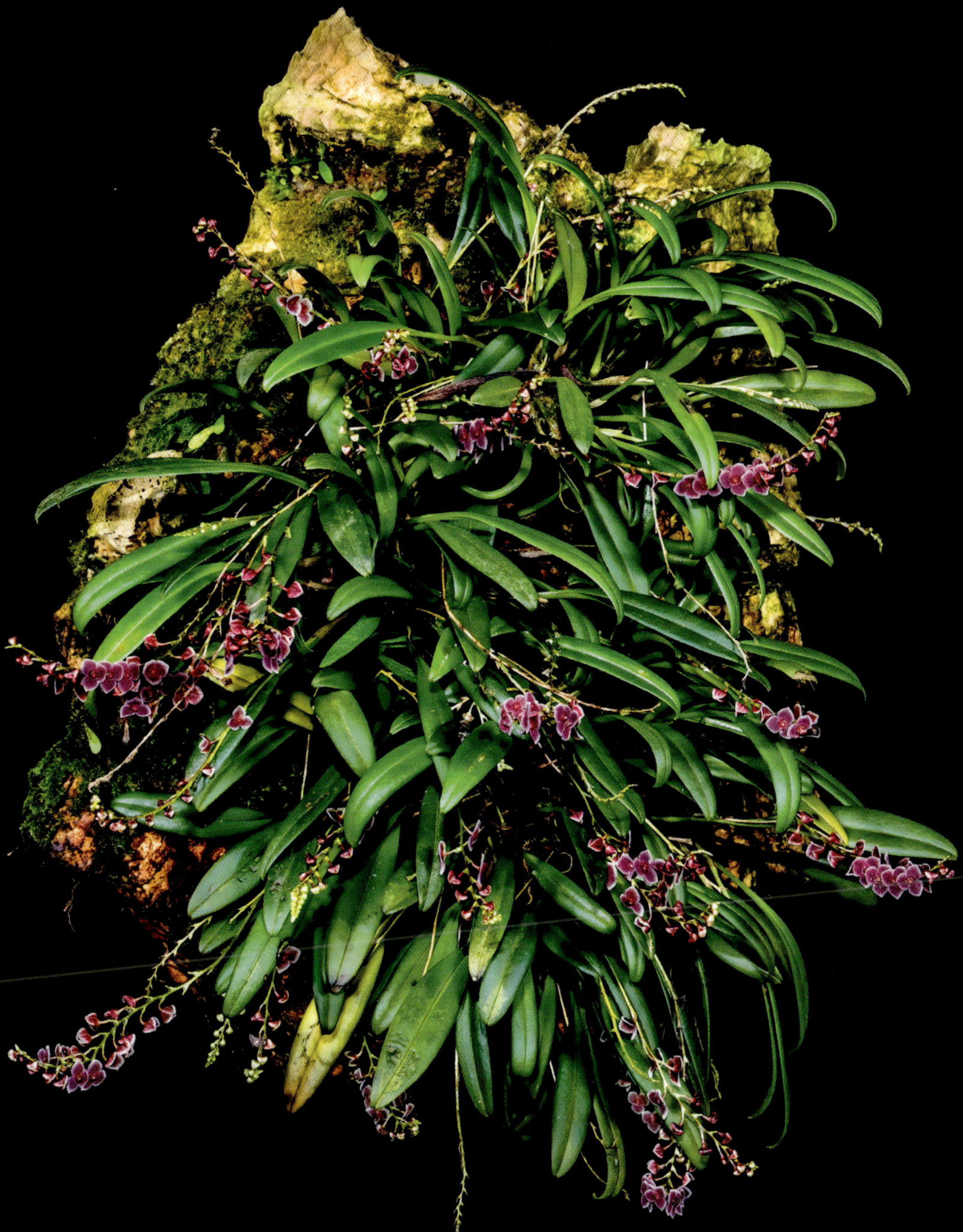

Stelis argentata

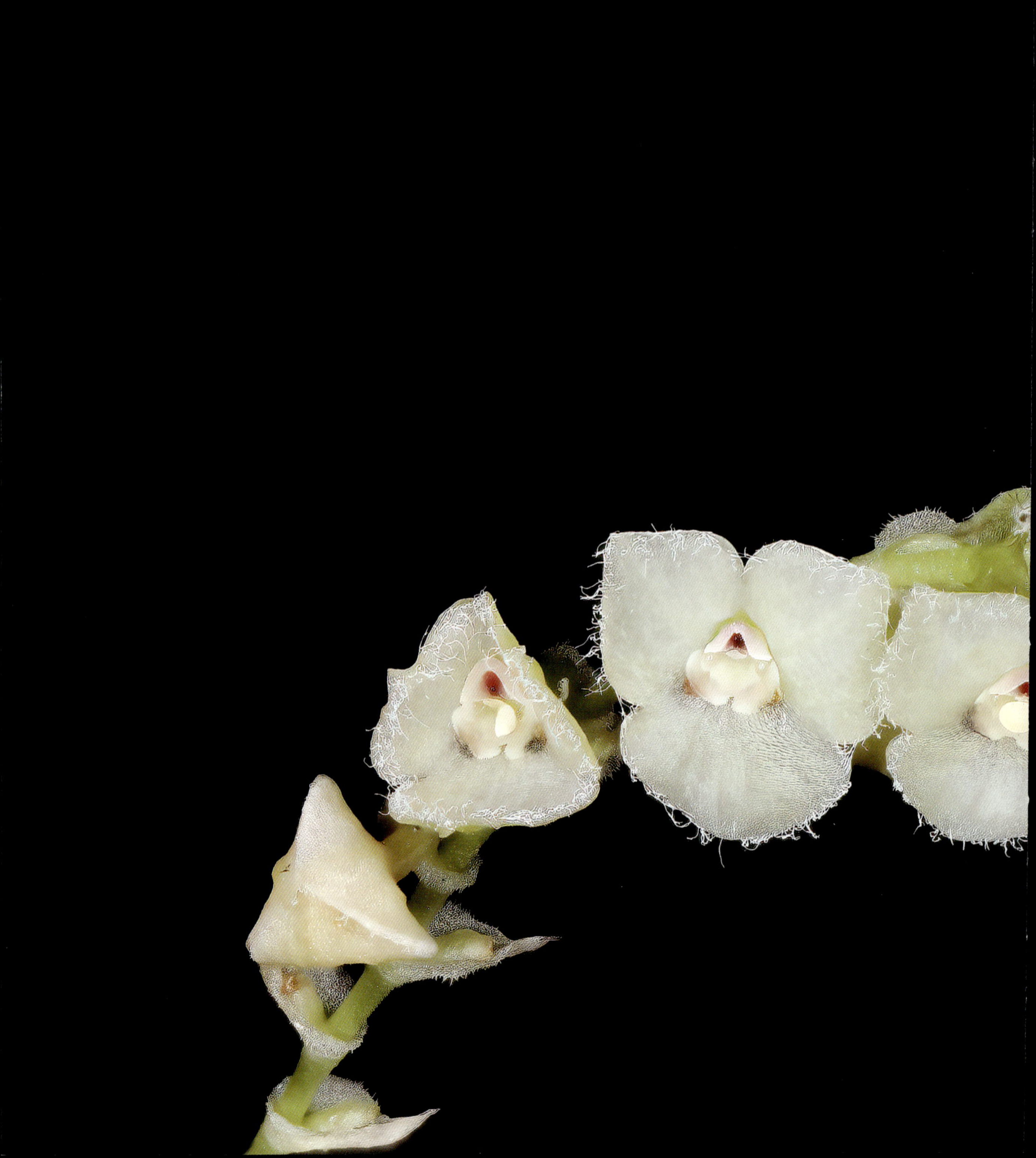

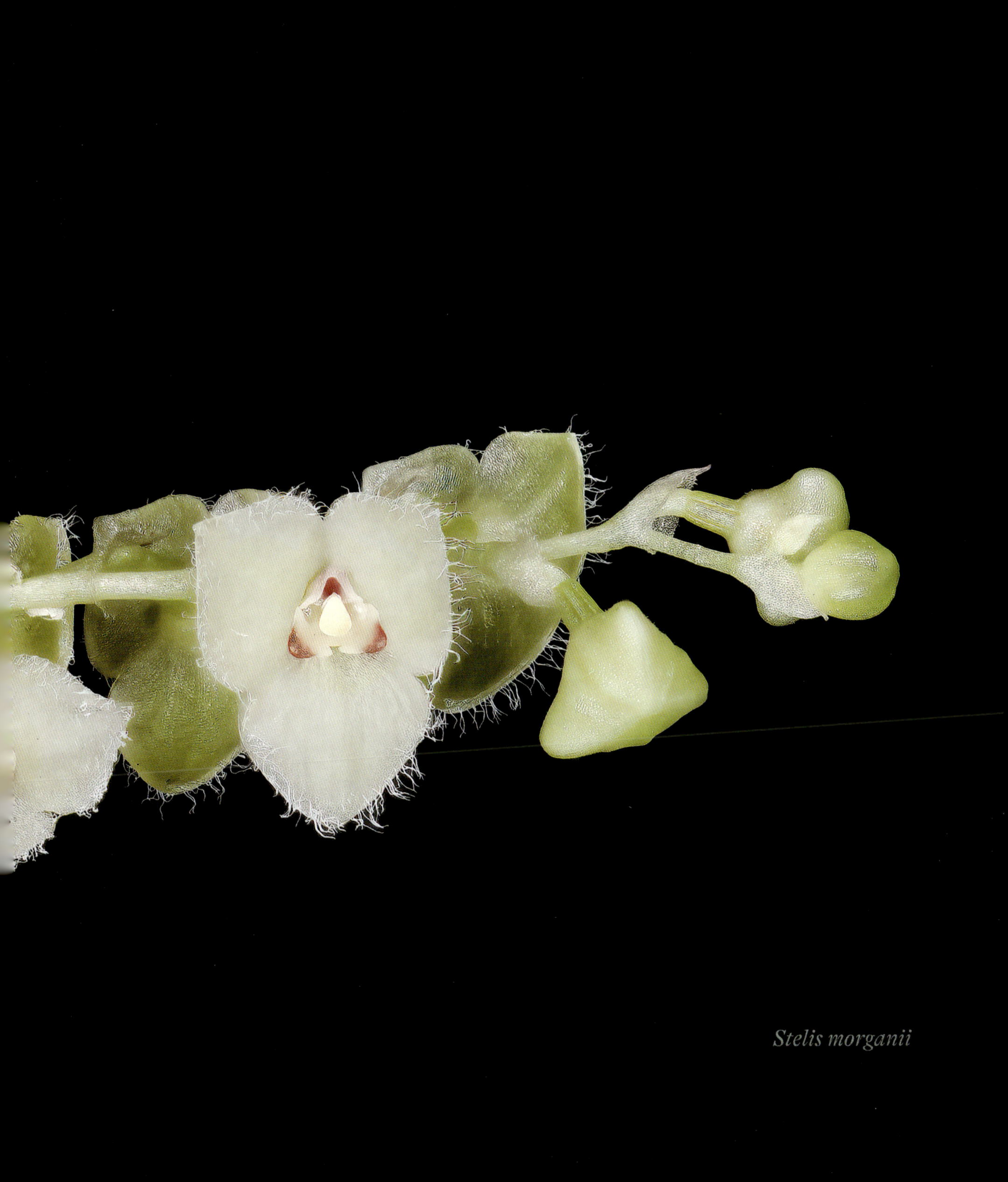

Stelis morganii

Trichosalpinx blaisdellii

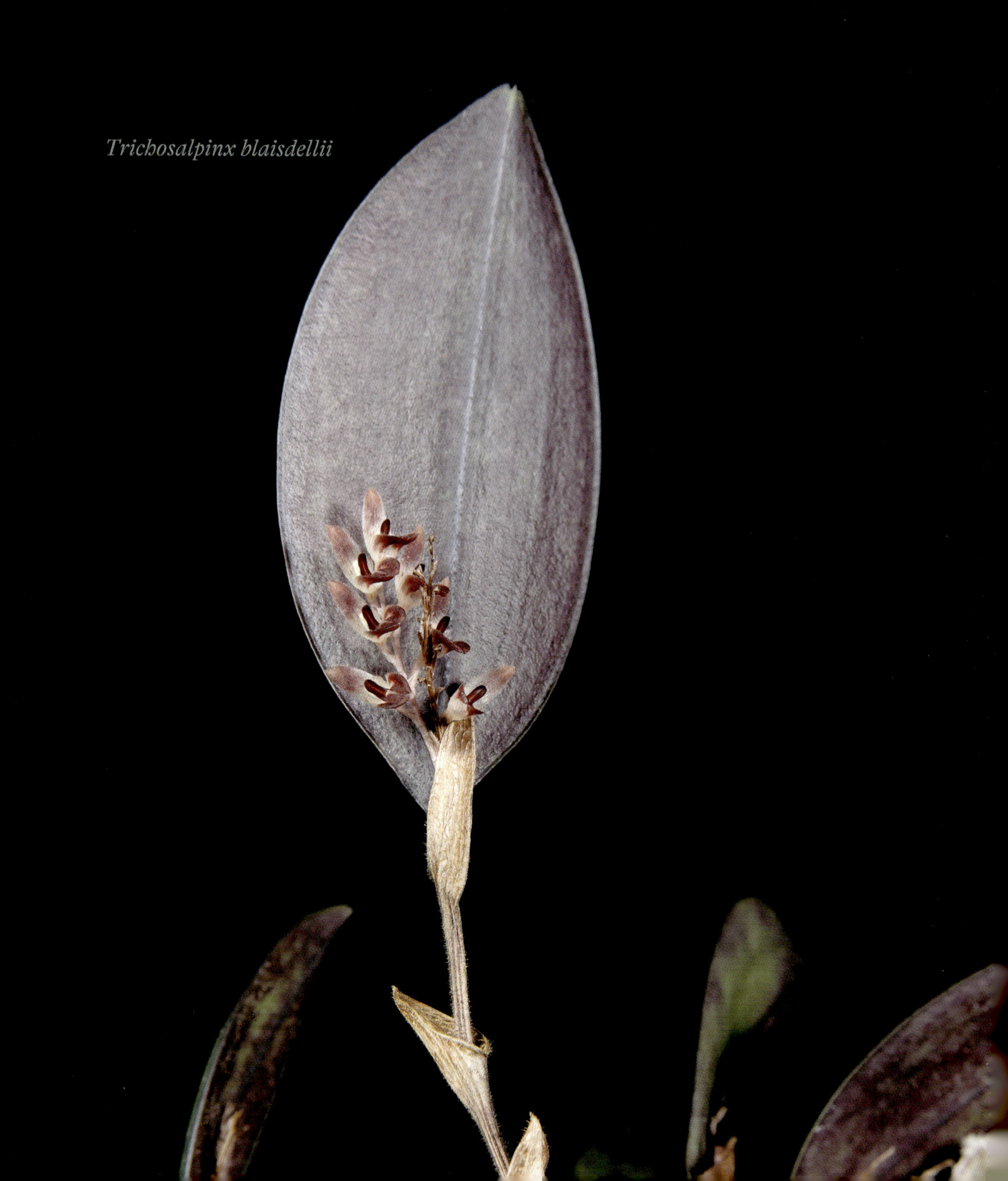

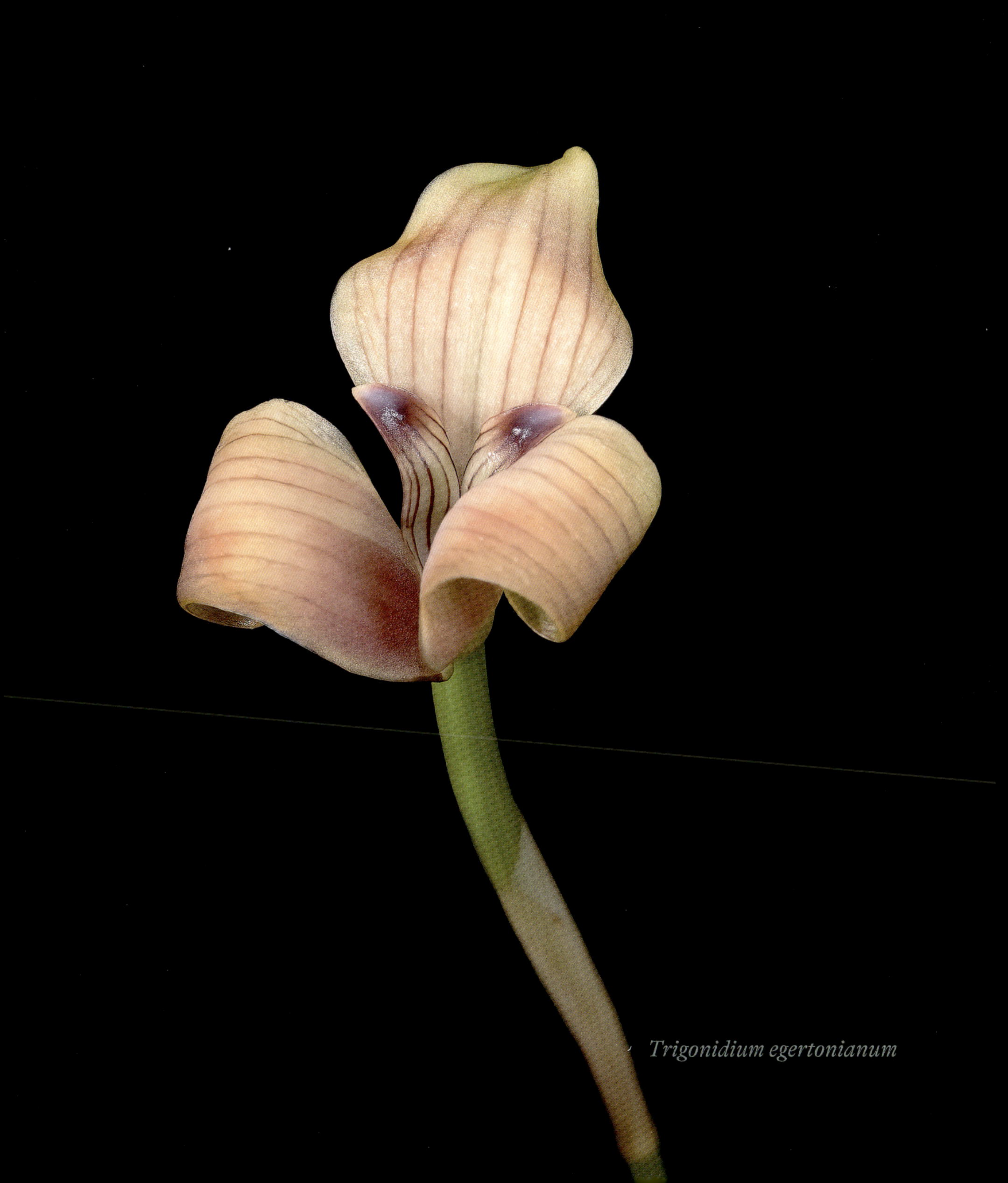

Trigonidium egertonianum

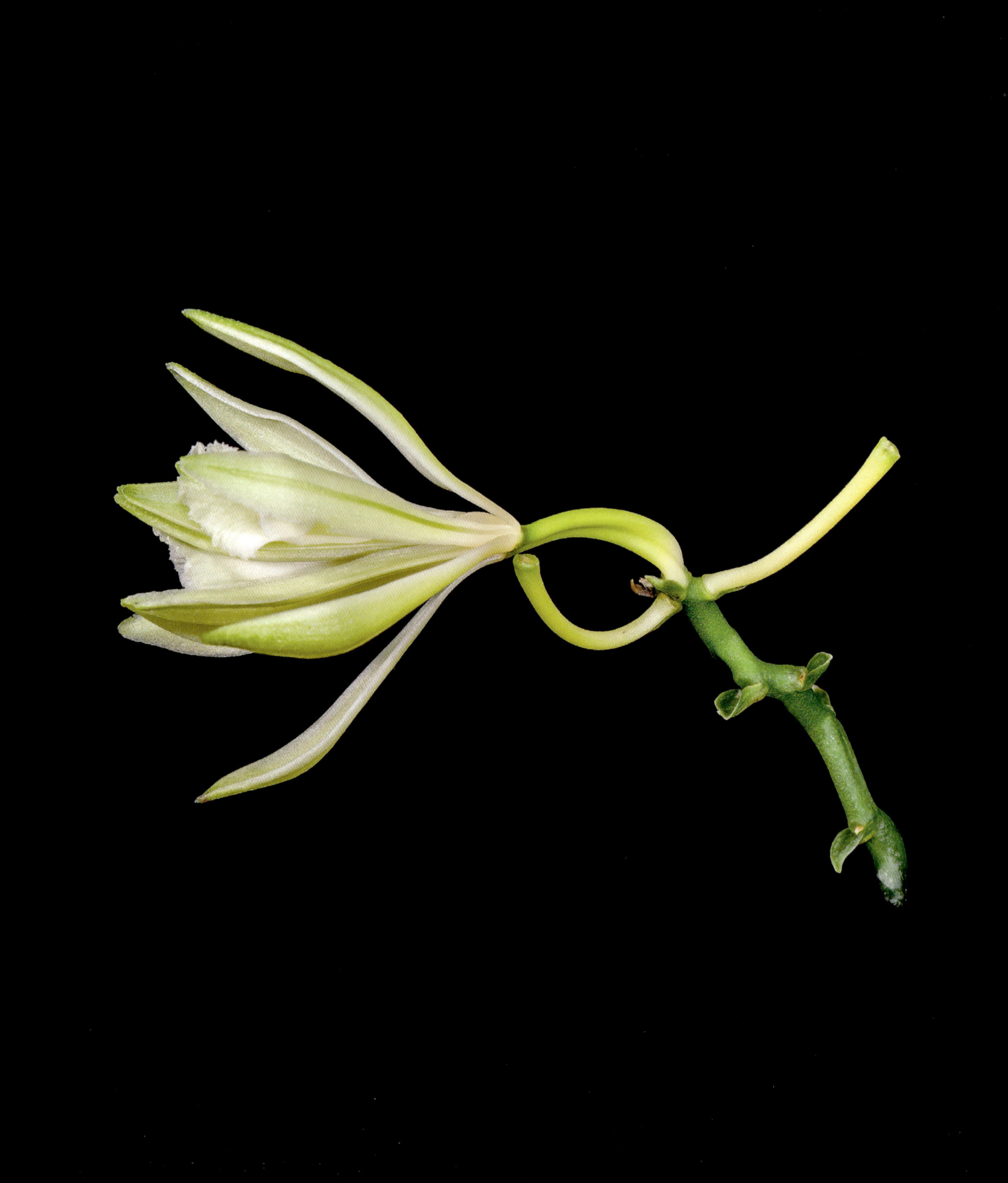

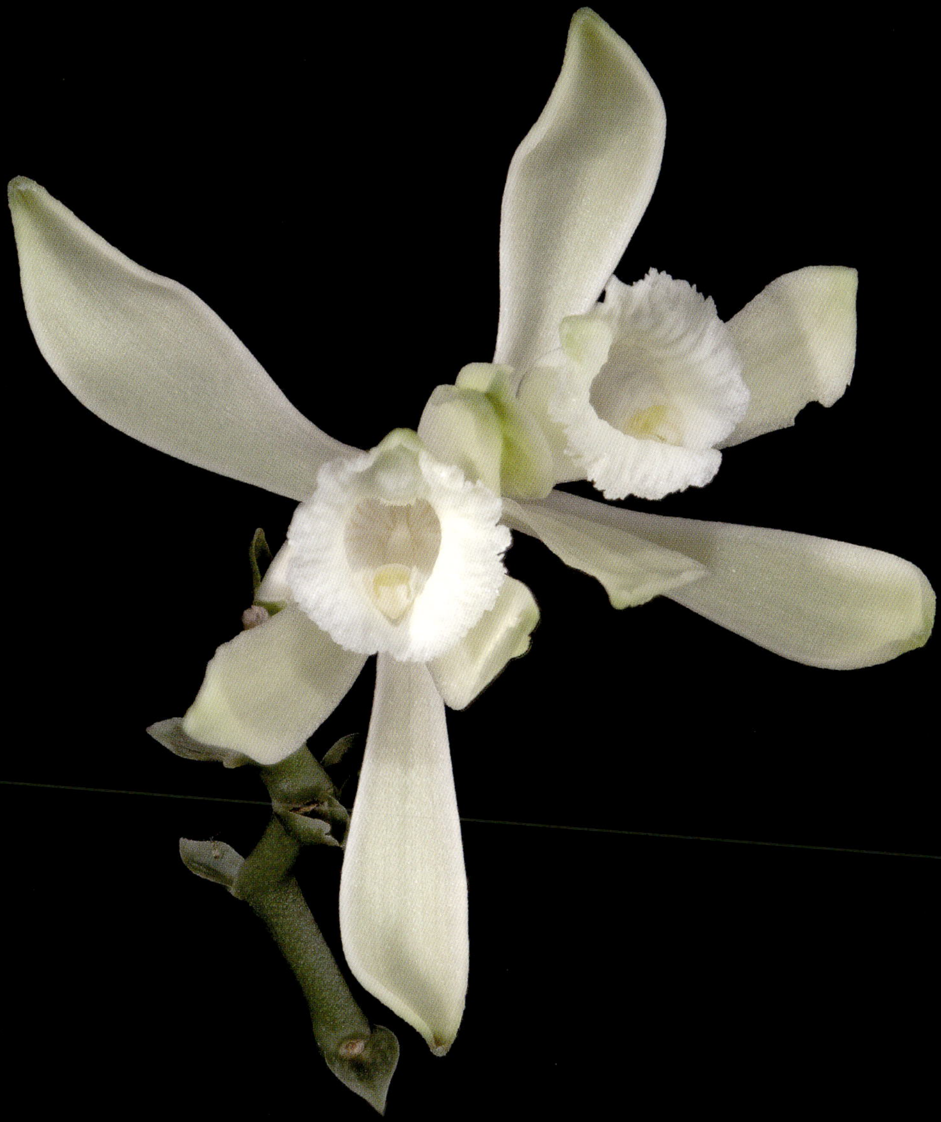

Vanilla hartii

CHECKLIST

The orchids referenced in the following checklist are all part of Selby Gardens' living orchid collection. The information provided for each orchid includes the full scientific name of the plant, the provenance of the plant, and the name of the photographer. The scientific name consists of genus, species, and author or authority credited as the first person to formally use the name. In some cases, the name includes the abbreviation sp., which indicates that the specific species cannot currently be identified. The provenance refers to the place of origin where the plant was collected in the wild, when known.

Acianthera sp.
Provenance: Brazil
Photographer: Wade Collier

Arpophyllum giganteum Hartw. ex. Lindl.
Provenance: Belize (Toledo, Bladen Nature Reserve)
Photographer: Sandra Robinson

Bletia riparia Sosa & Palestina
Provenance: Mexico
Photographer: Wade Collier

Brassia maculata R. Br.
Provenance: Belize (Orange Walk, Gallon Jug region)
Photographer: Wade Collier

Bulbophyllum fascinator Rolfe
Provenance: Thailand
Photographer: Wade Collier

Bulbophyllum lilacinum Ridl.
Provenance: Unknown
Photographer: Aaron Fink

Bulbophyllum longissimum (Ridl.) J.J. Smith
Provenance: Malaysia
Photographer: Sandra Robinson

Cattleya gaskelliana (N.E. Br.) B.S. Williams
Provenance: Venezuela
Photographer: Sandra Robinson

Cattleya lawrenceana Rchb. f.
Provenance: Brazil (Roraima)
Photographer: Wade Collier

Ceratostylis retisquama Rchb. f.
Provenance: Philippines
Photographer: Aaron Fink

Chysis bractescens Lindl.
Provenance: Belize (Cayo, Caves Branch Estate valley)
Photographer: Sandra Robinson

Coelogyne pandurata Lindl.
Provenance: Malaysia
Photographer: Sandra Robinson

Coelogyne parishii Hook., f.
Provenance: Unknown
Photographer: Sandra Robinson

Coelogyne tomentosa Lindl.
Provenance: Unknown
Photographer: Suzanne Havens

Coelogyne trinervis Lindl. 'Marie Selby'
Provenance: Thailand
Photographer: Sandra Robinson

Coryanthes macrantha (Hook.) Hook.
Provenance: Unknown
Photographer: Wade Collier

Coryanthes picturata Rchb. f.
Provenance: Belize (Cayo, Caves Branch Estate valley)
Photographer: Wade Collier

Dendrobium bifalce Lindl.
Provenance: Unknown
Photographer: Wade Collier

Dendrobium goldschmidtianum Kraenzl.
Provenance: Unknown
Photographer: Wade Collier

Dendrobium hancockii Rolfe
Provenance: China (Yunnan)
Photographer: Aaron Fink

Dendrobium malbrownii Dockr. 'Marie Selby'
Provenance: Papua New Guinea
Photographer: Wade Collier

Dendrobium pachyphyllum (Kuntze) Bakh. f.
Provenance: Malaysia (Selangor)
Photographer: Wade Collier

Dendrobium secundum (Blume) Lindl.
Provenance: Thailand
Photographer: Sandra Robinson

Dendrobium spectabile (Blume) Miq.
Provenance: Unknown
Photographer: Wade Collier

Dendrochilum cobbianum Rchb. f.
Provenance: Philippines
Photographer: Sandra Robinson

Dichaea muricatoides Hamer & Garay
Provenance: Belize (Toledo, Bladen Nature Reserve)
Photographer: Wade Collier

Dichaea sp.
Provenance: Belize (Stann Creek, Cockscomb Basin Wildlife Sanctuary)
Photographer: Wade Collier

Dinema polybulbon (Sw.) Lindl.
Provenance: Belize (Cayo, Sibun Forest Reserve)
Photographer: Wade Collier

Diplocaulobium hydrophilum (J.J. Sm) Kraenzl.
Provenance: Papua New Guinea
Photographer: Suzanne Havens

Embreea rodigasiana (Claess. ex Cogn.) Dodson
Provenance: Colombia (Antioquía)
Photographer: Phil Nelson

Encyclia bractescens (Lindl.) Hoehne
Provenance: Belize (Cayo, Caves Branch Estate valley)
Photographer: Wade Collier

Encyclia howardii (Ames & Correll) Hoehne
Provenance: Cuba
Photographer: Phil Nelson

Encyclia spiritusanctensis L.C. Menezes
Provenance: Brazil
Photographer: Sandra Robinson

Encyclia tampensis (Lindl.) Small
Provenance: United States (Florida)
Photographer: Aaron Fink

Epidendrum flexuosum G. Mey.
Provenance: Belize (Toledo, Bladen Nature Reserve)
Photographer: Wade Collier

Epidendrum galeottianum A. Rich & Galeotti
Provenance: Belize (Cayo, Chiquibul Forest Reserve)
Photographer: Wade Collier

Epidendrum ilense Dodson
Provenance: Ecuador
Photographer: Wade Collier

Epidendrum macroclinium Hágsater
Provenance: Belize (Cayo, Chiquibul National Park)
Photographer: Wade Collier

Epidendrum stamfordianum Bateman
Provenance: Belize (Orange Walk, Gallon Jug region)
Photographer: Wade Collier

Eulophia andamanensis Rchb. f.
Provenance: Unknown
Photographer: Suzanne Havens

Galeandra arundinis Garay & G.A. Romero
Provenance: Belize (Cayo, Pine Ridge)
Photographer: Wade Collier

Gomesa croesus (Rchb. f.) M.W. Chase & N.H. Williams
Provenance: Unknown
Photographer: Aaron Fink

Gongora leucochila Lem.
Provenance: Belize (Toledo, Bladen Nature Reserve)
Photographer: Wade Collier

Gongora portentosa Rchb. f.
Provenance: Unknown
Photographer: Wade Collier

Gongora unicolor Schltr.
Provenance: Belize (Cayo, Pine Ridge)
Photographer: Wade Collier

Guarianthe bowringiana (O'Brien) Dressler & W.E. Higgins
Provenance: Unknown
Photographer: Sandra Robinson

Guarianthe skinneri (Bateman) Dressler & W.E. Higgins "alba form"
Provenance: Unknown
Photographer: Wade Collier

Habenaria medusa Kraenzl.
Provenance: Indonesia (Sumatra)
Photographer: Sandra Robinson

Isochilus carnosiflorus Lindl.
Provenance: Belize (Cayo, Caves Branch Estate valley)
Photographer: Wade Collier

Kegeliella atropilosa L.O. Williams & A.H. Heller
Provenance: Belize (Stann Creek, Victoria Peak National Monument)
Photographer: Wade Collier

Lepanthes pan Luer & Dalström
Provenance: Ecuador
Photographer: Wade Collier

Lockhartia oerstedii Rchb. f.
Provenance: Unknown
Photographer: Wade Collier

Lophiarella splendida (A. Rich. ex Duch.) Carnevali & Cetzal
Provenance: Unknown
Photographer: Suzanne Havens

Lophiaris lurida (Lindl.) Braem
Provenance: Belize (Cayo)
Photographer: Sandra Robinson

Lophiaris oerstedii (Rchb. f.) R. Jiménez, Carnevali & Dressler
Provenance: Belize (Cayo, Hershey Citrus Field)
Photographer: Wade Collier

Lophiaris teaboanum R. Jiménez, Carnevali & J.L. Tapia
Provenance: Belize (Orange Walk, Rio Bravo Conservation Area)
Photographer: Wade Collier

Maxillaria acervata Rchb. f.
Provenance: Costa Rica (San Carlos)
Photographer: Wade Collier

Maxillaria fulgens (Rchb. f.) L.O. Williams
Provenance: Panama
Photographer: Wade Collier

Maxillaria porrecta Lindl.
Provenance: Costa Rica (Puntarenas, Coto Brus)
Photographer: Wade Collier

Maxillaria ringens Rchb. f.
Provenance: Belize (Toledo, Bladen Nature Reserve)
Photographer: Wade Collier

Mormolyca rufescens (Lindl.) M.A. Blanco
Provenance: Suriname (Wilhelmina Mountains)
Photographer: Sandra Robinson

Muscarella marginata (Rich.) Luer
Provenance: Mexico
Photographer: Wade Collier

Myrmecophila tibicinis (Bateman) Rolfe
Provenance: Unknown
Photographer: Wade Collier

Nidema boothii (Lindl.) Schltr.
Provenance: Belize (Cayo)
Photographer: Wade Collier

Octomeria juncifolia Barb. Rodr.
Provenance: Brazil
Photographer: Wade Collier

Ornithocephalus suarezii Dodson
Provenance: Unknown
Photographer: Wade Collier

Pabstiella tripterantha (Rchb. f.) F. Barros
Provenance: Panama
Photographer: Sandra Robinson

Paphinia herrerae Dodson
Provenance: Ecuador (Zamora)
Photographer: Phil Nelson

Paphiopedilum callosum (Rchb. f.) Stein
Provenance: Unknown
Photographer: Wade Collier

Paphiopedilum fairrieanum (Lindl.) Stein
Provenance: Unknown
Photographer: Wade Collier

Phalaenopsis amabilis (L.) Blume
Provenance: Indonesia (Sumatra)
Photographer: Phil Nelson

Phragmipedium longifolium (Warsz. & Rchb. f.) Rolfe
Provenance: Panama (Panamá, Cerro Jefe, Río Indio)
Photographer: Aaron Fink

Pleurothallis aspergillum Luer & Hirtz
Provenance: Unknown
Photographer: Wade Collier

Pleurothallis cardiothallis Rchb. f.
Provenance: Belize (Toledo, Columbia River Forest Reserve)
Photographer: Wade Collier

Pleurothallis luctuosa Rchb. f.
Provenance: Unknown
Photographer: Wade Collier

Pleurothallis ruscifolia (Jacq.) R. Br.
Provenance: Ecuador (Pastaza, Puyo)
Photographer: Wade Collier

Polystachya paniculata (Sw.) Rolfe
Provenance: Unknown
Photographer: Wade Collier

Prosthechea pygmaea (Hook) W.E. Higgins
Provenance: Belize (Cayo, Chiquibul National Park, Nohoch Che'en Cenote)
Photographer: Wade Collier

Prosthechea radiata (Lindl.) W.E. Higgins
Provenance: Unknown
Photographer: Wade Collier

Rhyncholaelia digbyana (Lindl.) Schltr.
Provenance: Belize (Corozal, El Tigre Preserve)
Photographer: Wade Collier

Sarcoglottis sceptrodes (Rchb. f.) Schltr.
Provenance: Belize
Photographer: Wade Collier

Specklinia brighamii (S. Watson) Pridgeon & M.W. Chase
Provenance: Belize (Cayo, Hershey Citrus Field)
Photographer: Wade Collier

Specklinia dressleri (Luer) Bogarín & Karremans
Provenance: Panama
Photographer: Wade Collier

Specklinia grobyi (Bateman ex Lindl.) F. Barros
Provenance: Belize (Toledo, Sarstoon-Temash National Park)
Photographer: Wade Collier

Specklinia pisinna (Luer) Solano & Soto Arenas
Provenance: Belize (Stann Creek, Sittee River Forest Preserve)
Photographer: Wade Collier

Stanhopea candida Barb. Rodr.
Provenance: Unknown
Photographer: Sandra Robinson

Stanhopea oculata (Lodd.) Lindl.
Provenance: Belize (Cayo, Chiquibul National Park, Nohoch Che'en Cenote)
Photographer: Wade Collier

Stelis argentata Lindl.
Provenance: Ecuador (Pastaza, Puyo)
Photographer: Wade Collier

Stelis morganii Dodson & Garay
Provenance: Unknown
Photographer: Wade Collier

Trichosalpinx blaisdellii (S. Watson) Luer
Provenance: Belize (Toledo, Bladen Nature Reserve)
Photographer: Wade Collier

Trigonidium egertonianum Bateman
Provenance: Belize (Toledo, Sarstoon-Temash National Park)
Photographer: Wade Collier

Vanilla hartii Rolfe
Provenance: Belize (Cayo, Pine Ridge)
Photographer: Wade Collier

GLOBAL PARTNERS

Selby Gardens would like to thank its many global partners in the fields of botany and conservation who have helped it to document orchids in the wild and to form its living orchid collection.

AUSTRALIA
Royal Botanic Garden Sydney

BELIZE
Belize Forest Department
Belize Zoo
Ian Anderson's Caves Branch Botanical Garden
University of Belize

CANADA
Montreal Botanical Garden

CHINA
South China Botanical Garden

COSTA RICA
Boracayán Wildlife Refuge
Lankester Botanical Garden

PANAMA
Smithsonian Tropical Research Institute

PAPUA NEW GUINEA
Lae Botanic Gardens

SINGAPORE
Singapore Botanic Gardens

UNITED KINGDOM
Royal Botanic Gardens, Kew

UNITED STATES
Atlanta Botanical Garden
Fairchild Tropical Botanic Garden
Longwood Gardens
Mildred E. Mathias Botanical Garden
Missouri Botanical Garden
National Tropical Botanical Garden
New York Botanical Garden
Phipps Conservatory and Botanical Gardens
San Francisco Botanical Garden
University of California, Los Angeles
University of Colorado Boulder
University of Connecticut
University of Florida

"I never was more interested in any subject in my life than this of orchids."

— Charles Darwin, 1861

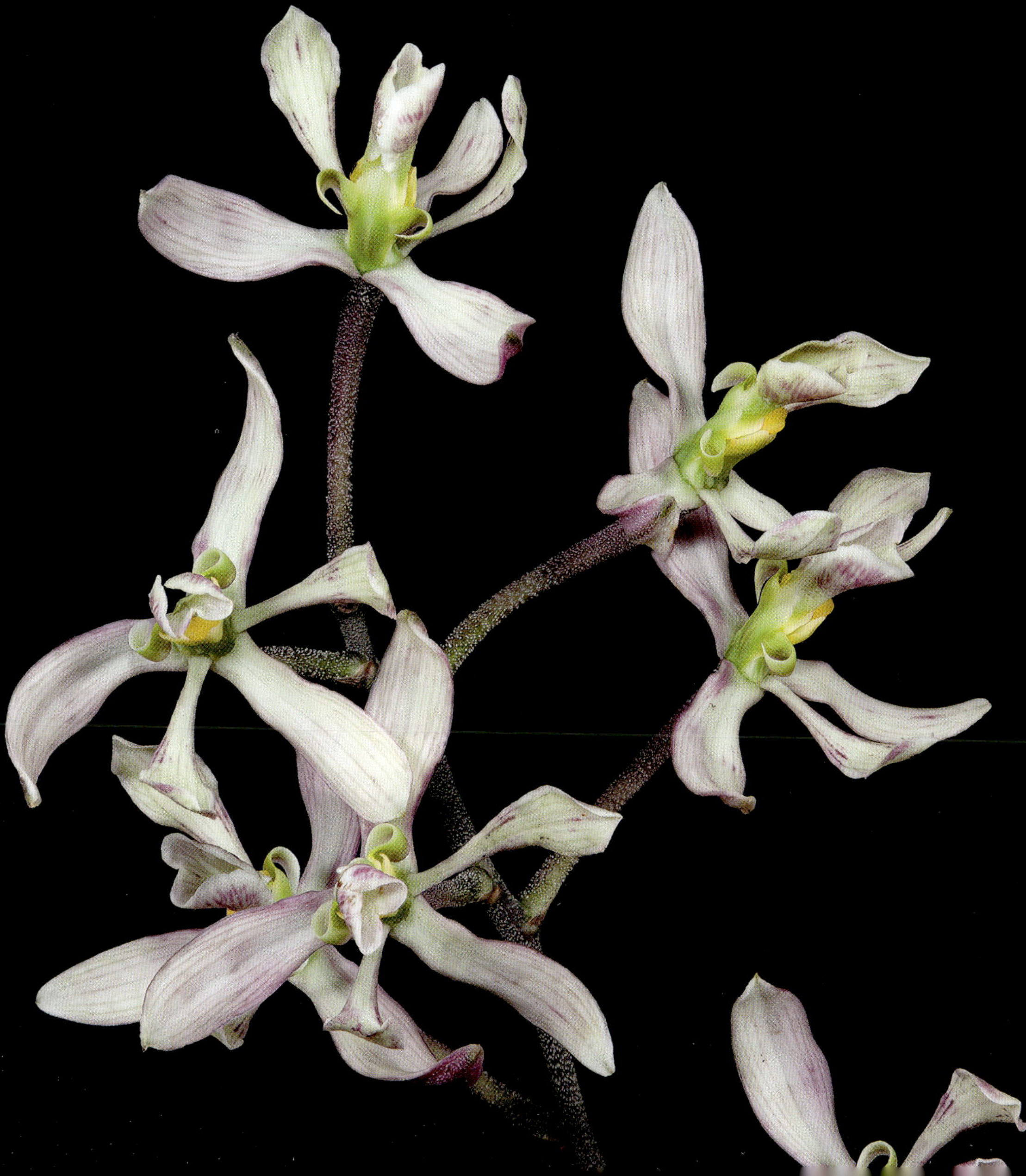

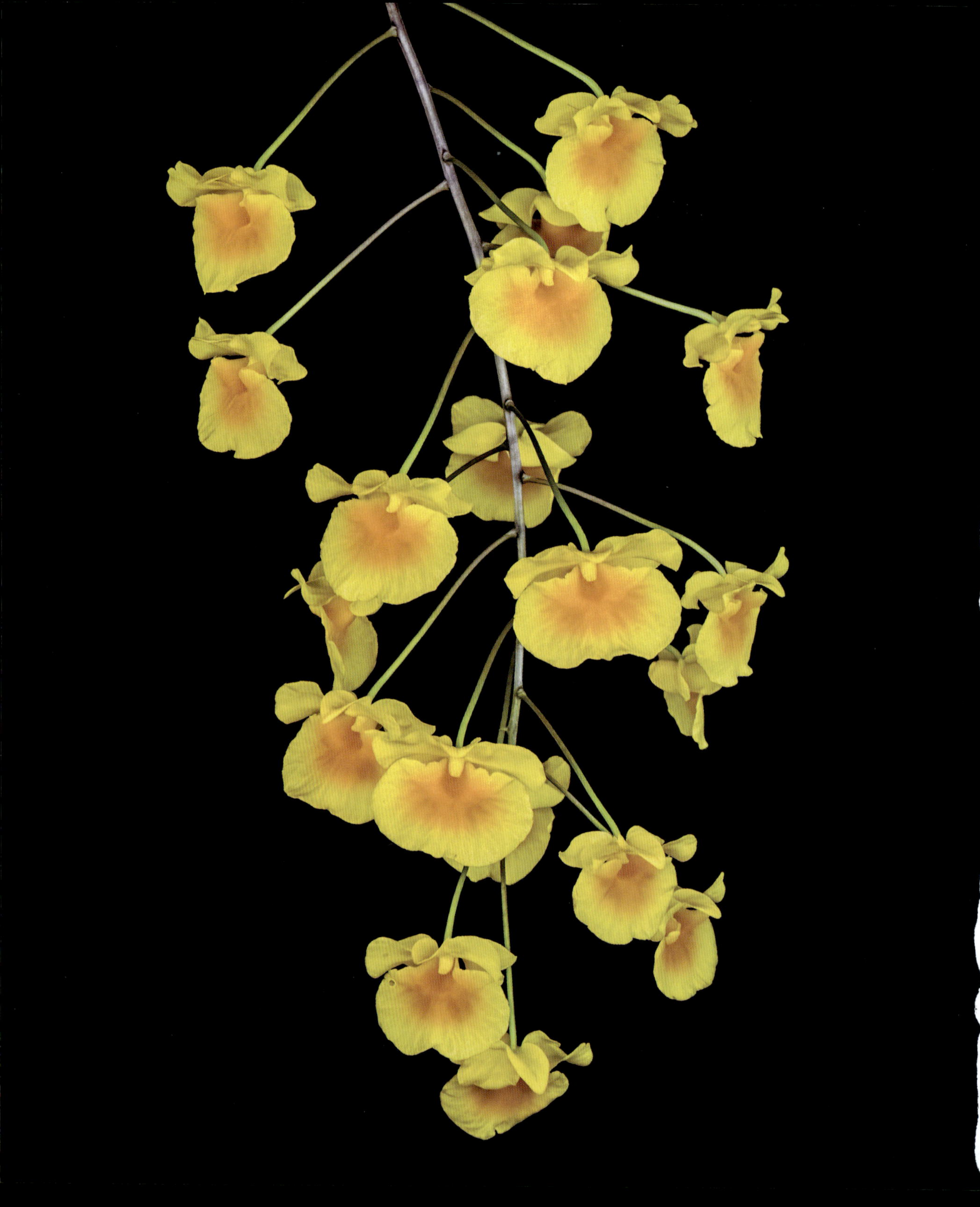